Design for
Operational Excellence:
A Breakthrough Strategy
for Business Growth

KEVIN J. DUGGAN

New York Chicago San Francisco Lisbon London Madrid Mexico City
Milan New Delhi San Juan Seoul Singapore Sydney Toronto

13 14 15 16 17 18 19 20   LCR   22 21

ISBN 978-0-07-176824-5
MHID 0-07-176824-6
e-ISBN 978-0-07-176856-6
e-MHID 0-07-176856-4

This publication is designed to provide accurate and authoritative information in regard to the subject matter covered. It is sold with the understanding that neither the author nor the publisher is engaged in rendering legal, accounting, securities trading, or other professional services. If legal advice or other expert assistance is required, the services of a competent professional person should be sought.
　　—From a Declaration of Principles Jointly Adopted by a Committee of the American Bar Association and a Committee of Publishers and Associations

Library of Congress Cataloging-in-Publication Data

Duggan, Kevin J.
　Design for growth : a blueprint for operational excellence in any business / by Kevin J. Duggan.
　　p. cm.
　ISBN-13: 978-0-07-176824-5 (alk. paper)
　ISBN-10: 0-07-176824-6 (alk. paper)
　1. Organizational effectiveness. 2. Organizational change. 3. Corporations--Growth. 4. Success in business. I. Title.
　HD58.9.D84 2012
　658.4'06--dc22　　　　　　　　　　　2011016485

Art credits or permissions info or referral to a credits section at the back of the book

This book is printed on acid-free paper.

I have chosen for my career to take the knowledge that I learn every day and to synthesize this knowledge into a teachable process that others can follow. I have strived to be a teacher as well as a guide to companies to improving their business performance. Perhaps one of the more difficult challenges is to apply the principles that you teach to your own company. Even with good education on the principles, it is of great help to have employees who are receptive, eager to learn, and enthusiastic, and who believe in functioning as more than just a team, but a team dedicated to growing the business. I have been fortunate to have this team at the Institute for Operational Excellence and Duggan Associates. Their hard work, efforts, and dedication have successfully removed management (that would be me) from the day-to-day operation of these companies, allowing me to spend a significant amount of time writing this text. More than just supporting me in this endeavor, the team provided me with the framework to dedicate my time and allow me to do what I enjoy doing most: teaching. For their efforts, I dedicate this book to the employees and thank them for the efforts that enabled me to achieve this accomplishment.

Contents

Foreword

As the lean movement evolved from learning about quality in the 1980s to learning about the Toyota Production System in the 1990s to the last decade's trend of Lean Six Sigma, it seemed to lose some things along the way. To put it simply, it lost people and it lost purpose. Certainly within Toyota, there have not been tool sets like lean and Six Sigma to "deploy," and there has not even been a continuous improvement culture to "implement." Within Toyota, if a young, ambitious professional proposes implementing *kanban*, using design of experiments, or using any of a number of other tools, a senior leader will ask the difficult question: What is your purpose? By asking the question, the leader is forcing the young professional to think: Why am I doing this? What will be the result if I am successful? Is this the most important result to be aiming toward right now? By forcing the young person to answer these questions, the senior leader is teaching him how to think.

Without focusing on developing people and having a clear understanding of where the business is going, we are left with deploying tools to get one-off results. We take out inventory here, we solve a quality problem there, we reduce changeover times, we organize the work areas, and so on. At some point, a senior executive asks: With all these "improvements" I hear about in Operations, why isn't our business growing?

Kevin Duggan's book, *Design for Operational Excellence: A Breakthrough Strategy for Business Growth*, addresses this important question. In his text, he teaches us that for true success, we need to connect our improvements so that we achieve a destination of Operational Excellence that will drive business growth. When this happens, there is an integral connection between what the leaders at the top care about (business success) and what is being worked on in the trenches to achieve Operational Excellence. There is alignment.

The foundation of Operational Excellence, as Duggan notes, is flow—the flow of value to the customer. That is why the organization exists.

When flow is interrupted, it reveals problems. In an organization without stable processes, the flow is interrupted so routinely that problems are a way of life, and management is needed to direct and support the flow. Management becomes embedded in the flow of product to the customer in a firefighting mode. We often suggest that management walk through the *gemba*, where the work is done, to understand the process and the problems. Neither is possible if, when you are "in the system," all you are seeing is chaos.

To get to the point where there is a reasonably stable and visible flow requires some work. The system must be properly designed. That does not happen by chance, and it does not come about simply by "empowering" the workforce. It takes significant expertise. It is a design process, like any other design process.

In this book, Duggan talks about designing lean value streams with a clear purpose in mind. He provides in-depth "design guidelines" that allow us to create a robust end-to-end flow in which the processes are robustly linked together, the first step in Operational Excellence. One powerful concept that Duggan introduces is "business in motion." He compares Operations to an aircraft in flight. An aircraft is designed to be in motion or in flight. Pilots are trained to use checklists while they are in flight to see problems. If they find problems, they also have standard methods for reacting to those problems. The analogy is brought into our operations, where we can design our operation "in motion" (when it receives an order from the customer) and then diagnose whether our operation is performing correctly by walking the *gemba* and creating a "visual checklist" similar to the checklist that the pilot would use. When problems do surface (and they will), Duggan provides the concept of "standard work for abnormal flow." With this method, not only are people willing and able to solve the problems, but they have a process or standard work that they should use to do so. Enabling people who work in the flow to do this requires a constant investment in training to develop the problem-solving ability of your team members—teaching them how to think. The willing part depends on the employee feeling truly like a part of the team, which includes feeling that she has a secure future. Job security is a noble goal, but it is difficult to ensure unless the company is growing. When it is, even major productivity increases are not threatening to the team members because they mean the capability to produce greater output while team members can all keep their jobs. And companies that are growing not only are more successful, but also provide a healthier environment for the people working there.

The final piece of the puzzle that is presented is that you need products that people want, and since technology and people's needs change over time, you must continually improve your products and services, and this is where Operations should spend its time as well. By having Operations integrated into the early stages of product development, not only do we eliminate waste but we also can create a flow in the product development process as well. As you will see in the case studies, companies have learned how to unleash human creativity and innovate through a formal process that involves Operations. As they have discovered, the creativity used to solve shop floor problems and reach higher and higher levels of excellence is actually not different from the creativity needed to design exciting new products that meet your customers' needs.

All of the case studies that Duggan provides are excellent examples of companies that have designed and implemented a lean flow, engaged their workforce, had a clear destination for the business, and were able to grow the business consistently over time. The design works! The results are clear! Companies that have committed senior leaders, establish flow, develop their people to high levels of capability to innovate and solve the most pressing business problems, and tie product and process improvement to a clear business strategy will grow and be the winners. It is a clear and simple recipe, but one that unfortunately few companies seem to be following. And this itself provides great opportunities for companies that do follow it.

Jeffrey K. Liker
Professor of Industrial and Operations Engineering
University of Michigan
Author of *The Toyota Way*

Acknowledgments

Having been formally trained as a mechanical engineer, I cannot say that my strength is in writing or in the English language. Trying to place my experience and knowledge into a readable format that one can follow, understand, comprehend, and apply is certainly a challenge to my writing skills. Therefore, I would like to acknowledge and thank Mr. James Marrese for his work on this text. While James has a degree in English, he has learned the technical principles of flow, has assisted in educational development, has traveled to many companies around the world, and can speak the language of Operational Excellence. It is with his assistance that this text was sculpted and put into the format that you, the reader, can learn from and enjoy. Thanks, James!

I would also like to thank the companies that opened their doors to us and allowed us to share their respective experiences with you. These companies include IDEX Corporation, Parker Hannifin Corporation, Hypertherm, Wood Group Turbopower LLC, VIBCO Vibrators, and GKN plc. A special thanks to all the employees at these companies, along with a hats off to them for the accomplishments they have made toward achieving Operational Excellence.

Introduction

The Return on Your Investment

You are about to make an investment, an investment of your valuable time. As a leader, you could spend your time on many different activities in order to grow the business that you work for. At this time, you have chosen to read this book. Like any good businessperson, you are looking for a return on your investment, an ROI. Here, the return is knowledge, but it is not historical knowledge of what other companies have done and what they believed in that led them to achieve their success, it is not management knowledge concerning leadership and other traits that have helped companies turn the tide and grow, and it is not academic insights that provide basic concepts along with simple examples. The return you will receive from reading this book is knowledge about how to *design the operation* of a company, not just to continuously improve the organization, but to create perpetual business growth.

For a minute, think about how an engineer designs a bridge, a building, an aircraft, or any other product so that it will perform properly and carry out its function. He uses the laws of physics, design criteria, and design principles to create something that, when brought to life, will function as intended. This design is given in detail in a blueprint, which provides the physical dimensions and tolerances for the product. It may also provide assembly instructions and notes on how to put the product together. Perhaps the design gets modified after testing, but the basic fundamentals—the laws of physics, the design criteria, and the design principles—do not change. Once the bridge, building, or aircraft is built, the people who operate and maintain it use it in the way in which it was designed to be used in order to achieve optimum performance.

Contrast the engineer's work and the resulting process with the way we design and run our business operations. We look for good people, leaders, and managers with knowledge and experience. Then we let them adapt their expertise to our specific corporate culture and the tasks that we carry out. Once we have hired them, we trust these new employees to redirect and reorganize our operations and make the changes that they see fit based on their knowledge and their previous experience.

Imagine what would happen if we hired engineers and allowed each one of them to design a bridge, building, or aircraft as she saw fit, ignoring the laws of physics, design criteria, and design principles. Then we let these engineers build these objects without a blueprint that shows the final product, its exact dimensions, and the construction notes. Suppose we hired these engineers because they interviewed well and their résumés stated that they had designed bridges in the past. We then let them design a bridge that they *thought* or *believed* could support eight lanes of traffic. Or maybe we let them design a building that they *thought* could be 20 stories high, or a jumbo jet that they *believed* could fly with only two engines, and we allowed them to build these designs because they were created based on the engineers' personal knowledge and experience.

Let's not forget the day-to-day operation of these devices, either. Without any design parameters governing how these items were to be built, each individual manager who worked with them would simply seek to improve his specific area the best way he knew how. If these items were not engineered to support the correct loads and were not operated as designed, would we want to drive on that bridge, live in that building, or fly in that aircraft?

The answer, of course, is no, and yet something similar happens when it comes to designing our business operations; there are no "laws of physics," design criteria, design principles, or blueprint to follow that enable business growth. In the past, there has been only the knowledge and experience of the people that we hire—until now.

In this book, we provide the laws of physics, design criteria, design principles, and, most important, the blueprint to follow in order to achieve Operational Excellence. When these are implemented, the result will be an operation that will drive overall business growth. We also provide the operator's manual explaining how to prepare people to jump to Operational Excellence and how to work in an environment of Operational Excellence in order to perpetually grow the business. As you can see in the case studies, the net result of designing operations using principles and teaching the employees how to work the operation as designed is quite powerful. Businesses have gone beyond continuous improvement and leapfrogged their performance (and their competition) by designing their operations to achieve Operational Excellence, and they have done so in a relatively short amount of time.

While we primarily discuss achieving Operational Excellence in companies that have manufacturing operations and office environments, the design principles can be applied to just about any business. This includes hospitals, banks, financial investment companies, service organizations, mining companies, process industries, insurance companies, logistics companies, universities, and even governments.

While we may use some engineering language to describe the content in the following chapters, the knowledge isn't technical; it's practical, and just about any company can use it. The information provided is a step-by-step process to follow, a methodology that enables a company to improve farther and faster, while creating a structure that perpetually enables growth. This methodology also provides substantial business results, which include

◆ A significant jump to true Operational Excellence in a short amount of time. Small companies can do this in months. Larger, multisite companies can do it in one or two years.

◆ For those of us who have embarked on a continuous improvement journey, the knowledge that programs that target waste elimination and cost reduction are a by-product of achieving Operational Excellence and creating *business growth*.

◆ An operation that will "start" every time it receives an order from the customer and will run smoothly from the time it receives the order to the time it delivers that order to the customer.

◆ A business that can adapt to changing markets and customer needs rather than react to them.

◆ A new concept and a new business growth model that is teachable to every (and we mean *every*) employee.

◆ A significant competitive advantage. As you can see in the case studies, it will be hard to compete with a company that has achieved Operational Excellence.

It may seem difficult to believe that there is knowledge that can deliver these results and more. Maybe it is hard to be convinced that by following a step-by-step methodology and implementing a design for business operations a company can achieve Operational Excellence and thrive in a short amount of time. It is possible to think that it is unlikely that business operations can be designed to enable business growth, but they can.

To help put the way we can design our operations to enable business growth into perspective, let's start by providing the four major concepts behind the process. The concepts are not difficult to understand. In fact, you'll probably agree that these ideas just intuitively make sense:

1. Continuous improvement is *not* about eliminating waste. It's about setting up an operation that will enable perpetual business growth. The process is *not* about creating a vision, then driving improvements toward that vision. It's about setting a *destination* and reaching it. Instead of continuously improving the company in the direction of a vision, we want to move the company from point A to point B in one large, quick jump. For those of you who know about lean concepts, you

may wish to think of it this way: *there is a destination to the lean journey, and that destination is Operational Excellence.*

2. There is a road map for getting to the destination. The road map comes with a compass that tells us whether we are heading in the right direction. There are also signposts along the way that let us know whether we are going in the right direction or whether we have gone off track. We simply have to know where to look for these signposts and how to read them.
3. Operational Excellence is not a myth. There is a clear-cut, practical definition of Operational Excellence, and there is also an "acid test" to let us know when we have achieved it. We will learn this practical definition and how to achieve it throughout the text.
4. The fourth and final concept is simple—if we know exactly where we are going and have a road map and directions that tell us how to get there, *we will get there a lot faster*.

With all this having been said, what's the true return on your investment? The true ROI for the time spent reading this book comes from implementing a design for business operations that results in increased market share, competitive advantage, business growth, and shareholder value. How do you get this return? By learning the operational design to grow your business presented in these pages.

PART

I

Destination: Creating Operational Excellence

1

The Engine of the Business

In the early 1970s, there probably was a day in most people's lives when there was an important event that they had to attend in the morning, let's say an interview or a final exam. They were probably nervous about the event, having studied or prepared for it the entire night before. When they got up that day, they were apprehensive. Over and over again, they ran through the information they had studied and how they expected the events of the day to unfold. They left their house promptly, walked out to their car, and got in. Suddenly, they were no longer nervous about the obstacle that was ahead of them that day. The apprehension, however, did not leave them. Instead, their focus had shifted and their worry intensified: they wondered whether their car was going to start to even get them to the interview or exam.

The car had had trouble starting in the past, and they hoped that the engine would not be finicky again today. They tensed up as they put the key in the ignition, saying things like, "Come on, baby, you can do it," then turned the key and perhaps said a silent prayer all in hopes that the engine would fire up (and continue to run). Once they turned the key, the ritual would begin by pumping the gas pedal or pulling a choke, and cranking the engine again and again. Soon, the battery would drain of its power and they had to use their last resort: push the car (hopefully downhill), jump in, shift into gear, then pop the clutch!

Hopefully, this ritual would get the car started, but there was no guarantee of success. The engine might rev up for a few seconds and then die. If the car finally started and ran smoothly, the driver would breathe a long sigh of relief and go on his way, his thoughts (and apprehension) returning to the event that was ahead of him.

Fast-forward to the present day. When you go out to a late-model-year car, do you have any apprehension about whether it will start? Do you find yourself nervous? Do you even give it a momentary thought? Would you ever even think about pushing your car downhill, jumping in, and popping the clutch to get it started? Your answer to these questions is probably no. You simply turn a key or press a button, and the engine magically starts the first time, every time. You have no worries that it won't start consistently every time. *And that's exactly how your operation should run: it should start every time.*

When customers give us orders, we should not have to think about, worry, or wonder whether those orders will be finished on time, with perfect quality, and delivered to the customer when the customer wants them. The order comes in from the customer (that's the start button), and the operational side of the business processes the order with no interruptions and then delivers the product. We shouldn't have to think about it or worry about it. Without flaw, the process should take place when we get an order. Just as today's engine starts every time, our operations should start every time, and like the modern engine, they should be smooth and seamless, without any managers pumping the gas pedal or pulling the choke, or management teams pushing the car to jump-start it.

While the concept of a smooth, seamless operation delivering product to customers without management intervention may seem implausible, as was the concept of starting a car on the first try in the 1970s, it is entirely attainable. Of course, we may think it was technological changes that allow today's engines to start every time. The advances in electronics and microprocessors played a big role in this, but technology is not the only reason why the modern car engine starts consistently every time. The main reason that today's engines start every time is that someone at a car manufacturing company, perhaps in Sales or Marketing, decided that the company needed an engine that would start consistently in order to be competitive in the marketplace. This challenge was then given to the engineers. To be successful, the engineers could not simply keep tinkering with, adjusting, or continuously improving the engine as it was. They had to redesign the engine. In other words, the reason the modern-day engine starts the first time, every time, is that *it was designed that way*. So why won't our operations start every time? *They are not designed that way.*

THE BUSINESS IN MOTION

When an engineer designs something that is in motion, such as an aircraft, an engine, or an elevator, she considers both a static design with the object at rest and a dynamic design with the object in motion. For example, the static design of an aircraft at rest is the size of the wings, fuselage, landing gear, windows, seats, and other such things. The dynamic design of an aircraft is the design for its performance in flight: the cruising speed, center of gravity changes, slipstream effect, drag characteristics, and other related aspects.

When we use the words *business operations*, we are talking about the dynamic side of the business. Think of it as *the business in motion*, or the day-to-day activities that a business must carry out in order to get its products or services to the customer. Most companies spend quite a bit of time and do a good job on the static design: the necessary building size, the right equipment to meet production capacity, the physical layout of the factory and offices, the number of shipping and receiving doors, the number of parking spaces for employees, and so on. All of this is well planned and well laid out.

When they are considering the physical layout, more progressive companies have even thought about creating "flow,"[2] and have therefore designed their facilities to support flow. They have connected processes, created cells, moved heavy machinery, eliminated inventory storage locations, and streamlined their factory layouts to provide products to customers in an efficient manner. Some companies have even rearranged their *offices* to support flow. While these initiatives are good and are heading in the right direction, they are still just dealing with the physical layout. They involve where machines will be placed, how wide the aisles will be, where conference rooms will be located, and so forth. What they don't cover is the dynamic side of the business, meaning what they will do when the customer calls, or when things are *in motion*.

While the static design of business operations is typically carried out with great care, many questions in the dynamic design often go unanswered or even unasked. For example, is your office layout designed to flow information to production when it needs it? Or, more important, does it flow information to the customers when they need it? In your office, how will everyone know what to work on next? When will information flow? How will we know whether the office is on time? On the manufacturing floor, similar questions apply: Sales may know what the customer wants, but how will each operator know what to work on next? How will we know whether the operation is on time? How often will we know that it's on time? What will we do if there is a problem?

While the static side of the business is clearly planned and thought out, the more important *business in motion* side is left up to management. Managers are charged with making decisions to steer the course and keep things moving in the right direction. Every day, they manage the operation and at the same time try to continuously improve it.

Rarely do we step back and think about an actual dynamic design in our operations. If we do, we find that developing and implementing the improvements in the operation that are needed in order to achieve the company's preset goals are left up to individual managers. Yet the operations side can have a direct impact on the profitability and growth of the business. Just think about what happens when Sales works for months to take clients away from a competitor, we finally get an order, and Operations ships it three weeks late.

In most operations, quality, reliability, cost, delivery, profitability, and many other aspects of performance depend on good management and leadership to procure parts and produce products when the customer wants them, at or below cost. We rely on people with strong management skills and a leader who can drive the management team to work in concert to bring raw materials together, then fabricate, assemble, ship, and deliver a high-quality product to the customer on time. In fact, in most cases, how an operation is run is left up entirely to the leader in charge. If a leader leaves and a new one comes in, the new one may run the operation in a completely different way. For example, one leader may focus on improving unreliable processes by implementing a Six Sigma program. When he leaves, whoever fills that position may drive an outsourcing program and move production to suppliers who can produce good quality.

In most cases, the profitability and growth of the operation, along with its ability to contribute to shareholder value, depend primarily on the leader's background, management experience, and leadership style. Therefore, the success of the design depends on our hiring the right person for the operation. Companies go so far in trying to find the right person with the exact credentials they are seeking that they spend a great deal of money hiring executive recruiting firms. The cost of finding the right person is worth it, as it is imperative that this person not only be a perfect fit for the existing organization but also have the right skill set to improve the company and grow the business.

In fact, operations are so dependent upon management for success that if an operation is not successful in delivering product to customers over time, eventually the "right person" or even the entire management team gets revamped. The products we're delivering or the machines we produce them on are not altered; we simply swap out the people in charge. We seek out a new leader or manager, one whom we hope has more experience and more knowledge than the previous one, to help us correct the underperformance by applying her skill set. We then rely on her to do her job and deliver product to the customer in order to return profit and shareholder value. She must do this on her own, without any laws of physics, without any design for the business in motion, without any design for the aircraft once it is in flight.

2

The Myth of Improvement

Imagine that you are boarding an aircraft. You take your seat and relax as the other passengers get on board and the doors are shut. The plane begins to roll down the runway and then takes off. While it is cruising, the captain comes out and gathers the flight crew in the galley. He holds a meeting with them and asks if there are any issues he should know about. After they tell him that all is well, he informs them that they have to find ways to reduce the operational cost of this flight. He asks the crew members for suggestions, and they brainstorm answers such as, "Move more people to the back of the plane for better balance," "Try 10 percent flaps for more lift at slower speeds," "Transfer fuel to the aft tank to move our center of gravity, we may get more speed," "Trim the nose down; we should get better fuel economy that way," and "See if we can change our route." You soon realize that the captain and his team are using their experience and knowledge to improve the performance of the aircraft in flight. They are trying to reduce the cost of the operational side of the flight. Sales and Marketing got the people in their seats, but if they want the flight to show a profit (and perhaps keep themselves employed), everyone needs to make sure that the plane is flying and also improve the performance of the plane at the same time.

As strange as it sounds, this same phenomenon happens every day in many operations. Like the aircraft, our business takes flight when we get a call from the customer, and activities are set in motion. As managers, we do what we must to get the orders to the customer, but we also have to improve the overall operation to keep it profitable with the same people delivering the product.

There is a significant difference between the two examples, however. In real life, every captain goes to flight school. He learns how the plane has been designed, the engineering behind aircraft performance, and how that design can be maximized in flight. Therefore, he does not need to assemble a team to look for trouble spots and try to improve them. Instead, he follows a checklist to see that everything is done right and in the proper sequence to ensure safety and maximize the performance of the aircraft. The optimization of the flight is based on the design specifications of the aircraft. Back to our company: Do we have a checklist to follow? Is it based on a design? Most likely, the answer is no, and without a design to follow or a checklist to use, improvement is left up to leadership and management.

THE NEVER-ENDING JOURNEY BEGINS

Over the past few decades, just about every company has embarked on a journey of continuous improvement. Led by management, companies are seeking to improve their operations and their business by creating a goal or vision toward which to lead people. These visions are usually motivational and inspirational. They excite employees about business growth in the future. For example, statements such as "Be the global leader in precision measuring" or "Delight customers with superior performance and quality" tell the employees what the company is striving for. They may say what is good for the company as well as the employees. A good vision statement can fire up the troops to help move forward and improve the performance of the operation.

Once the vision statement is sent out, the next step is to embed continuous improvement into the operation to achieve the vision. In this step, we challenge teams to make the business operations more efficient. We provide them with improvement tools, benchmark other companies, seek the knowledge used by the best companies, shamelessly steal ideas from other industries, and perhaps even hire consultants to help us. Armed with this knowledge, and perhaps with someone to guide us along the way, we start teaching employees how to continuously improve the operation. (See Figure 2.1) We

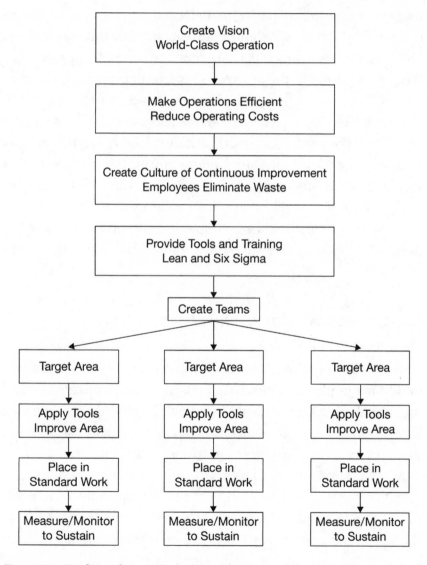

Figure 2.1 *Traditional Continuous Improvement*

challenge them to eliminate waste, or the non-value-added activities, in order to make the operation more efficient each day. The goal of this effort is to have an army of people who improve the operation each day, or to *create a culture of continuous improvement.*

The improvements are done through many techniques, such as value stream mapping, *kaizen* (rapid improvement) events, and action workout events, where team members target an area of the operation in which to make an improvement. They then present the proposed improvement to management, management approves, and the team implements the proposal. Once the improvement is implemented, it needs to be embedded into the standard work in order to sustain it. Then management monitors and measures the results to ensure that the results do not drift backward. Each day, this process continues: find areas that need improvement, improve them, and then embed the improvements into standard work. If management is successful, in the end, we will have an army of people that work for us who not only do their own jobs but also make the operation more efficient by finding waste in the organization and striving to eliminate it.

SEEING THE MYTH OF IMPROVEMENT

The journey is under way. Management sets a vision and charges Operations with becoming efficient. Operations seeks to create a culture of continuous improvement, so it provides training and tools, creates teams, and selects target areas to improve. Improvements are made, the new process is documented in standard work, and management monitors and measures the results to ensure that they are sustained. The organization follows a process of improve, sustain, measure, and monitor, then repeats that cycle over and over again to create a culture of continuous improvement. The end result of this process, or the best possible outcome we can have using this process, is a "staircase of continuous improvement." (See Figure 2.2.)

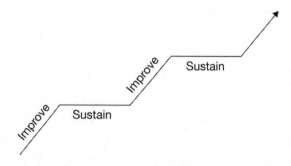

Source: *The Office That Grows Your Business: Achieving Operational Excellence in Your Business Processes,* Institute for Operational Excellence, North Kingstown, R.I., 2009.

Figure 2.2 *Continuous Improvement*

Improve, sustain, improve, sustain. As this process continues over time, the cycle repeats itself, and the operation progresses; teams make improvements in one area and then embed the changes into the standard work in order to sustain them. But often, the pattern of improvement does not look like a staircase at all. In many cases, sometimes the operation moves forward, sometimes it slides backward, and sometimes the company regresses and possibly even abandons its improvement efforts altogether. (See Figure 2.3.)

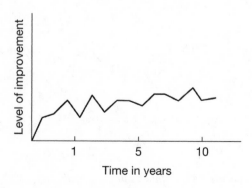

Figure 2.3 *The Continuous Improvement Journey*

Even if you apply the best tools correctly, if you make an improvement and sustain it, then make another improvement and sustain it, the best you can achieve over time, *the best result this design will yield*, is a slow, steady climb up the staircase of continuous improvement, as shown in Figure 2.4.

Why do some companies have erratic performance when they try to make improvements, as shown in Figure 2.3, while others have more of a perfect staircase look, as shown in Figure 2.4? The answer is a common one, and for this method of ongoing improvement, it is also correct. The answer is leadership. Strong leaders have made companies successful in applying day-by-day continuous improvement. Why? *Because strong leadership is needed if this method is to be successful.*

This approach needs to be driven. It takes quite a bit of *management energy*, and strong leaders can inspire, create, and harness that energy for extended periods of time to lead the company through this long-term process of change. Companies without energetic leadership stumble and move backward during those periods when leadership and management are distracted by other business issues. The message here is that this approach to improving operations

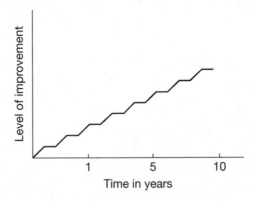

Figure 2.4 *The Staircase of Continuous Improvement*

involves providing employees with tools like problem solving, *kaizen*, value stream mapping, and others and guiding them to use these tools to eliminate waste every day. The product of this will be a culture of continuous improvement.

However, in order for this approach to be successful, embedded in it is the need for strong leadership and an abundance of management energy, and this is the area that countless books have made their focus. Companies seek to improve by hiring the right leader. In other words, the best method that we know of making improvements requires strong leadership, and because of this requirement, this is where we put all of our efforts. If ours is one of the lucky organizations that happens to be successful, the best it will ever get is a never-ending journey in which employees try to improve the operation each day.

THE PROCESS OF "IMPROVEMENT"

The word *improvement* means many different things to many different people. It is a subjective term that is sometimes defined by measurements, such as lower operating cost, reduced inventory, reduced lead time, increased efficiency, increased productivity, better quality, or better on-time delivery. It can also mean whatever the current leader decides it means, and the process of improvement is often one of management setting goals and employees making changes in their respective areas to achieve these goals. Once a particular goal has been achieved, management can set a new one. This cycle of goal setting and achievement continues as management finds new areas to improve, sets goals, and motivates teams to achieve these goals. Teams then strive to achieve these goals, and if they do, even if the goal is achieved for only a short period, management acknowledges the accomplishments (perhaps even with a small celebration), then assigns a new area to improve along with new goals.

If the goals are not achieved, management dives in to find out why and to reenergize the team; it may even give the team a new negotiated goal so that it can be successful. It is important that the team be successful in achieving the goal in order to keep the cycle going and build momentum. This process of improvement relies on quite a few things going right in order to keep the improvements continuous. And if all the ingredients are right (the right people, the right leaders, and the right knowledge) and if everything goes right, the *best* this process will yield is a climb up the staircase of continuous improvement year after year.

But if this process takes so long, then why do we do it? Why do we strive to improve, then sustain, improve, then sustain, over and over again in a staircase fashion? Why do we strive to create a culture that will do this perpetually? The answers are really quite simple: first, because this is the only design we know about, and second, *because we have been taught this design over and over again.* It has been well documented that a continuous improvement journey should go on forever, that it's a never-ending journey with no destination, a journey in which we strive to eliminate waste each and every day to improve our operation.

But think back to our aircraft example and imagine if the captain said to the crew, "We need to make this aircraft fly higher, since higher altitude gives us more efficiency," and then challenged the crew to find ways to make the aircraft go a little higher or perform a little better each day. Wouldn't we think that this approach was strange? Wouldn't we intuitively feel that there should be a better way, a more formal and process-oriented way that would deliver repeatable results time after time? Would we feel comfortable sitting on the aircraft while it was in flight—while it was in *motion*—and watching a team brainstorming where to improve, then trying a rapid improvement or *kaizen* event to make the improvement? Or, would we feel more comfortable watching the captain use a checklist to ensure that the aircraft is performing correctly, in accordance with its design specifications, along with a predefined checklist of adjustments to make as needed? Most of us who travel would probably vote for the latter.

With all this having been said, *the myth of improvement is that it's a continuous journey of finding and eliminating waste, but in reality, it's not.* If we follow this method, then we are incapable of knowing whether the operation is performing as designed because a design never existed in the first place. Our thoughts on improving the operation are that it is an endless journey, and if we think this way, that is exactly what our efforts will be. Our operation will improve its performance at the rate it's pushed by the current management team, and we'll plod along up the staircase.

We can break this myth by thinking differently, by thinking that improving operations is *not* about *continuous* improvement but about designing the performance of the operation and then ensuring that the operation is performing in accordance with the design specifications. Once the operation is performing in accordance with the design, further improvement comes from *updating* the design. The result is that the performance of the operation goes from point A to point B in one big step or jump, not incrementally. Another way we can break the myth is to stop giving people tools to improve the operation and then letting them loose to find areas to improve. Instead, we should *design* the operation to run in a certain fashion and then provide a checklist to optimize the performance of the design, and that is just what companies have done to leapfrog their performance to Operational Excellence.

3

The Leapfrog

There are many companies that have aggressively pursued continuous improvement for more than 20 years, using the staircase approach that we described in the last chapter. There are other companies that started their continuous improvement efforts only two or three years ago, and yet some of these companies are much farther along than the ones that embarked on a continuous improvement journey more than 20 years ago.

Some of these recent adopters have gone farther and grown their businesses faster than some of the veterans. They have done much more than just create employees who eliminate waste everywhere they see it. They have gone beyond having process control and connecting value-added activities so that they flow at the rate of customer demand. They did not stop once they had created a *lean enterprise*. In fact, they were not even trying to create a lean enterprise. These companies leapfrogged their competitors by taking a different approach and using an engine with a different design, resulting in operations that have exceeded the boundaries of what Six Sigma and lean tools can yield. And they did it faster, too. (See Figure 3.1.)

What made the difference? How were some companies able to leapfrog their competitors and reach new levels of performance without going through years and years of traditional continuous improvement? How did they evolve so quickly? Their first step was to break the myth of continuous improvement and set an exact destination for the operation, then they put a design in place to get there.

Figure 3.1 *The Continuous Improvement Journey*

The Destination

Let's go back to our aircraft analogy, but now from a different angle. Imagine that you're boarding an aircraft. You take your seat and relax as the other passengers get on board and the doors are shut. You hear the captain's voice say, "Thanks for boarding Flight 102 heading west." How would you feel about the "heading west" part? Would you be comfortable knowing that the plane is heading west, or would you be more comfortable knowing exactly where the plane was heading? Even if the captain said, "This plane is heading west to California," California is a big state. Wouldn't you wonder exactly where the plane was going and what its exact destination was?

When we tell employees that continuous improvement is a never-ending journey, a journey without a destination, we are essentially telling them that their plane is heading west. And since the employees are along for the ride, they never ask questions such as: Where will all these improvements take us? Where will this journey take us? What is our destination? What does it look like? What route are we taking? How will we know if we are going in the right direction? What are the signposts along the way? How will we know when we have arrived at the destination?

Without answers to these questions, we just seek to improve every day and learn new tools that help us do it better. We read books, visit other companies, and perhaps hire consultants. We try to learn how to "head west" from many different sources instead of setting an exact destination for our operation.

SETTING THE DESTINATION

We have been fortunate that we have not had to answer the question, "Where will this journey take us?" as it is one of the toughest questions for anyone who has embarked on a lean or continuous improvement journey to answer. It is not an easy question to answer, but how we answer this question has a dramatic impact on the performance of the company one way or another. The companies that answer this question correctly shorten their journey significantly because they know where they are going. They save years of learning from experience, bypass years of evolution, skip years of pain as they struggle to improve, and eliminate the years of trial and error on new initiatives and strategies as new leaders come and go. The right answer to this question separates companies that have a *vision* from companies that have an *exact destination*. Companies that answer this question correctly also establish a design that enables their business to grow, which we will discuss in later chapters.

The correct answer to this question is key, as companies with an exact destination are able to plot an exact course and get to their destination quickly, while others try to improve each and every day in order to achieve a vision. When we design our operations to grow our business, there is a strong difference between a vision and a destination.

WHAT'S YOUR VISION?

Company visions are usually intended to be inspiring. They are intended to motivate the workforce to achieve an objective set by the company. Visions also tend to convey what the company wants to become and achieve at some point in the future, and this is often stated in competitive terms. For example, a car company may have the vision to become the world's leading consumer company for automotive products and services. A beverage company may have the vision to be the number one worldwide distributor and provider of low-salt, high-energy drinks. Visions are usually passionate and are geared toward rallying the people in the organization to achieve the stated goals.

Typically, visions do not tell employees at each level of the organization, in practical terms, what *they* need to do to achieve the organization's goals. The members of senior management are usually given the task of using their knowledge and experience to guide their respective areas to achieve the goals set in the vision. Each manager below them does the same, each trying to achieve the goals in the best way he knows how. Everyone does his best to drive his area forward toward his *perception* of how the vision applies to him.

We typically leave it up to each manager, or each person in the company, to determine how she will help us reach our target. To help her do this, we try to hire the best people we can. This requires us to always be seeking out new people and new talent to move the company forward. Again, each person does what she thinks is best and uses her knowledge and experience to help her attain her objectives with the company's objectives in mind. Even though managers are doing what they think is best for their area, the sum of their efforts is that the company is constantly being tugged in countless different directions, requiring even more meetings and direction setting from the top to keep the company somewhat on course.

As a result, the company changes through evolution. Usually, it can evolve only at a slow pace because each manager is trying to improve his area to attain the company vision the best way he knows how. Sometimes, the evolution can be fast if there is a strong leader in place. A strong leader who keeps the course constant and drives people toward the vision may get results. However, this does not ensure that the results will be *consistent* or *sustainable*, nor does it ensure that the company will get the results that the leader is seeking. Why? Because if a leader seeks particular results, people will usually find a way to report those results. But if a leader installs a process to achieve the desired results, then either the results will be consistent or the process will be adjusted.

WHAT'S YOUR EXACT DESTINATION?

When we say *exact destination*, we are not seeking a definition in terms of results. We are seeking to have every employee understand exactly where the company is going *and how to get there*. We want all the employees to understand where the company is going in practical terms from their viewpoint. We want them to not only understand where the company is going but also want to get there. They all know the exact heading that will get them there. They know the steps along the way. They can see for themselves the signposts that tell them that they are going in the right direction—they are on course. And they know when they have arrived at that destination. In order to do this, we need to describe where we are going as if we were physically standing in the operation a year or so from now. Imagine that you are standing on the shop floor. You can't talk to anyone. You can only see, listen, and observe. What do you see? What do you hear? What is happening? What can you tell about the shop floor just by standing there and observing?

What if you are in the engineering department? What do you see? What do you hear? What is happening? What can you tell about Engineering just by standing there and observing? Imagine the same scenario in Sales, Finance, Production Control, and every other department. We want all the employees to understand the destination: what it would look like, what activities would be taking place, and how it would operate. The destination we are seeking is one that everyone can understand and know how to apply to her particular area. The sales office is different from the manufacturing floor, so these areas would be described differently. The destination is one that people can internalize as it applies to their specific area, and it even applies to the executive offices.

If the destination is conveyed correctly, not only can each employee understand it but he can see the benefits of it and will want to create that environment in order to work in it. When we describe the destination in this manner, we are clearly defining the performance specifications of the business in motion. We are providing the "flight characteristics" or dynamic design of the aircraft while it is still on the ground, thereby telling everyone who will operate the aircraft exactly how the whole thing will behave while in it is flight, not just what his particular department will do. Once the destination has been clearly defined in these practical terms (and I will help you do this in the upcoming chapters), each employee will be taught what the destination is on two levels: the destination to which the company as a whole is going and how he can achieve the destination in his particular area.

Finally, achieving the destination, meaning how the company will actually get there, must be based on a process, not on an opinion or brainstorming. It needs to be based on a process for one simple reason: *so it can be taught.*

It's not left up to each manager or individual to decide how she will get there. It's not left up to people who have new and innovative ideas that they will apply in their area. It's not left up to evolution. We convey the exact destination and we provide a detailed process or road map for getting there, and each employee knows exactly where she is going and how to get there. The result is that the company leapfrogs the traditional staircase of continuous improvement and leaves its competitors behind as they try to improve a little more each day. Once we achieve our destination and sustain this new level of performance, we ensure that we do not slide backward while we continue to try to move the company forward; the upcoming chapters describe how to do this.

It's All about Teaching

Perhaps the most important distinction between a vision and a destination is this: employees are *told* what a company vision is. They don't know the why or the how behind it; they know only what the company wants to achieve. A destination, however, is *taught*. We need to teach employees exactly what the destination is and the step-by-step process for getting there. When we teach the destination and the process for getting there, we skip years of evolution on the staircase of continuous improvement, years of learning through trial and error, and years of management trying to sustain any improvements that have been made. The information that we provide must be crystal clear at all levels and must be presented in a simple, concise, and practical manner. In fact, when it comes to teaching the destination, *we should ensure we also establish a process on how to teach it.*

The key to establishing the destination is that it must apply to every employee in the company. Not only should each employee understand where the company is heading, but she should also know what to do in her particular area to help achieve that destination. The destination has to have a common denominator that describes this type of operation and that applies to Manufacturing, Engineering, Purchasing, and Sales. It has to be one simple statement that we can teach at all levels, to everyone in the organization, a statement that will organically embed the destination into the company's culture and be instantly transferable to new employees.

The intent is not just to motivate people, with the result that the more motivated an individual employee is, the more that particular area moves forward, but to move each area forward in synchronization with all the other areas of the company. We want to describe what we are really trying to do with all of our continuous improvement efforts; we want to describe what we are really trying to do with our lean journey, and that description would probably go something like this: We are trying to create an operation where

> *Each and every employee can see the flow of value to the customer, and fix that flow before it breaks down.*

In other words, our destination is to create *Operational Excellence.*

4

Defining Operational Excellence

Operational Excellence is a term that is often defined in many ways. Excellence in everything we do. A world-class operation. The best an operation can be. The ability to manage value creation processes without waste better than the competition year after year.[1]

In practical terms, the words *Operational Excellence* try to convey the idea that the operation is at the very highest level of performance. It has reached the pinnacle; it has set the standard; it is the best an operation can be. The difficulty with this description is how to define "the best." If an operation always delivers product 100 percent on time, with perfect quality, at or below cost, is it necessarily performing the best it can? The answer is no. Even if the metrics are perfect, the operation may be consuming a large amount of management resources to obtain the performance. For example, in order to get this performance, management might have to meet every hour to manage resources and set priorities, which takes time away from other important activities.

In reality, Operational Excellence is not about performance or even financial metrics, although it will have an impact on them. It's about *how the operations side of the business supports business growth*. It's about more than just having an operation that can deliver products to customers on time and with perfect quality. It's about understanding that Operations is a strategic part of the business that can have an impact on market share, break into new markets, adapt to changing markets, keep the business ahead of the competition, and return sustained shareholder value.

For this concept to mean something to our employees, it is important that we describe Operational Excellence in a way that each employee can understand from a practical standpoint in his day-to-day environment. The definition should also be *visually measurable.* We should be able to see it when it has been attained. It should also be *binary*, meaning that either we have attained it or we have not. And finally, it should be defined in such a way that each employee knows exactly what to do every day in order to help grow the business. That's why we defined Operational Excellence in a way that is practical, easy to understand, and teachable at all levels of the company. As a reminder, Operational Excellence is defined as when

> *Each and every employee can see the flow of value to the customer and fix that flow before it breaks down.*

This one simple sentence, which is easy to remember and easy to share, provides each employee with the destination not only of his efforts but of the entire organization's efforts when it comes to operational improvement. It lets each employee know what the company is trying to accomplish and what he needs to do in his specific area if he is to contribute. It clearly identifies that waste elimination and a culture of continuous improvement are not *goals* of Operational Excellence but rather *products* of it. It also identifies continuous improvement along a set path, a road map to get somewhere. It lets employees know that improvement efforts are not ambiguous (seek out waste and eliminate it); they are focused on an end result.

Whether you work on the factory floor building products, in Engineering designing products, in Sales taking orders, or in any other area, the definition holds true. "Each and every employee" means that everyone understands that her activities provide value to the customer. Each employee understands how her activities flow the necessary material or information through several processes to the customer. Each can see whether the flow is working normally or abnormally, and each knows what to do when flow starts to become abnormal. For now, think of this concept as self-healing flow, or flow with an immune system.

By now, you should have a basic understanding of Operational Excellence. But before we do a deep dive into the concepts and how to apply them, it is important that we take some time to learn about the "why" of Operational Excellence. Ironically, understanding why companies should choose to pursue Operational Excellence is what keeps them off the staircase of continuous improvement and enables them to leapfrog the competition, and it's analogous to the design of the modern car engine.

WHY OPERATIONAL EXCELLENCE?

As mentioned earlier, the current design of many operations requires management to run the operation and also improve the performance of the operation while it is in motion. As difficult as it may seem, management has done exactly that. Over the years, management has improved operations by using various programs and tools like SMED (Single-Minute Exchange of Dies),[2] poka-yoke,[3] 5S,[4] and others, spreading them across the operation like peanut butter. Other tools like SPC (statistical process control) and Six Sigma have focused on improving quality and have been used to make each process repeatable, predictable, reliable, and dependable.

Over time, management has directed its attention toward improving flow. Cells have been formed in order to create one-piece flow through a process. In the past 10 years, with the advent of lean, management has begun driving improvement by connecting the upstream and downstream processes, such as fabrication, machining, and packaging, to the cells. Managers have learned about value streams[5] and have begun implementing them from the receiving deck to the shipping deck.

Value streams have also been driven into the office in order to streamline the business processes. Improvements have been focused on the supply chain as well, as it was discovered that even the most robust value streams in the operation do not flow if just one component in the supply chain is missing. Improvements even have been made in the product development processes, where ideas for new products are generated and then brought into production. Improvements have been made everywhere in the operation, and many success stories have been widely published. However, even though managers have worked hard to make improvements in the world of operations (and they have), this progress has been limited by the maximum performance that the design of the operation will allow.

THE BEST OUR ENGINE CAN DO

If managers could successfully implement all the improvements that are currently being driven using the improve, sustain, improve, sustain approach, as described in Chapter 2, the best the operation could yield would be end-to-end flow through the factory, support groups, and supply chain. In doing so, they would have taken the basic engine and improved it to the point where product flowed to the customer, perhaps even at the rate of the customer demand. Let's not downplay this, as it's quite an accomplishment. Companies like Boeing have put in a moving line to produce large aircraft in a continuous, end-to-end flow fashion. It has been quite an undertaking, and Boeing has been successful. Toyota has been working at this for more than 50 years and has put in end-to-end flow from stamping through final assembly, not for one product but for a mix of products flowing down the same line. Toyota is ahead of the curve when it comes to flow and has set the benchmark in the automotive industry for many years.

Companies are seeking to use continuous improvement to create end-to-end flow, but the process takes many, many years if it is done using the staircase of continuous improvement. Still, this result would be a significant improvement and a major accomplishment. If you have created end-to-end flow in your company, then congratulations, as this is not a small task, and you have accomplished quite a bit. Companies that have accomplished this are held in high regard and have become showcases for others to benchmark. However, you have also reached the limit of the current design of our "operation engine." You have attained the best performance that the current design of the operation can ever yield. It is the best, but have you reached Operational Excellence? Unfortunately, even after all the work that has been done and all the improvements that have been made, the answer is no.

WHY OUR OPERATIONS WON'T "START"

Let's go back to our car engine example. Today's car engine starts every time, while the engine of the 1970s did not. Why? In the 1970s, engines used mechanical distributors that provided electricity to the spark plugs and carburetors that provided fuel. In order for the engine to start or run, the right amount of fuel had to be atomized with the right mixture of oxygen and had to be present in the right volume at exactly the time when the spark plug fired to combust the mixture. The fuel would be atomized in the carburetor, then travel through a manifold that fed each cylinder to power the engine, and all of this was happening about 900 times per minute at engine idle, or about 15 times per second!

Since the carburetor and the distributor were 100 percent mechanical devices, engine vibration, heat, and high velocity of movement led to wear over time, and eventually they became unreliable. Hence, the engine wouldn't start every single time. We could have improved the materials that these devices were made of or added more controls to make them perform a little better, but there would still have been no guarantee that the engine would start every single time.

This is the exact approach we have taken in our operations. Our operations don't start every time, so we've tried to change the materials or add more controls. In other words, we've upgraded the education of our people and added more leaders and management, or we've changed the leaders and management, and perhaps purchased new systems in order to get the operation to perform. Remember, companies seek out leaders who have innovative ideas and experience that will help lead them to be more competitive in the marketplace. Often, a new leader will bring in some of his previous team to help him make changes in the operation more effectively. As with the old car engine, though, this is also no guarantee for success, as all we have done is added more controls to a system that was never designed to start every time in the first place.

MUSCLING FLOW

In Operational Excellence, we do not create flow to increase productivity or efficiency. We create flow so that we know whether the flow of value to the customer has been broken. It's about everyone knowing whether things are normal or abnormal, and making abnormal flow stand out. When the aircraft line at Boeing stops moving, everyone can see it; everyone knows. If a line stops at Toyota, everyone knows. Most manufacturers that have put in flow, and maybe even your company, have a way of letting people know when flow has stopped. That's the first step toward Operational Excellence: having a good, robust flow, which means a flow with very little waste, or a *lean flow*, that every operator can see and understand from end to end. Operators can see and understand the difference between normal and abnormal flow, and this applies in business processes in the office as well.

Contrast this with companies that have put in flow to eliminate waste or become more efficient. Eventually, if they are good, they will create end-to-end flow. *But what happens when flow stops?* Somewhere in the operation, in support groups, or in the supply chain, flow inevitably stops; in fact, it tends to stop often. When this happens, it's time for management to get involved and *muscle the flow*.

Somewhere in the company, in some fashion, a support group jumps in to fix the problem and determine why it happened in the first place. Group members come up with quick decisions to keep the line running or keep people busy. They use problem-solving tools to search for answers. They work with teams and do root-cause problem solving to implement long-term solutions. If they cannot fix the problem quickly, they escalate it to the next level of management. Managers contact other managers. E-mails and voice mails are exchanged. Managers begin making decisions to try to solve the problem and restart the flow. Each person works independently until all the managers realize that they need to get everyone on the same page, and there is only one way to do this: have a meeting.

Meetings are held for one reason: to correct flow—the flow of product to the customer; the flow of information to support product flow; the flow of information needed to do business, such as taxes, accounting, and other such functions; the flow of information in product development; and so on. Meetings are set up with the intention of making a decision that corrects flow. They are intended to set a course of action that everyone will follow. In these meetings, we arm-twist, negotiate, cajole, and find ways to get our ideas heard and implemented. After a good amount of time passes and we wear out one another, perhaps a decision gets made, actions are assigned, and priorities and dates are established. Everyone goes back to work, but we're not done yet. Meetings spawn requests for more information or generate immediate priority changes that cause interruptions in office workflow and, most likely, requests for other meetings. A ripple effect is sent through the support groups that breaks down any preestablished flow that has been set up in business processes. One way or another, eventually a decision is made, issues are resolved, and flow to the customer resumes.

In our "engine of the 1970s design," we strive to eliminate waste and create flow. However, when flow stops, even the best-performing operations still depend on management or support groups to fix the problems in both the short term and the long term. Every time we seek to improve, we start this cycle again: somehow we find a way to create flow, and then we use management to keep it running. We do this year after year and get a little better each day, although we sometimes slide backward in the process. Our operations design relies on management to start the engine, warm it up, and *keep it running*. If these things don't happen, the flow of product to the customer slides backward and deteriorates, and it becomes solely dependent upon management muscling the flow of product to the customer every day. When the operations design stutters and stalls, we use more layers of management, or perhaps change the management, to start it again. Different managers come in with different experiences and styles that can affect the performance of the operation, but the original design retains its performance limits.

THE PARADOX OF MANAGING FLOW

It's a paradox. The current design of our operations requires management to "manage" the delivery of product to the customer, even in the best-performing operations where we have flow. Yet that same management can make many decisions each day that introduce variations and disruptions into the flow. Supervisors reprioritize products and direct people to expedite shipments. Planning revises schedules after they are issued. Management has meetings, and plans and schedules change. The very same people who strive to implement flow are the ones who oversee it and have the ability to disrupt it easily.

Another paradox: meetings are held to make decisions when flow is broken, yet those decisions kill flow! In the office, decisions run rampant; anyone can make one. The more we make them, the more variation we allow to enter into our business processes. Imagine for a minute what would happen if your company never held a meeting. How much more work would get done in the office? How much more productive would your office be? This is just one of the paradoxes that leads to a slow, steady climb up the staircase of continuous improvement. This is why this climb takes many years, and why the potential of the system is inherently limited. And the situation won't change, because the need for management to control the system and fix it when it breaks down has been *accepted and embedded into the design of the system*, and herein lies the flaw.

Even if we are good enough to go beyond a culture that eliminates waste and creates end-to-end flow, that flow will still break down someplace, whether on the shop floor or in the office, and the answer will be to see the supervisor or alert management. If there is no quick fix, we put together a team to review and solve the problem. The team members apply their training and work hard to eliminate the problem, but since they need to work with other employees in other areas, such as Engineering and Purchasing, a meeting is needed. Meetings interrupt the flow of other activities, spawning more meetings. While this is happening, another problem occurs somewhere else in the company, and the cycle repeats. Why? Because we set out in the beginning to continuously improve and to create flow that gets fixed by management *when* it breaks down. We didn't set out to create flow that gets fixed by the employees *before* it breaks down.

It comes down to this: understanding what Operational Excellence is and why we should pursue it are the keys to keeping us off the staircase of continuous improvement. This understanding will enable us to design our operations to support business growth because we will understand exactly what Operational Excellence is and why we should attain it. With this knowledge, we will understand that it's about more than eliminating waste and creating flow. Operational Excellence can eliminate many of the endless meetings and office disruptions to which we've grown accustomed. We will understand that everyone should see the flow of value to the customer and be able to fix it before it breaks down.

We will understand that Operational Excellence means that the people who work in the flow each day are responsible for the flow, and that flow happens without management, even when it becomes abnormal. We will understand that a visitor should be able to tell whether we are on time with regard to customer demand or whether there is a problem by following the flow and telling normal from abnormal. A visitor will also be able to see the standard work for situations in which flow becomes abnormal. This is important, because if a visitor can tell, then so can every employee. Finally, we will understand all of these things and more about where we are going on our continuous improvement journey *before we even start it*!

With this knowledge and this understanding of what the destination is, we will know exactly where we are going, and we will be able to choose a different track to get there, a different path of improvement that does not follow the improve/sustain staircase. It's a path that goes directly to the destination and follows a road map to get there. With this information, our course is direct, our heading is set, and our destination is unambiguous. And from all of this knowledge, we have the *ability to leapfrog.*

5

Creating the Road Map to Operational Excellence

How do we get to our destination? The traditional way would be to put a plan in place and let management drive the plan, altering it as needed. We have learned that planning is everything; in fact, the process of planning is more important than the plan itself because the plan changes. The ability to create a good plan is a necessary skill for a leader. However, with the traditional approach, we are trying to create a plan that can be changed by management when we should be trying to create a road map, or perhaps it's better to think of it as creating the road itself. The key thinking here is that a road is a *physical pathway* to move something along, and in this case, that something is the company. If we want to move the company quickly to the destination of Operational Excellence, we need to carve a pathway or create a road to get there, and carving that pathway includes carving up the operation into true value streams that not only have flow through assembly departments but also flow through fabrication steps, shared resources, inspection areas, Engineering, Purchasing, Accounting, and anywhere else that a series of activities takes place. This type of flow is also not a standard type, such as one-piece flow or a first in, first out (FIFO), that we typically think of. We want to create self-healing flows, or flow with immune systems, and, more important, *flow without management*.

Creating our road map means creating the physical pathways through which material and information will flow to the customer according to the principles of Operational Excellence. These pathways are created through formal education, starting with developing true product and process families. Much more detailed education on mixed-model flow, shared resource flow, flow in the office (business process flow), flow in the supply chain, and flow in product development is required. Having each employee understand the physical pathways of flow is the first fundamental of our road map. It is also the foundation block of our new engine design for Operational Excellence. We will explore these concepts in more detail in future chapters. At this point, the key is that the road map is created through education on exactly what Operational Excellence is, the principles of creating Operational Excellence, and truly understanding how to design for self-healing flow.

THE ACID TEST

Unlike a vision that motivates the employees and inspires them to attain a goal, we have set a destination. One of the key advantages of having an exact destination is the ability to know when you have gotten there or reached that destination. Since we have defined Operational Excellence as when "each and every employee can see the flow of value to the customer, and fix that flow before it breaks down," we can now test whether the operation is capable of doing this. The test is a simple one as we progress along our road map.

In a typical rapid improvement or *kaizen* event, a team is chartered to improve an area, maybe Shipping, for example. Management sets goals and challenges the team to increase the number of cases it can ship, perhaps by a hundred, without increasing labor. The team works frantically for a week, brainstorming and coming up with different ideas on how to improve the area and achieve the management goal. At the end of the week, it typically reports to management, with the leaders of the operation gathering around and the people who performed the improvements showing their before-and-after case along with the savings, answering a few questions, showing their remaining to-do list, and celebrating the achievement. As time passes, management may check in on the progress of the changes, but the employees' energy seems to fade. Therefore, more management energy is needed to get the tasks accomplished, which means that the ultimate success of the result relies on good management to provide resources and drive people to complete the tasks. Again, this method has worked in the past, although it usually works more successfully when outsiders are hired to bring a sense of shock value to the team.

The Operational Excellence approach is different. First, the team is chartered not to improve an area but to create flow through an area. It is asked to carve its first pathway where material can flow, not just a typical flow, but a robust flow where each employee knows

- What do I work on next?
- Where do I get my work from?
- How long will it take me to do my work?
- Where will I send it?
- When do I send it?

The employees would know all of this information without a schedule, without a dispatch or expedite list, without a supervisor telling them, and without management telling people what to do. Once this charter has been determined, the next step is to provide *formal education* to the team members. They go to college. The improvement or design of flow is not left up to brainstorming; it is done by following hard and fast principles of flow (we will discuss these in more detail in later chapters).

An important point here: if outsiders are brought in, they are brought in to *educate*, not to *facilitate*. Education is done first with formal books in a classroom environment, then later out on the shop floor in the targeted area. Finally, the team applies its recent education to implement self-healing flow, or flow without management, in the first section of the pathway. At the end of the implementation, the team does not present to management; it presents to the other employees who are in other areas of the flow (leaders should attend, however). The team members present what they have learned and how they have applied the principles of flow and Operational Excellence to the first section of the pathway. And before the debriefing concludes, someone has to make sure that the area passes the acid test.

The acid test is done simply by selecting someone in the operation who was not at the presentation of the report and did not hear the team members discuss what they had done and how they had done it. Think of it as keeping a person "locked away" in a side room so that he cannot possibly know what the team has done. A good way to do this is to wait until the team has finished showing what it has done, then walk into the office and get a worker, perhaps an engineer or an accountant, anyone who is not familiar with the area in which flow was implemented. Bring this person out to the area and ask her a few questions:

◆ Can you tell whether this area is on time with respect to customer demand right now?
◆ Can you tell whether things are going right or whether something is wrong?
◆ Can you tell whether the employees know what is normal flow and what is abnormal?
◆ Can you tell whether the employees know what to do when things are abnormal?

Listen for the answer. If there is hesitation, or if the worker has to ask questions back, or if she just says no, then the team has failed the acid test and has not installed Operational Excellence in the area. While having a team come up with ways to create Operational Excellence in an area and then having an independent person test the results to see whether the team has been successful may sound a bit like a cat-and-mouse game, it is quite the opposite. It is more like going for your pilot's license. You will know the test questions, and therefore you will be better at designing the flow so that you pass the test the first time. The team knows the design principles and how the design is supposed to perform, and therefore it can usually past the test the first time. This means that as we implement sections of the road map, the design is robust and performs to robust standards the first time. Teams create flow without management, flow where the employees know what to do when it starts to break down, and flow that self-heals at its first implementation. Contrast this with companies that strive to put in flow and feel that they are successful when they finally do it. Of course, that flow soon breaks down and management has to step in, forever leaving these companies on the staircase of continuous improvement.

CASE IN POINT: WOOD GROUP TURBOPOWER LLC

Rana Das is the vice president/general manager at Wood Group Turbopower LLC. The operation in Miami Lakes, Florida, overhauls turboprop engines for military and civilian aircraft. Rana was well educated in lean and was in the midst of implementing lean concepts when he attended an aerospace conference in November 2008. After learning about Operational Excellence and understanding that the key is not just to establish flow but to know whether the flow has been on time, Rana went back to his organization and began looking at its improvements in a new light.

He quickly saw that the focus of the firm's improvement efforts was only on eliminating waste. The improvements that the teams made did affect productivity, but Rana knew that there was much more. When he was called to attend the report of a kaizen event, he would listen patiently while the team presented what it had done and why the new method was better. After listening patiently, he would turn to one of the team members and ask, "Can you tell if we are on time just by watching?" Of course, the team member's heart sank a little as he replied, "Well, no, not really."

"Then keep trying," Rana would reply, heading back to his office. Soon, teams got the message that there was more to this than they had first thought. And while Rana was more enlightened concerning the concepts of Operational Excellence, he knew that his entire operation needed to know these concepts as well. Therefore, he brought in outsiders, not to facilitate and run kaizen events, but to run formal education on how to achieve Operational Excellence in an operation as complex as jet engine overhaul.

Within six months, Rana reported that not only had the operation reduced its turnaround time (which is the lead time to repair an engine and return it to the anxiously awaiting customer, the standard by which all overhaul operations are judged, along with quality) by 45 percent, but profits had gone up significantly. More important, the firm was attracting new customers and getting more orders, growing the business.

THE RESULTS OF ACHIEVING OPERATIONAL EXCELLENCE

When we set our destination as Operational Excellence, we create a road map. We design the operation to "start every time." We formally educate our employees on how to execute to the design. Each employee understands how to create true flow. The employees also understand what normal flow is, and therefore they understand what abnormal flow is. They know what to do when things are going right, and they know what to do when flow starts to break down. Very little management is needed to deliver the product to the customer, and a visitor can walk into the operation and tell whether it is on time. When this happens, we have reached the destination of Operational Excellence. Good things should be happening. The question is, exactly what are the good things, and how are they affecting the business?

Let's put aside the traditional financial measures for a minute. While Operational Excellence affects these very positively, there is much more to see from an operational standpoint. The impact of reaching Operational Excellence may be different from what you expect. While I stated earlier that at the destination of Operational Excellence each employee would see the flow of value to the customer and be able to fix it before it breaks down, that is about only half of what the destination is really about. What we are really after by achieving Operational Excellence is a positive impact on the business, or, more specifically, sustained business growth.

How will achieving Operational Excellence in the operational side of the business affect business growth? Here's the link: if the employees who build the product can also adjust and fix the flow before it breaks down, and do all this with little or no management, then what will the managers be doing, since they are not chasing parts, people, and suppliers; managing resources; and so on? In a world of Operational Excellence, managers will be busy with what's probably the first line on their job description: *growing the business*.

The concept is simple: we cannot grow the business *unless we have time* to grow the business. Where will executives, managers, and all the employees get the time to grow the business to its fullest extent if they are busy managing or maintaining the business every day? In order to grow the business, each employee should be spending time on *offense*, rather than spending time on maintenance and defense. Think about how your employees spend their time. Think about how much *management intervention* is needed to get an existing order or product to a customer each day. Think about what you could do with this time if it were dedicated to offense, or business growth.

A good way to explain this concept is to think of a soccer team. There are eleven players on the field. There is always one goalkeeper, who is on defense; and then two to four defenders; two to four midfielders, who shift between offense and defense; and anywhere from one to three strikers on offense (additional players like stoppers and sweepers might be part of the defense, too). However, if you could design the team any way you wanted, what would you *want* the configuration of the team to be? Perhaps ten players all working on offense, kicking the ball at the opponent's net, and one "super goalkeeper" who can block any shot sent his way. This "super goalkeeper" can take any order from the customer and deliver it without assistance from the other members of the team, which frees them up to score more goals.

OFFENSE AT ALL LEVELS

Although Operational Excellence will reduce the management intervention needed in the operation and allow the managers to spend their time working on offense, it's not just management but everyone in the organization to whom this applies. Each employee at every level should be working on offense. A supervisor can work with Engineering on product design changes that the customer requests; Purchasing can spend time sourcing materials for new product development; administrative assistants can research and provide contact management information for salespeople and executives. Even if employees work in a support group such as Finance and prepare tax statements each month, they must be aware that the activities they are performing are not creating offense, so these activities must be streamlined in order to allow others to have more time to work on offense.

CASE IN POINT: VIBCO VIBRATORS

VIBCO Vibrators is located in Wyoming, Rhode Island, and produces industrial-strength construction vibrators, which "are mechanical devices designed to generate a proportioned amount of vibration."[1] The vibrators do this either mechanically, hydraulically, or via alternating or direct current. The company maintains a service, production, and engineering department as well as traditional services such as customer service and reception.

While VIBCO thrives on lean production and Operational Excellence (its president even has a weekly two-hour radio show on the subject to assist other companies in Rhode Island), of special interest is how it applies these principles to its receptionist position. At most companies, the typical receptionist's job is to greet visitors, answer phones, schedule conference rooms, and perform other maintenance or perhaps even defense activities, such as updating employee records and maintaining spreadsheets. Some companies have attempted to reduce the overhead cost of the receptionist by purchasing automated phone answering systems that require customers to go through seemingly endless menus before being able to talk to an actual person, even when they are calling to purchase something. Of course, this is a barrier to both existing and potentially new customers.

VIBCO's approach is different. It is centered on offense. VIBCO values the customer contact and believes in having zero barriers between it and the customer. It is VIBCO's policy that the customer always gets a live voice when he calls; the company never wants a customer to get someone's voice mail or be put on hold. It has a receptionist who is very busy answering calls from all over the world, quickly assessing the caller's needs, and putting him through to the appropriate resource to make the sale. This might sound pretty standard, but there is much more to the activities that the receptionist does than simply answering and transferring calls with a friendly voice. She is also one of the key contributors to offense.

VIBCO values any contact with a potential customer, and the first point of contact is the receptionist. Trained well beyond transferring phone calls, the receptionist actively seeks to learn more about the potential customer while she is on the phone with him. Once he gives his company's name, she searches the Internet to research *the company to find out exactly what its business is and which of VIBCO's products it might use. While these are common client or sales management techniques, they are typically performed when a sales associate answers the phone, not by the receptionist.*

While the receptionist is performing offense activities during calls, even more impressive are the activities that she is performing when the phone is not ringing (although this is a rare occurrence at VIBCO, as its business continues to grow). These are the times when she is reviewing the companies that called and researching them further, or formally capturing the knowledge of clients' needs and potential future needs in a database. She also searches for various other locations or sites that a client may have. This information is then passed on to Sales, which contacts these other locations to let them know that one of their divisions is using VIBCO products.

In fact, just about everything that the receptionist does is fo-cused on offense, or growing the business, while other companies try to eliminate the receptionist position to save money or give the receptionist busywork to do when she is not answering calls. The learning here: offense activities can be performed at all levels of the organization once we understand the value of freeing up time and focusing our efforts on business growth.

THE OFFENSE METER

How many conference rooms are there in your company? How many offices are there where two or more people can meet and talk? How many meetings take place each day? Each week? Each time people are gathered in a room, what are they discussing? Is it offense, main-tenance, or defense? This is exactly the thinking we want each em-ployee to be aware of. Are we meeting to grow the business? Are we meeting to maintain the business, or perhaps even defend the busi-ness? Remember, most meetings are held because somewhere in the corporation, in the offices or in manufacturing, *flow is broken*. We need to have a meeting to fix the flow of information or the flow of the product.

Therefore, one of the more significant benefits of Operational Excellence is that there are very few (or perhaps zero) meetings to fix flow! Since this is one of the expected results, we should measure it. One way to do this is to put an "offense meter" outside of each conference room (see Figure 5.1). The offense meter is a simple pie chart diagram and can be broken into a few categories: immediate offense, long-term offense, maintenance, defense, flow is broken, and other. Offense is direct business growth, or activities that generate revenue. There may be subcategories or layers in a hierarchy based on the return of cash. For example, reviewing the needs of a potential new client prior to the final sales call may result in revenue being generated that day, while a meeting on a new market venture may not return cash for a year. As employees enter the room, they adjust a movable pointer on the chart to the appropriate category, thereby allowing everyone in the office to see what type of activity is happening in that room in terms of business growth.

Maintenance covers meetings that you may have to hold but that do not generate revenue—human resources, employee reviews, new policies, accounting, things like this. Fixing flow means that something has gone wrong with the delivery of a product or information, and we have to meet to reset priorities, expedite the product or information, or patch flow back up. Defense occurs when we have to make up for something that has gone wrong: quality problems reached the customer, the wrong items were shipped, or rework of any kind, including reworking of information, is needed. A category of "other" might also be needed, depending upon your business. One of the necessary attributes of an offense meter is that it is color-coded. The "offense" section should be colored green, with the brightest green representing the most immediate generation of revenue, while darker shades of green are reserved for offense that will take more

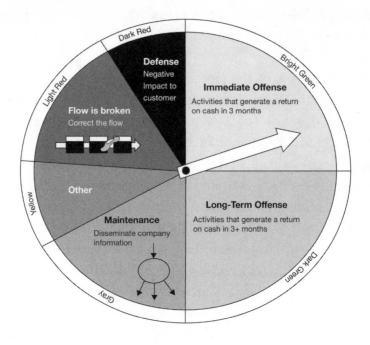

Mtg. Color	Color Type	Mtg. Type	Date	Duration	Details
○	Bright Green	IO	4/5	30 min.	Conference call with customer
○	Dark Green	LTO	4/7	45 min.	Update marketing literature
●	Light Red	FIB	4/8	15 min.	Mtg. on late quotes
○	Gray	M	4/14	30 min.	Review health-care plan
○	Bright Green	IO	4/17	20 min.	Develop new client list
○	Dark Green	LTO	4/22	25 min	New article for website

Figure 5.1 *The Offense Meter*

time to turn into revenue. Make maintenance gray or neutral, "flow is broken" light red, and defense dark red.

Beside the offense meter, there is a blank chart. On this chart, employees indicate why they met. They enter a colored dot that indicates the category on the meter, along with the date, duration, and subject of the meeting. All of this means that a quick walk by the conference rooms and a glance at the offense meter and the history chart can let us know how much meeting time we are spending on growing or repairing the business. Companies that achieve Operational Excellence will see a red dot on their sheets only about every two or three months.

LEADERSHIP IN OPERATIONAL EXCELLENCE

Leadership is considered one of the key ingredients of business performance. The subject of leadership has been covered in many books and articles, has been the theme of many conferences, and much, much more. As mentioned earlier, leadership is also considered to be the driving force behind continuous improvement. Without strong leadership, the organization goes up and down the staircase of continuous improvement. The subject of leadership gets a lot of attention, and with good reason: it is needed. People need to be led, and some people are naturals at leading, while others can learn to become good leaders. While leadership is key to achieving Operational Excellence, the type of leadership may not be the type of leadership that companies are used to, nor is it the traditional type of leadership that we hear or read about.

There are significant differences. Let's think about leadership in the sport of American football. In American football, there are many leaders for a team of 52 active roster players. There are offensive coordinators, defensive coordinators, quarterback coaches, and, of course, the head coach. They devise strategy and orchestrate plays in order to move the ball forward through the opponent's defense.

Plays are written down in playbooks, and everyone has a role in each particular play: whom to block, what pattern to run, where to look for the hole or gap in the line. Leaders drive heavy "standard work" through the use of the playbook, and when a play is not executed correctly, there has usually been a breakdown in the standard work, which means more practicing of the plays during the week.

During the game, the plays are sent in to the quarterback, as he is the front-line leader, the one who is charged with making it happen. He shares the play with the rest of his teammates, they go to the line, and then he double-checks to make sure that everyone is in the right position. He reviews the defense and, if necessary, can adjust the play by shouting instructions to the team. When everything is set, he initiates the play by signaling to the center to hike the ball. He tries to execute the play like what was done in practice as possible, but he makes adjustments as the defense closes in. Sometimes the quarterback has to improvise and do what he can in order to achieve the objective of a first down, or just to move the ball forward as far as he can. His teammates react to the improvisation, too.

The point here is that, as in a business organization, there is a leader, or the head coach. He leads his staff members, who are the other coaches, and they work in their respective areas, then meet with other coaches to determine the game plan. They develop standard work, then lead the players to carry out their roles in each play (or follow the standard work). In the end, they give the quarterback the responsibility for leading the team through each play during the game. They also provide the quarterback and other players with guidance during the game.

Contrast this to rugby; it's a different game altogether. While the premise is the same (move the ball past your opponents to a goal line), the style of play is completely different. The player who is carrying the ball must try to penetrate the line on his own. His teammates cannot block for him. The player can pass the ball backward to another player, but he cannot throw the ball forward. While there are set plays that have been developed, there is no stoppage of play during which coaches send in plays, nor are there huddles in which a quarterback tells everyone what to do. There are strategies, and players know where to be in order to be ready to receive a pass from a teammate in case he decides to pass to them. However, the intent is to move the ball through the defensive line, and being able to take advantage of that line at any moment is the key. (See Figure 5.2.)

In American football, there are leaders off the field (the head coach and the other coaches) and a leader on the field (the quarterback) who executes the plays. In rugby, while coaches develop skills and strategy, who exactly is the leader on the field? The answer is, *whoever has to be.* American football is more "command and control," where management sets the plays and trains the players to execute them. After each play, management makes the decision on which play to execute next. The managers do not want or expect the players to make decisions on their own. Maybe some small decisions are necessary as the play progresses, but the players are still following the play and the standard work that they were trained to do by management (the coaches).

Rugby is more fluid. The expectation is that each player will be aware of what is going on in terms of the progress of the ball through the opponent's line. The players will adapt their position as needed to

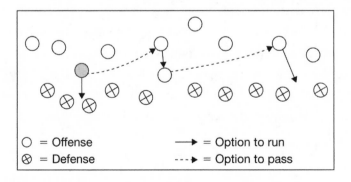

Figure 5.2 *The Rugby Line*

best assist in moving the ball through the line. Sometimes they lead (when they have the ball), and other times they are supporting the movement of the ball. They are not "empowered" to make decisions, as that would imply that management has passed the right to make decisions down to the players. Management has not done this, as the game of rugby is played by having the players make decisions out on the field while they are playing the game. In other words, managers never had control of making decisions in the first place because of the design of the game. They are not capable of making decisions because the structure of the game or the system does not allow them to do this.

Instead, each player learns how to lead when it's his turn, when the ball comes to him. Each player also knows where to be to best support the movement of the ball (again, not necessarily supporting the current leader) through the defense. And whether he is the player with the ball and leading or just positioning himself to help the team move the ball forward, each player *knows the destination* to which the ball is supposed to go (the goal line), and all the players work to move the ball to that destination.

In our operation, if we depend on the leaders to develop the plays, provide the strategy, and come up with a plan, then assign people and manage resources, and finally adjust the plan and resources as they see fit to reduce cost and continuously improve, we will forever be dependent upon management to determine where we should improve and how we should improve, and management will be responsible for sustaining the improvements. As in American football, we won't be able to move the ball forward without our coaches (management) and huddles after each play, which are also known as meetings in the world of operations.

Nine Tough Questions
on Continuous Improvement

CHAPTER

6

↓

Preparing People to Jump

There are companies that have applied the principles of Operational Excellence and "jumped" their operational performance to support offense quickly. Some have achieved the results previously described, while others are well on their way. We will review some of these companies in Part IV of this book, our case study section. While these companies have used continuous improvement to transform their operation to support business growth in a short amount of time, most companies are working on eliminating waste to increase productivity and efficiency, and they are bound to the staircase of continuous improvement.

All companies have the same goal: to make money, grow, and be profitable. The reason why we should strive to make our operations perform better is the same for all companies. In general terms, *how* to make our operations better is the same for all companies as well. We use tools, change the culture, and add strong leadership. If *why* and *how* to improve are basically the same for the operational side of most businesses, what separates the ones that have jumped from the ones that are on the staircase? If the tools are similar, and the focus on culture change is there as well, why do some operations perform significantly better, support overall business growth, and do it in a shorter amount of time than other companies using basically the same tools? The answer is that the companies that jumped were able to answer nine tough questions about their continuous improvement efforts, and some of them were able to answer these questions even before they began a formal continuous improvement program, which substantially increased the rate at which they jumped and the height they achieved.

Why are these nine questions so important? What is so significant about having the right answers to them? How do they get companies off the staircase of continuous improvement and enable them to jump to Operational Excellence? Because in order to *do* things differently, we first have to *see* things differently, and that is exactly what these nine questions allow us to do.

These nine tough questions, correctly answered, get people to see. They allow the employees to see where the operation is going and where they are going, too. They also create the foundational thinking behind continuous improvement and Operational Excellence. They provide the insight, the awareness, and the change in thinking that are needed to enable the jump. They shape the need for a new engine design for operations that starts every time. They allow each employee to see the flaws in the old design and the higher performance in the new design. They also allow each employee to understand the need for a new design in order to get this performance, as the present approach to improvement will not yield it.

But the design alone is not enough. People will be working to the design specifications, or the principles of Operational Excellence, which means that a good deal of formal education will be needed. And since we will be unveiling a new kind of engine, not just an update of the existing one, we will also need to change the thinking of each employee in order to support the design. In other words, we need to address the culture, too. The design will be forever debated unless everyone understands the why behind the design. Explaining the why in very simple and practical terms is the key to preparing to jump to Operational Excellence. It sets the foundation or provides the alignment that allows each employee to understand and want to contribute to the improvement of the operation *in a specified manner*.

While employees are often enthusiastic about performing *kaizen* events, eliminating waste, and increasing productivity, this enthusiasm is created by giving them free rein to brainstorm and create ways to do these things. This is very rewarding. However, we are now going to teach the employees a set method to follow to make the improvements, similar to an engineer designing a new engine. They will have to do some homework, study, and challenge themselves to follow a process to make the improvements. We want to make sure that they fully understand why they are doing this in order to keep the enthusiasm going forward.

These questions should also give the employees another very important insight. They will become aware that there will be no change of direction and that Operational Excellence is not the new flavor of the month. They will become aware that the things they have done in bringing about continuous improvement will not be undone, and that they will still need the tools that they are using. What they have learned is still applicable and is needed if the operation is to achieve Operational Excellence. They will learn that if they have an existing continuous improvement program, these questions will clarify it and give it a direction and purpose other than just to reduce cost or eliminate waste. They will learn that the correct answers will give their continuous improvement program a turbo boost, not slow it down in any way. They will add significant momentum to the continuous improvement effort, along with new energy and a robust path for that energy to follow.

These questions will certainly generate good discussion and will provide insight into the current continuous improvement program. Most likely, there will be many different answers to these questions. The various answers will demonstrate that each person in the company has a different concept of exactly where the operation is going and what he is supposed to do in his specific area to help move the operation in that direction. Although I am asking these questions of you, the reader, I suggest that you also ask them of your own people as an exercise in order to provide the most effective learning.

Start with the senior staff members, and then have them share this exercise with the rest of the organization. Facilitate the session and record the answers on a flip chart. In order to guide you through the process, I have provided the typical answers that you may hear. The answers to the nine questions will help you diagnose whether your company is following the staircase of continuous improvement and getting a little better each day, or whether it has an exact heading and a foundation to jump to Operational Excellence. If it turns out that you are climbing the staircase and trying to improve each day, don't worry; I will provide the answers that will help enable the operation to jump. By going through the questions, we are taking the team through a process. The questions need to be asked in sequence in order to follow the process. To help understand how this process will work in real life (and I do suggest that you do it with your team), I will first provide a list of typical answers to each question in order to contrast them with the answers that enable Operational Excellence.

Here is how you can get started: Bring your team into a conference room. Assign one or two people to be scribes (they can participate as well). Hand each of them a stack of sticky notes. Pick a few areas of the company that have representatives present. For our example, we will use Manufacturing, Engineering, Purchasing, and Sales. Tell the team that you are going to write a question on the board and ask the same question for each area. You want each person to give as many answers as she can. Each answer will be written down on a sticky note and placed on the board.

There are some rules. No one can comment on or ask questions about any of the answers given. No one can talk unless he is giving an answer. No one except the facilitator can question anything, and she can do so only to clarify a statement from the person who gave it. There are no right or wrong answers, and no answer gets judged. With all this having been said, let's get to the questions. Ready?

7

The First Question: Why Do We Do Continuous Improvement?

Inside the operation, we seek continuous improvement. We drive continuous improvement to eliminate non-value-added activities. We target areas such as cost, lead time, quality, on-time delivery, inventory, and other measurements, usually dictated by the finance department. It all makes sense. If we go into an operation, pull the senior staff—supervisors, management, continuous improvement people, Engineering, and other support groups—into a conference room, and ask them, "Why do we do continuous improvement?" we will probably get answers similar to these:

- Eliminate waste.
- Improve productivity.
- Improve quality.
- Increase efficiency.
- Increase capacity.
- Promote teamwork.
- In general, foster a continuous improvement culture.

If we could summarize all the answers given in one statement, perhaps it would go something like this: "The reason we do continuous improvement is to make our operation perform better each day." This may seem like an excellent answer.

However, this means that each person in the operation should look at his area or span of control and make it perform better. The operations leader looks at performance from one perspective (inventory turns, performance to budget, and so on), the operations management team looks at it from another (lines running, good quality, quick changeover times, and so on), and the operators on the floor have a different view altogether (just make sure the parts are here). "Making the operation perform better" also assumes that the right measurements are in place to guide each individual to make the right decisions based on her specific role. The result is that we drive people to do what they do as efficiently as possible and hope that their collective activities will make the overall operation more efficient. Management coordinates all the departments to make sure that our islands of efficiency result in the entire operation being more efficient.

In some companies—the ones with strong leadership and management—this does work to some degree. However, even if the overall operation continues to perform more efficiently than it did the day before, this does not mean that the right product is being shipped to the right customer at the right time. It could just mean that the operation is more efficient in financial terms or that we have succeeded in reaching an arbitrary goal set by management. Maybe we have succeeded just in making our resources more efficient. But did these activities provide a short-term gain for tomorrow, or have they contributed to the growth and profitability of the company for years to come?

While some of our continuous improvement activities might perhaps improve our *operation*, how many of them actually improve our *business performance*, whereby "improve our business performance" we mean getting more money to the bottom line, increasing our market share and business growth, and continuing to increase shareholder value?

If we answer the question, "Why do we do continuous improvement?" by stating, "The reason we do continuous improvement is to make our operation perform better each day," we are bound to climb the staircase of continuous improvement year after year.

The right answer in this case, or the one that enables us to jump to Operational Excellence, is, "The reason we do continuous improvement is to grow the business." Business growth comes in the form of increased market share, increased top-line revenue, more profit, and increased shareholder value.

Let's dive into this answer a little further. While we may commonly think that we do continuous improvement for the purpose of making our operation more efficient, the question really is, "Efficient to whom?" We can make our operation seem more efficient in terms of what *we* see every day: labor utilization, machine utilization, and so on. But in reality, we should be striving to be efficient to our *customers*, providing them with what they want, when they want it, and how they want it, in order to achieve growth within our existing customer base and grow by gaining new customers. The intent is to have the operation be so good that our customers enjoy doing business with us because our operation "starts" and delivers their order every time, without interruption. With this engine embedded in the business, we use it to grow our market share and maybe even branch into new markets or make acquisitions.

This way of thinking is critical, because we want each employee to understand that continuous improvement is not about *getting a little better* each day, but about *growing our business* each day. It's about bringing more money to our top *line*, as well as our bottom line, each day and enabling our business to grow each day. That's why we do continuous improvement. We are trying to get each employee to thoroughly and completely understand that this is a business, and that its success is measured by its growth, its capture of new market share, and its ability to sustain top-line as well as bottom-line results. We are trying to change the current thinking that continuous improvement is about waste elimination and efficiency to the idea that continuous improvement is about business growth. Eliminating waste and improving efficiency is a by-product of continuous improvement. After all, does it really matter how much waste we eliminate or how efficient we are if the revenue does not come in on the top line?

8

The Second Question: What Is the Best Way to Improve?

There are many tools, methods, and approaches to improvement. Most of these methods center around continuous improvement. Some of them have been developed recently, but most of them have been around for many years. Most companies that are very active in continuous improvement use just about all of them in one form or another. How do we decide which approach to use? How do we know which one is right? Who decides? Most leaders go with what has been successful in the past, perhaps even with the things that were successful at a previous company for which they worked.

If we were to ask what is the best way to continuously improve, we would probably get the following answers about he best way to improve:

- ◆ Have a burning platform.
- ◆ Do *kaizen* events or rapid improvement events.
- ◆ Educate people in the latest tools and techniques of continuous improvement.
- ◆ Empower each employee to see waste and eliminate it.
- ◆ Have leaders drive continuous improvement.
- ◆ Monitor and measure results.
- ◆ Motivate people by rewarding them for their improvements.
- ◆ Get everyone involved.

If we ask our group to summarize all of these answers in one statement, perhaps it would be something like, "The best way to improve is to create a culture of continuous improvement." This might seem to be a good answer because it doesn't talk about tools or leadership. It talks about everyone's way of thinking, about ways to improve the operation using tools to implement changes. By answering this question in this manner, the mindset of the operation's management team is that we have to change the thinking of every employee so that the employees always see waste, seek out waste, and find ways to eliminate waste each day.

This means that we want everyone to be thinking about continuous improvement. We want people to have improvement tools such as 5S, SMED, *kaizen,* and poka-yoke and use them to seek out waste and eliminate it. The thought is that we will create an army of people who find ways to continuously improve, and thus continuous improvement will happen everywhere. Each person will have the tools and knowledge needed to improve his own area. Each person will constantly challenge himself to come up with *ideas* for improving, or brainstorm with others in order to come up with *ideas* for improving. Think of it as a wildfire of continuous improvement. The fire of improvement creates momentum. It spreads, burning fast. However, it can also burn out of control, going in whichever direction the wind blows it.

Even if we are successful in creating a culture of continuous improvement, when we have no strategy or plan for how our efforts will drive business growth, our initiatives will create islands of efficiency that have a limited impact on the ability of our continuous improvement program to lead to increased market share and an increase in shareholder value. Creating a culture of continuous improvement is like scattering seeds throughout the company and simply hoping that they take root and grow.

The real answer to the question, "What is the best way to improve?" is a little bit different. The answer is to communicate to each employee exactly where the operation is going *from a business perspective,* thereby providing a *destination* for our continuous improvement efforts. Then, we want to provide all the employees with a "road map" or process that will guide them to this destination as it relates to their environment.

Therefore, the best way to continuously improve is to educate each employee on exactly where we are going, provide him with a process for getting there, and then guide him through the process. By doing this, not only will we be able to get the results that we seek, but we'll be able to get them much faster than we would by simply scattering seeds throughout the company and hoping that those seeds take root and grow. If we answer the question, "What is the best way to improve?" by stating, "The best way to improve is to create a culture of continuous improvement," we are bound to climb the staircase of continuous improvement year after year. If we provide the answer, "The best way to improve the operation is to set a destination and provide a road map for getting there," then we have begun to educate the workforce with the idea that improvement means following a predefined road map that will yield an overall improvement in the operation and the business. In other words, if we follow the road map step by step, we move the performance of the operation from point A to point B, which will also affect our business performance and enable us to grow the business.

CHAPTER

9

The Third Question: How Do We Know Where to Improve?

Even if we have educated our workforce about the tools needed to eliminate waste and our people are motivated to improve the operation, how do they know where in the operation they should apply their tools and efforts if they are to make improvements? Who decides? Should we empower everyone who has been trained to decide for himself? Should it be up to the leader or a steering committee? Should we target quick wins so that our efforts build momentum? How we approach the topic of *where* to improve next is directly related to how fast the operation improves. The question of where to improve next may be a little more interesting than the previous two, and it is likely to provide insight into how the team views the need for improvement. It will also stir up some good debate and provide insight into the team's thoughts and feelings on who decides where to improve and how. The list of typical answers to the question, "How do we know where to improve?" may include responses such as

- ◆ Wherever we can show results fast to build momentum.
- ◆ Wherever the boss tells us.
- ◆ Wherever we can get quick wins.
- ◆ Wherever the biggest problem lies. We use a Pareto analysis (see Figure 9.1) to find the biggest problem. We solve that problem and then tackle the next biggest one.

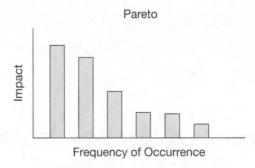

Figure 9.1 *Pareto Analysis of Problems*

◆ Using impact vs. effort charts (see Figure 9.2), whatever area would give the biggest impact for the least amount of effort.
◆ We review customer feedback and target areas that show problems.
◆ Wherever we will get the best financial return.

Summarizing these responses in one statement is a little more difficult. Perhaps it would be something like, "We decide where to continuously improve based on where performance is lacking and the resources that are available."

Typically, the people who decide where to continuously improve are the leaders of the operation, since they are in charge of the operation's overall performance. Usually, they are senior people with vast

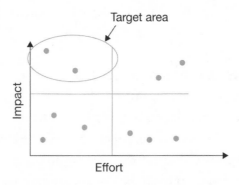

Figure 9.2 *Impact vs. Effort Chart*

experience. They receive information from various sources and decide where improvements should happen next to benefit the operation, usually focusing on the biggest problem in the operation at the time of the decision. However, as this happens over and over again, it often turns into the Whac-A-Mole® method. (Whac-A-Mole is an arcade game in which a mallet is used to hit plastic moles popping out of different holes at random and in rapid succession. As soon as one mole is hit, another one pops up someplace else right away, and the player is forced to attack whichever one comes up next over and over again.) Wherever the biggest problem is right now, go attack it. When the next one pops up, we'll attack that one.

This approach drives our continuous improvement efforts toward fixing the largest problem or the largest cause of pain to the operation *right now.* Essentially, we are seeking to plug holes in the operation. Even if we apply root-cause problem-solving tools to plug the holes permanently, the approach is still to seek out and plug the holes to get better, to "whack the mole" that happens to appear at the time.

Contrast this with having a process to follow that guides us on how to design the operation in order to contribute to business growth, which results in increased market share and more available cash to make acquisitions, all of which are part of growing the *top line.* For example, part of the design for our operation would be to implement end-to-end, self-healing flow that does not require daily management. The result of this would be to reduce lead times and inventory (cash) and to free up management to work on offense and grow the business (market share). The design for our operations includes the office, or business process, too. This needs to be synchronized with the flow of manufacturing, similar to electricity flowing to a spark plug at the correct time in order for a car engine to start.

If we continue to use the approach of finding the biggest problem, we find the areas of opportunity that management identifies as being biggest, then begin attacking these areas without first aligning the effort with the end goal of Operational Excellence and business growth. In fact, making the connection at all would be difficult. Even though more progressive companies have adopted a value stream approach, seeking to implement flow from the receiving deck to the shipping deck (which is a step in the right direction), the intent here is typically to eliminate waste and reduce cost. Value streams themselves are designed with a set of principles (and these will be outlined in future chapters), yet companies still map out the flow of their current state, then brainstorm what they can do to design their future state *without applying these principles*. The result, again, is incremental improvement.

For example, a company may prepare a current-state map of its parts flow from Machining to Assembly. People brainstorm and decide to put in a *kanban* or pull system between Machining and Assembly. They decide that one of the biggest problems in Machining is downtime. Therefore, they plan a *kaizen* event to reduce downtime. They perform the *kaizen* event, reduce downtime, install a pull system, and get rewarded for it. Soon, the pull system requires daily management to produce what Assembly needs because of erratic downstream demand from Assembly, where there is no flow. The pull system itself eventually fails because it is unable to respond to the volatility in demand from Assembly. Management is back to expediting and setting priorities in the Machining area, destroying the improvements that had been made earlier.

This result, two steps forward and one step back, happens when we try to "assess" where improvement is needed and apply it there. The result is slow improvement. To avoid this, we need to set a destination, or how the new operation engine should be designed and should perform. And when we think about the performance of the operation, we are not talking about financial measurements; we are measuring whether it is performing as designed, something that each employee should be able to see. These are measurements that the employees can do something about in each of their respective areas, even the office.

Having a road map tells us exactly how to get to our destination. The road map is based on the principles of Operational Excellence, which we will cover in detail later on. Educating people on the destination, the principles of Operational Excellence, and the road map for getting to that destination will keep us from the "two steps forward and one step back" approach. It will also keep us from brainstorming and creating the next target area to improve, and also negate the urge to just eliminate waste wherever we see it. The road map not only should provide the method at a high level but also should outline the step-by-step transformation of the operation at all levels and in all areas. In manufacturing, the plan is broken down by product families; in the office, it is broken down by process families, right down to the process level so that each employee knows how her specific area is connected to the overall road map. The road map should show us signs along the way, letting us know that we are going in the right direction, we are getting there.

The correct answer to our question, "How do we know where to improve?" is, "By following the road map." If we answer the question in a way similar to the summary statement, "We decide where to continuously improve based on where performance is lacking and the resources that are available," we are again bound to climb the staircase of continuous improvement year after year.

So far, we have answered three questions about continuous improvement. These initial questions are key if we are to align our improvement efforts. Not only do they allow us to move quickly, but they are also laying the groundwork that will enable us to leapfrog the staircase of continuous improvement. Let's recap our starting questions and answers to build a strong foundation before going further. The questions we asked were

1. Why do we do continuous improvement?
2. What is the best way to improve?
3. How do we know where to improve?

The typical responses to these questions that we gave, the ones that cause us to climb the staircase of continuous improvement year after year, are as follows:

1. Why do we do continuous improvement? "The reason we do continuous improvement is to make our operation perform better each day."
2. What is the best way to improve? "The best way to improve is to create a culture of continuous improvement."
3. How do we know where to improve? "We decide where to continuously improve based on where performance is lacking and the resources that are available."

Again, while these might seem like good answers, at best they will drive us up the staircase of continuous improvement year after year. The right answers to these questions, and the ones that lay the groundwork that will enable us to leapfrog the staircase of continuous improvement, are as follows:

1. Why do we do continuous improvement? "The reason we do continuous improvement is to grow the business."
2. What is the best way to improve? "The best way to improve the operation is to set a destination and create a road map for getting there."
3. How do we know where to improve? "We know how to improve by following the road map."

The first three questions set the stage for rapid improvement by letting each employee know that our improvement efforts will not be subjective. They will not be based on management goals and brainstorming. Improvement does not mean just getting better; it means moving the company from point A to point B. To do that, we describe exactly what point B is and provide a road map based on principles for getting there. With that in mind, our next set of questions will break down the myths of flow and begin to shake out exactly where each employee thinks his continuous improvement program is taking him. We will most likely find that there is some confusion about flow, and that each person, even in management, has a different idea of exactly what the company is trying to accomplish with its continuous improvement program. Let's start by understanding the true need for flow.

CHAPTER
10

The Fourth Question: Why Do We Strive to Create Flow?

From lean teachings, we have learned that the best way to eliminate waste is to create true value stream flow. Flow means building a product in progressive steps from raw material to the customer without stopping, without interruptions, without any rework loops, and without any steps backward. This includes the flow of material from our receiving deck to our shipping deck, the flow of information in our business processes, the flow of material in the supply chain, and even the flow of knowledge in our product development processes. In all cases, we strive to create flow, as it is crucial to improving the operation. The question is, why? Some of the typical answers

- ◆ Eliminate waste.
- ◆ Increase throughput.
- ◆ Increase efficiency.
- ◆ Respond better to customers.
- ◆ Reduce inventory.
- ◆ Reduce lead time.
- ◆ Increase productivity.

The theme in these answers is to do more with less—to achieve more production with less inventory, labor, and time. We might summarize these statements by saying, "We strive to create flow because it is the most efficient way to produce."

In the last decade, creating flow has made a significant impact in terms of reducing lead times and inventories, as well as increasing inventory turns in many operations. Companies have placed a great deal of emphasis on creating flow in their operations, no matter how big or cumbersome their product may be. In the 1990s, Boeing management made history by cutting a channel in the production floor, installing a chain conveyor in it, and building aircraft by actually pulling them through the factory as they were being built. They created a moving line so that they could apply the concept of flow in building a product as large as a jet airliner. It was a huge undertaking, yet Boeing knew that flow was the best way to produce, so the company took on the challenge and was successful. This was touted as a model of efficiency, and many companies that produced large products also began to follow suit and install moving lines.

Again, the question is, why? Why did Boeing spend the money, time, and effort to install a moving line for a product as big as a jet airliner? Financially, this had to be justified. Did the payback from the increased productivity support the expense? Why did other companies follow suit? To improve efficiency, increase their productivity, or better utilize their resources? While many companies have created flow for these reasons, that's *not* why we strive to create flow. There's really only one reason we strive to create flow in our business processes or manufacturing operations, and that reason is simple: *so we can see when flow stops.*

What separates a good operation that applies lean principles and achieves value stream flow from a great company that achieves Operational Excellence is knowing what to do when flow stops, because it will. No matter how good the value stream design is; no matter how we size and resize pull systems or supermarkets; no matter how much we work on uptime, setup reduction, and process control; no matter how much we train the operators; and no matter how much we work on the supply chain to get material to the right place at the right time, eventually flow is going to stop. And what we do about it counts.

However, if we don't build a robust system of flow in manufacturing, the office, and the supply chain, we cannot recognize that flow has stopped, and herein lies the fundamental difference between the traditional thinking about lean and Operational Excellence. In lean, we build flow to eliminate waste and deliver product at the rate of customer demand. In Operational Excellence, we build flow at the rate of customer demand to see when flow stops. *Eliminating waste is a by-product of creating this flow.*

Let's go back to our large jet airliner example. When a jet airliner was built in a large bay with hundreds of workers, it was a scene of heavy activity. However, although quite a bit of activity was taking place, it was impossible for an operator, supervisor, manager, executive, or anyone else to tell if everything was going right or if something was wrong just by looking at the aircraft. No one could tell if the aircraft was being built on time to customer demand, if it was being built in the proper sequence, if the exact number of people were working at the right positions, or if the right material was being delivered at the right time. No one could see the disruptions to production, and disruptions occurred, as getting the right parts to the right place with the right people was always a challenge.

While the disruptions were being dealt with, the managers would redirect workers to work someplace else so that they remained productive. It was the job and the responsibility of the manager to handle disruptions in her particular area. She would handle them in the best way she could, even if what she did affected another area. In short, there was no visibility of the disruptions that stopped production. The aircraft was buried in a sea of activity that left the overall operation blind to the lack of progress. The only people who knew about issues in the overall production were the managers, and most of the rest of the organization found out through meetings, where managers tried to patch up or redirect the flow and get it back on track.

When we talk about creating flow in order to see when flow stops, we mean that everyone in the organization should be able to see when it stops, no matter what position he holds or what job he does. Anyone can walk through the area, just look at the process, and tell if it is on time to customer demand, if it is ahead or behind, or if it has stopped. And he can do this just by looking at and watching the process, without asking any questions or reviewing any computer reports.

By creating flow, we are essentially applying the age-old adage, "Lower the water to see the rocks below." We cannot have flow if we have disruptions, and we cannot solve disruptions if we cannot see them. We try to expose the disruptions that stop flow so that we can see them, similar to seeing the rocks below the water. As Boeing has proved, the size of the product does not matter; we need to be able to see the flow of product to the customer so that we can see when flow stops.

However, this does not mean that we should necessarily build large products on moving conveyors in order to create flow. Quite the contrary, in fact. If we know that the intent is to see when flow stops, this opens up other methods of creating flow that are just as effective and avoid the expense of putting in large mechanical conveyors. One method is to break up the material that the operators use to build the equipment into carts, with each cart representing a preset amount of assembly time. For example, let's say that a cart has four hours' worth of material on it. By presenting a cart of material every four hours and removing the empty cart from the previous four hours, we would know whether the large product (which might take weeks to build) is on time within four hours. How? Because at the end of every four hours, we should be able to take away an empty cart; if we cannot, then we know that the process is behind and flow has stopped.

The ability to see when flow stops is crucial in our business processes, too. Here, the flow of information is often very difficult to see, and it is often difficult to tell whether our business processes are on time. But we should still strive to create flow in our business processes so that we can see when the flow of information has stopped.

Just as in manufacturing, there are principles for creating flow in the office. The concept of a workflow cycle (which I will describe in later chapters) sets physical pathways along which information flows, and also gives the timing of the information flow down these pathways. The result is that workers in the office know where and when information should flow, and they can tell whether this flow is on time.

For example, suppose the final step in preparing a quote for the customer happens during a workflow cycle that begins at 1:00 p.m. and is completed by 2:30 p.m. each day. At the completion of the workflow cycle, finished quotes are sent to Sales (the information flow) via a standard e-mail (a preset pathway). If work backs up to a predetermined point during the workflow cycle, the workers see that the flow is becoming abnormal, and a signal is sent to bring in another engineer to assist them. The flow is adjusted by the people in the flow to ensure that customers gets their quotes when promised in a short amount of time. And by the way, Sales won't have to be making phone calls during the day to chase the status of the quote, and they won't have to make excuses to the customer at the end of the day for why the quote wasn't completed on time. A salesperson can tell the customer to expect a phone call or e-mail at 3:00 p.m. with the finished quote, and the customer receives the quote by then. Of course, being dependable with accurate quotes in a short amount of time is a competitive advantage when it comes to winning business and customers, as well as growing the top line along with market share as we capture new customers with a robust quoting process that does not rely on management to set priorities and expedite certain quotes.

The same holds true in the supply chain. We want the supply chain to flow at the rate of customer demand, and we want to be able to see when that flow stops. We want to know whether the supply chain is on time or whether there is a problem before there is a disruption to the flow in our facility. Yes, this is much more challenging in the supply chain. For example, when we are working with new suppliers, how much time and effort do we put into determining whether the supplier will be on time? And not through management and phone calls, but through a system that everyone can see. Yet, to build a robust supply chain, this point needs to be emphasized.

If we just negotiate a price and a delivery date, then leave it up to the supplier to deliver to that date, we usually find out at the last minute that there is an interruption to our flow in the supply chain, and management is forced to react. If we had a binary signal that told the supplier send or don't send, if that signal originated from a single source and was received at the supplier by a single receiver, with standard work for both the sending and receiving of the signal (similar to an electric circuit), and if this signal was visual, then anyone could tell if our flow was broken simply through the signaling method used.

While creating flow is very effective in eliminating waste, reducing inventory, and reducing lead times, companies that achieve Operational Excellence know that the true reason we create flow is to be able to see when flow stops. We want to see when flow stops so that we can educate and enable the people in the flow to correct the problem before it becomes catastrophic and customers do not get their orders. We also do not want management jumping in to correct flow by making decisions; we would like to correct the flow using some type of standard work that the workers in the flow follow. Remember, we want managers and everyone else in the company working on offense, not sitting in meetings trying to get orders to customers.

If we answered our question "Why do we strive to create flow?" by stating something along the lines of, "We strive to create flow because it is the most efficient way to produce," then once again, we are on the staircase of continuous improvement. The correct answer here, the one that enables us to jump to Operational Excellence is, "to see when flow stops."

11

The Fifth Question: What Causes the Death of Flow?

As mentioned earlier, a value stream is defined as all the activities, both value-added and non-value-added, that are required to bring product from raw material to the customer. One of the most emphasized guidelines in creating a lean value stream is continuous flow, which we will discuss in future chapters. Why is this guideline discussed so much? Because a value stream that flows at the rate of customer demand is a healthy value stream. A value stream that can adapt to changing customer demand is a healthy value stream. Value stream health is derived from flow. In other words, *flow gives the value stream life.*

Value streams that have constant interruptions in flow are not as healthy as they could be; in fact, they are ill. Some value streams that become ill get better. They receive the attention of management. Those in management get together, they have a meeting, they make decisions, they set direction, and the value stream is given treatment. It heals, and flow resumes. Other value streams become ill and do not survive. The flow that gave the value stream life is no longer present. Processes are no longer robustly connected to each other through binary signals. Schedules, priority lists, expedites, supervisors, and the outcomes of endless meetings now tell each process what to make next. The activities and processes required to build the product still exist, but management oversees and directs them in order to deliver the product to the customer. Only the shell of the value stream remains. For all intents and purposes, the value stream has died.

Why does this happen? Why do value streams that took a great deal of effort and many months, if not years, to implement become ill and die? In some companies, why were value streams the way of the future years ago, only to fall apart under the pressure of cost, outsourcing, and other management initiatives? What would cause all this? It is important that we learn from this; after all, if we're going to spend a lot of time designing a value stream with robust flow, shouldn't we understand why it fails prior to designing it? There will probably be a long list of answers that will mention leadership, management, and changing priorities. Some of the typical answers you may get when you ask, "What causes the death of flow?" are

◆ The leader who drives it leaves the company.
◆ There is no buy-in from the top.
◆ There is no support from the top.
◆ Other projects take priority.
◆ There is a lack of leadership.
◆ There is a lack of resources.
◆ It's the flavor of the month.
◆ There is no end-to-end value stream manager.
◆ There is no continuous education.

Let's summarize these into one concise statement: our value streams die because of a lack of long-term commitment from the top. Improvement is most successful when it is driven from the top. Leaders try to embed it in the culture. If the leader's emphasis goes somewhere else before improvement has been embedded in the culture, then the improvement initiative slides backward. When this happens, the focus of the leader's attention moves away from value stream flow and instead is placed squarely on finding ways to get the orders to the customers, make the budget, or make his boss happy. The commitment to value stream flow seems to fade, and eventually things revert back to the way they were before value stream initiatives.

As discussed earlier, value stream flow is created by connecting processes with fixed pathways and binary signals. Essentially, we design a system for the flow of material and information by creating flow paths with binary switches, similar to those in an electric circuit. Material and information are moved based on signals (send/don't send), and material is moved along fixed pathways. It is a good system, and one that is disciplined and has standard work for flow. It takes quite a bit of time to design robust value stream flow, and even more time to implement it. By contrast, how much time do we spend on what to do when flow stops or there is a failure in the system? What about what to do when a signal is not sent or the pathways are full? In short, what design do we have for when flow breaks down?

We spend months, if not years, implementing our design in order to achieve our vision of end-to-end flow at the rate of customer demand. Then, the first time flow stops, what happens? Management (which is precisely what we tried to design out of our process by creating end-to-end flow) is called in to take action. Why is management called in? Because the people building the product have not been educated on what to do when flow becomes abnormal or stops altogether. Slowly, the flow becomes dependent upon management to keep it alive, and without the constant attention of management, it dies.

Here is how this happens. Typically, when value stream flow stops, supervisors or managers begin to make decisions. They use their knowledge and experience to make a decision that responds to the stoppage in flow and gets the product to the customer. If they cannot come up with a solution, the problem gets escalated. Phone calls get made to the office so that managers can start investigating. Perhaps, if the problem escalates up to the operations manager, she may get involved in order to find out what the problem is and what is causing it. In the end, once the managers discover the source of the problem, there is only one way to solve it: have a meeting. After much negotiating and influencing, someone in the meeting makes a decision and states, "Here is what we're going to do." The managers and supervisors go off and inform their people of the decision, and then try to figure out exactly how they are going to execute their part in it.

This all seems like the right thing to do. If there is a problem, we try to solve it on the front line. If we can't, then we escalate it to the next level. We discuss the problem with other managers, make a decision on how to correct the problem, and provide direction so that the decision can be carried out. Managers and executives at each level make decisions that are within their sphere of authority and use influence where they do not have authority. However, each decision has an effect. A decision made by one manager has a ripple effect, causing other managers to make decisions, and this can keep managers busy all day. Each manager is trying to do the right thing: get the product to the customer on time. The managers are supposed to manage people and resources, make appropriate decisions to utilize them effectively, and get the product to the customer. They make many decisions each day. Why? The answer is simple: it's in their job description; we expect them to make decisions. There is no limit to the number of decisions that can be made, it is infinite, *and each independent decision erodes value stream flow a little more.*

When a decision is made, it is probably because the flow has become abnormal. To get the flow operating normally again, supervisors and managers effectively "take control of the flow." They can make practically any decision that is needed to get the order to the customer, which, it is important to note, is not necessarily the same thing as fixing the flow. They can break down the standard work that has been established for the flow. For example, they might issue priority lists, expedite certain activities, rearrange products in FIFO lanes, and instruct operators to run different products that have "higher priorities" than the visual signals indicate.

When the flow is operating normally, only one decision is made, and that decision is always the right one. Why is it always the right one? Simple: we give the operators only one choice. They build the next product that comes to them in the FIFO lane, they set up the next job on the machine as indicated by the visual signal from the supermarket, and so on. The standard work for the system of fixed pathways and binary connections provides each operator with only one choice for what to build next. The result is the flow of the right material and information at the right time to deliver the product to the customer.

When a breakdown of this standard work occurs, value stream erosion begins. The eroded value stream flow becomes dependent on the decisions of supervisors and management for life. Soon, this way of doing things replaces the normal value stream flow altogether and simply becomes the way things are done. At this point, management has taken control of getting the product to the customer. Binary signals and pathways for the flow have been degraded or destroyed outright, or they are being ignored because they no longer have any integrity. The rules of value stream flow no longer have any significance, as the management team now decides what operators should work on next and where material should go. The standard work that was put in place to create flow has all but evaporated; *management decisions about the flow have killed the designed value stream flow.*

Another way to think of this is by way of analogy. Think of a decision as a virus. When someone makes a decision or provides his input or direction with regard to value stream flow, when he prioritizes, expedites, or does something similar, a virus has crept into the system, and the value stream starts to become ill. The virus penetrates the very standard work, the very binary signals and fixed pathways, upon which healthy value stream flow is based. The virus can enter the value stream easily because the value stream has no defense against the attack, no immune system against the virus. As more decisions are made, the virus replicates itself and spreads throughout the value stream. Eventually, the virus runs rampant through the system and simply *becomes* the system. Management must now make decisions and "muscle the flow" each day to get product to the customer. It must tell each process what to work on next and try to direct the movement of product through the operation so that it gets to the customer.

Managers are now the "life support" system for the value stream. They are the doctors and nurses that closely monitor the health of the value stream by monitoring its flow. The value stream depends on them. When flow stops, an alarm goes off, and the doctors and nurses are called in to diagnose the problem quickly and resuscitate the value stream. When this happens, the value stream is terminally ill. It constantly needs the attention of its life support system (management) to keep it from getting any sicker. The value stream remains alive only as long as it receives high-quality care from the life support group, and management must now make many decisions every day in order to get the remains of the value stream to deliver product to the customer. Over time, if our doctors and nurses cannot resuscitate the value stream, we simply get new doctors and nurses and hope they do better.

In manufacturing, some companies have done a better job of limiting the spread of this virus in their system. They have been much more progressive in handling front-line decision making. They have figured out how to put together a process to support value stream flow. Sometimes these processes are known as "response teams" or "help chains." When an operator has a problem and the flow stops, she can press a button to send a signal or pull a cord to stop the line. When this happens, an established team of people responds to the problem. Since something critical has happened to the flow of product and must be corrected immediately, the team's response time is established and measured. This team is armed with a good level of education in problem-solving tools, and the team members have standard work on how to use them. They use a set of diagnostic questions to formally investigate and solve the problem.

This is a step in the right direction, as it is a process with standard work. It is a formalization of the emergency response system that responds to the value stream when it has a problem. It is similar to a 911 call. The call is made, and there is a formal process to follow once the call is initiated. However, while this response may be good, the continuation of value stream flow still depends on external resources. We still need doctors and nurses to keep the value stream healthy. The doctors and nurses may use better tools and a better process to make better decisions that limit the potential for the virus to spread, but the virus can still creep into the system and potentially wreak havoc.

Remember, we also want to create flow in the office as well. And if decisions are the virus that erodes and breaks down value stream flow in manufacturing, then think about what happens in the office where the business processes are performed. Here, decisions are made every minute. For example, how do the people in the office know what to work on next? Everyone in the office, at all levels, has to constantly decide what to work on next. People are directed by supervisors and managers, who make many decisions each day to determine how best to utilize the office resources. With so many decisions, how much true flow really exists in an office? Usually, very little or none. Meetings take place in an attempt to set direction and resume the flow. Meetings are an attempt to get a group of people, each of whom would otherwise make an individual decision, to all make one decision collectively. But meetings usually cause rework, reprioritization, and other wastes. In fact, *meetings kill flow*. While their intent is to correct and reestablish flow, most likely they cause flow somewhere else to stop, wait, and get reanalyzed, reworked, and redirected. If decisions are the virus that kills the flow in manufacturing, then that virus is always present in the office. However, in the office, the "virus" is part of the way the office functions, and because we have accepted that, we don't even know that the virus exists. In the office, we live in a world where we constantly make decisions, even though *decisions kill flow*.

Although decisions kill flow, there is certainly a need to make decisions, or rather, to make good decisions. Exactly how do we know when we have made a good decision? If we are striving for normalcy and not having to make decisions, then *a good decision is one that does not spawn other decisions.* It puts us back on track to the original premise of having flow without decisions. A good decision would reflect back to why we implemented flow in the first place, not provide an opportunity for management to take over the operation. When a problem that *does* need management attention arises, we should think in terms of how we already answered some of the previous questions: achieving a destination, following a road map, making sure each employee can see why flow stopped, and then getting the employees involved in the process of fixing the flow so that management can back out again and not become more involved.

For example, let's say we have a fabrication process, such as a stamping press, feeding parts to an assembly area. If Stamping didn't stamp the part that Assembly needed, then management should *teach* the rules of flow and then back out and let the employees solve the problem now that they have been sufficiently guided. Management should then monitor what happens and check progress regularly, thereby supporting the system, not creating workarounds or exceptions that eventually destroy it.

When we have true flow, what *don't* we have? If product or information is flowing through an operation the way it should, what is *not* happening? There are no disruptions, direction changes, interventions, reprioritizations, or course corrections. No one is trying to manage people or resources just to get product out to the customer. And the decisions that management has to make should keep such activities from entering the value stream flow.

The point we are after is this: Why is there a need to make decisions in the first place? Why do value streams need external resources to patch them up when something goes wrong? Why do they have to be managed? The answer is simple: *because they are designed that way.* Why are they designed that way? Because we thought we created flow for the sake of efficiency, and the focus is on eliminating waste and being efficient. When flow stops, management is called in to "regain" that efficiency. Since we thought we created flow for the sake of efficiency, over the years, whenever someone has another way to be efficient, we debate the method. A new manager may find it more efficient for his department to run things in batches based on economic order quantities rather than put in a formal flow system, and since this is more efficient in terms of the measurements established at his organization, flow dies.

So, what causes the death of flow? The reason flow dies is that we don't truly understand why we created it in the first place. If we knew that we created flow just to see when it stops and the inherent value that provides in all areas of the operation, then we could teach the people who work in the flow what to do in order to correct it. We would also understand that flow *will* stop and not be surprised when it does, deem it a failure, then call in management to fix the failure.

If the answers you received are along the lines of lack of leadership, lack of support, or lack of commitment from the top, then you are bound to climb the staircase of continuous improvement. The correct answer here, the one that enables an operation to "jump" to Operational Excellence, is, "we don't understand why we created flow in the first place."

Before we go much further, let's be clear about decisions. Again, even in the best operations, they still need to be made. We have no magic pill that will eliminate the need for them. We can, however, provide some knowledge on how to reduce the number of decisions we need to make and how to ensure that the decisions that we do make are in the direction of moving the company forward. We can also move a lot of the decision making to the front-line employees who build the product and provide them with standard work on how to make their decisions.

With that in mind, let's revisit our statement "decisions kill flow." Why would anyone make a decision that kills flow? What is the real reason this happens? If we kept asking why until we discovered the root-cause answer, that answer would come down to this: an inability to answer our next question.

12

The Sixth Question: What Would the Shop Floor Look Like if We Did Everything Right?

If some hypothetical business has done everything right in its continuous improvement program, what will its operation look like? If we successfully apply the tools of continuous improvement to their fullest extent, what will our operation be like once we're all finished? Think about a company that has mastered and applied every single continuous improvement tool imaginable. The management team and workers both know about them and use them to their fullest extent. They perform *kaizen* events, apply the concepts of SMED, 5S, visual systems, cells, value streams, pull systems, and all the rest. They have done these successfully, they have done everything right. Imagine you are standing on their shop floor once this is done. What does the shop floor *look like*? You can't talk to any managers, ask any questions, request any computer printouts, or access any computers or reports to inform you of what's going on. You can only look, listen, and use your senses as if you were physically standing there. What do you see? What do you hear? What's happening around you? What would this shop floor be like? What are you observing? What is the environment like? How would you describe it?

When you ask the question, "If we applied every continuous improvement tool to its fullest extent, what would our shop floor look like?" the following are some typical answers that you will probably get:

- We would be a world-class manufacturer.
- We would be a company that has very little waste and lots of value-added activities.
- Any employee could stop production.
- We would be very profitable.
- We would have less inventory.
- We would have high inventory turns.
- We would have perfect quality and 100 percent on-time delivery.
- We would have the latest problem-solving tools available to our employees.
- Our employees would do root-cause problem solving as problems arise.
- We would be the benchmark for our industry.
- We would have a highly trained, highly efficient, very productive workforce.

All of the answers here are good, but none of them describes a destination. They describe *the results* of years of hard work in continuous improvement, but they don't really give us an overall picture that describes exactly where our journey of continuous improvement is taking us as if we were standing on our shop floor observing it a year from now. Some of the answers here are subjective, opinion-based, or things that we could not actually *see* or *hear* if we were walking through the shop floor. For example, "efficient" is a subjective term, not something that we can see on the shop floor. "Being productive" is also subjective. Having "less inventory" just assumes that we will have less inventory than we have today, without saying how we will know that we are carrying the *right* types and amounts of inventory. Again, these answers are *the results* of our continuous improvement efforts, but they do not describe what we would see if we were standing on our factory floor or walking through our operation.

Let's ask our question again, but this time, we'll provide answers that indicate a destination. The answers we are seeking are more binary in nature. They give us an accurate description in a yes/no format. They don't speak to results; instead, they speak to what the operation would look like and how it would run each day in order to *get* those results. The right answers are difficult to come up with, so I will provide some insight into what is being sought by giving some answers here. The answers I provide may be a little bit different than you would expect, so I encourage you to look at them and think about whether or not they apply to your continuous improvement destination. If they do, then the following list may contain some good answers to teach your people.

Pretend we are walking through the factory a year or so from now. "If we applied every continuous improvement tool to its fullest extent, what would our shop floor look like?" Remember, you cannot "see" perfect quality, 100 percent on-time delivery, or reduced lead times.

- ◆ I can look at any process and tell whether it is on time to customer demand, without asking any questions or seeking out any information.
- ◆ I can pick any process, look at the part the operator is working on, and know when that exact part will ship to the customer.
- ◆ I can see that each operator knows how long it takes for the product to move from Receiving to Shipping.
- ◆ I can see that each process is connected to the next process through binary signals that indicate send or don't send.
- ◆ I can see whether the product is flowing normally.
- ◆ I can see standard work at each workstation.
- ◆ I can see standard work for the flow of material and information between workstations.
- ◆ I can walk the flow from Receiving to Shipping without a tour guide assisting me.
- ◆ I can see whether the flow has started to become abnormal.

◆ I can see operators following standard work to correct the flow when it starts to become abnormal.

◆ I can see whether we have the right amount and the right kind of inventory needed for today's production.

◆ I can see very few management or supervisory personnel on the shop floor.

◆ The small number of management personnel I do see are teaching, not directing.

◆ I can hear almost no discussions or debates.

◆ I do not hear any questions being asked; everyone seems to know what to do.

◆ The small amount of discussion I do hear is employees working to improve the standard work used to correct abnormal flow.

◆ I can see operators moving to different areas on their own to adjust the flow.

◆ I can tell whether the flow of product is under control and working naturally or whether supervisors have stepped in and taken control by giving people direction.

When comparing the first list with the second, notice that the answers on the first list cannot be seen or observed out on the shop floor; we cannot tell whether they are happening. The second list indicates what we would be able to see if we set an exact destination for our continuous improvement journey. We can go out to the shop floor and determine whether these things are happening, and thereby judge whether we are making progress.

Let's push our comparison of these two lists a little further. How difficult would it be to teach the answers on the first list? Could we teach the answers at all, or would we essentially have to dictate them to everyone? We could probably teach people the reasoning for or justification behind why we want to achieve the goals on the first list, but could we teach people what their respective environments would be like if we *did* achieve those goals? Now, think of yourself as the person given the task of achieving the goals on the first list. How would you make them happen? Are there guidelines or processes for everyone to follow, or is everyone left to achieve the objectives any way he can? How would we be able to tell if we were getting close to achieving our goals?

Let's ask the same questions about what we see on the second list. How difficult would it be to teach these concepts? How easy would it be to tell if we were approaching or had in fact achieved any of the answers on this list? Remember, successfully changing an organization hinges on the *ability to teach*. It is easy to set a goal and tell people that they must attain it. It is much tougher to develop a process and then teach it to everyone. Difficult as it may be, developing a process and teaching it to everyone will provide sustained results that then can be continuously improved on for many years.

13

The Seventh Question: What Would the Office Look Like if We Did Everything Right?

Manufacturing is only one part of the operation. We also have to have a flow of information in order to support the flow in manufacturing. Therefore, we have to provide the same thinking for the business processes done in the office as well. The office may involve a wide variety of activities in many different areas. We want to think about what would happen if we applied every continuous improvement tool to its fullest extent in each of these areas, and we applied them correctly. While we cannot cover every different type of office, we will survey a few main areas that should be common to most companies, such as Engineering, Purchasing, and Sales. With that in mind, let's take a look at our engineering offices. If we asked, "What would our engineering office look like if we did everything right?" some typical answers might be

- ◆ Engineering provides timely responses to questions.
- ◆ Engineering always finishes quotes on time.
- ◆ All engineering changes are done on time.
- ◆ Engineers are always prepared at meetings.
- ◆ Engineers always show up for meetings.
- ◆ Engineering management will get involved and help solve problems.

◆ Engineering has the latest tools to help it develop and design our products.

◆ Engineering designs products for efficient manufacturability.

◆ Engineering gives the same attention and priority to production problems as it does to new product development.

Although these answers may be typical, they are not very practical; it would be very difficult, if not impossible, to walk through the engineering department and see or observe the answers on this list, let alone try to teach or learn them.

Let's rethink our question in terms of how we would describe the environment in Engineering if we applied every continuous improvement tool to its fullest extent. This description would include the flow of work, what the engineers are doing, and what management is doing. This description should speak to a destination for the engineering department, that is, we can or cannot see or observe certain things happening. "If we applied every continuous improvement tool to its fullest extent, what would our engineering office look like?" Some of the answers would include

◆ I can walk into the engineering office and tell whether it is on time right now to the workload it has.

◆ I can tell that each engineer knows what to do next based on FIFO lanes and binary connections to the next process in the workflow, not through management meetings and direction.

◆ I can see Engineering receiving binary signals and following standard work to sustain flow.

◆ I can see that Engineering has preestablished guaranteed turnaround times (GTT) that ensure that work will flow through the department at a certain rate and by a certain time under normal conditions.

- ◆ I can see when the next workflow cycle will start and when information will flow through Engineering.
- ◆ I can see information from Engineering moving forward to the next department through integration events, where the outputs of Engineering are matched up with the inputs of the next process.
- ◆ I can tell when the next integration event is going to happen and whether or not the engineering department is on time for this event without asking any questions.
- ◆ I can see that the only reason people are getting together in a conference room is to flow information and to capture and retain knowledge.
- ◆ I do not see any meetings in which management tries to re-arrange, redistribute, or reprioritize the flow of information or work.
- ◆ I do not see managers prioritizing work or negotiating with other managers on what the engineers should work on next.

To reiterate, this list gives us answers that can be used to teach exactly what the engineering department would be like when we have successfully applied continuous improvement to it. It also helps us know whether or not we are heading in the right direction as we progress.

Let's move on to Purchasing. "If we applied every continuous improvement tool to its fullest extent, what would our purchasing department look like?" Some of the typical answers we might get would be

- ◆ Purchasing uses strong negotiating skills to get the best possible price and delivery terms from our suppliers.
- ◆ Purchasing monitors supplier deliveries and ensures that our suppliers are always delivering on time.

- ◆ Purchasing calls suppliers prior to any shortages to get material delivered on time.
- ◆ Purchasing researches many different supply sources, not just looking for the best price but finding the supplier that has the best quality, the best delivery terms, *and* the best price.
- ◆ Purchasing attends daily production meetings so that people there are aware of any potential production problems that may exist.

These are the typical answers that we might expect. Next, we have a list that describes what we would be able to see or observe if we had an exact destination for what we want our purchasing department to look like:

- ◆ I can see that flow has been established to move information through Purchasing at preset times.
- ◆ I can see whether Purchasing is on time for all the workload it has right now.
- ◆ I can see Purchasing following standard work in order to source parts from suppliers.
- ◆ I can see Purchasing establishing binary connections with suppliers.
- ◆ I can see preset days and times at which knowledge transfers with our suppliers take place.
- ◆ I can see which suppliers have established flow and can support the flow of our products to customers.
- ◆ I can see Purchasing formally sharing knowledge with other departments.
- ◆ I do not see any management intervention with the purchasing agents; no one is asking them questions or telling them what they should be doing.

- ◆ I can see that Purchasing has established workflow cycles and guaranteed turnaround times at which information flows and knowledge is captured.
- ◆ I can see purchasing people preparing knowledge and information for upcoming integration events.
- ◆ I can see work flowing into and out of Purchasing through the use of a FIFO sequence.
- ◆ I can see Purchasing receiving binary signals and following standard work to sustain flow.
- ◆ I can hear Purchasing teaching suppliers how we measure capability in terms of mix and volume.
- ◆ I can see Purchasing receiving binary signals when suppliers trigger their early warning system to identify a potential upcoming missed shipment.

Like our other lists that describe a destination, note how this one defines and describes things that we would or would not be able to see or observe happening after we successfully applied continuous improvement.

Let's move on to the sales department. "If we applied every continuous improvement tool to its fullest extent, what would our sales department look like?" Again, let's take a look at some typical answers first:

- ◆ Sales provides an accurate forecast.
- ◆ Sales no longer calls and drops in orders at the last minute.
- ◆ Sales sells evenly and eliminates the usual end-of-the-month or end-of-the-quarter rush.
- ◆ Sales sells only to the capacities that we provide. Sales does not promise the customers something that we cannot do.
- ◆ Sales is not present in operations meetings, trying to set priorities and expedite products to key customers.
- ◆ There are no scheduling changes.

- ◆ Sales spends more time with customers.
- ◆ Sales provides timely information when needed.

This might seem like a wish list for the sales department, and perhaps for Operations as well, but none of these answers describes for us what the work environment of Sales would look like if we applied every continuous improvement tool to it. As we've done with our other departments, let's take another look at the question and see if we can describe what an exact destination for Sales would look like in terms of what we would or would not be able to see or observe:

- ◆ I can see that Sales has preset times at which information flows to Operations.
- ◆ I can see Sales delivering the information to Operations in the format required for Operations to procure raw materials.
- ◆ I can see Sales using capability charts for the operation in terms of volume *and* mix and selling to that capability when dealing with customers.
- ◆ I can see Sales displaying the true customer demand for the next scheduling interval.
- ◆ I no longer see a forecast posted. Sales has eliminated forecasting by understanding our true capability and alerts us only when our capability in terms of mix and volume is going to be exceeded.
- ◆ I can see Sales teaching customers how our flow works and how we can guarantee their delivery.
- ◆ I can see Sales giving customer tours and asking the customers if they can tell whether we are on time.

Now that we've looked at some of the individual departments that support Operations, let's take a look at all business processes in general. "If we applied every continuous improvement tool to its fullest extent, what would our business processes look like?" In keeping with our format, let's first take a look at some typical answers we might expect:

◆ Our offices are clean and very well organized.
◆ Every item in the office is labeled and identified so that anyone can easily find what she is searching for.
◆ People in the office communicate effectively.
◆ All meetings start on time and have an agenda to make them effective.
◆ Fewer approvals are needed.
◆ Our systems never experience downtime.
◆ People work together toward a common goal.

Now let's take a look at our business processes and see if we can describe what an exact destination for them would be like. "If we applied every continuous improvement tool to its fullest extent, what would our business processes look like?"

◆ I can see whether the office is on time without asking questions.
◆ I can see preset flow paths in the office that provide the formal route along which information flows.
◆ I can see that everyone knows what to work on next based on flow, not based on management reshuffling priorities.
◆ I do not see any meetings taking place to decide priorities.
◆ I can hear very few decisions being made on what to work on next.
◆ I can see and hear almost no guidance on when and how to do something being given to employees by management.
◆ I can hear very little noise; everyone is working, not influencing or negotiating his or her point of view.
◆ I can see people sharing knowledge and information at preset times during the week or during the day.

- ◆ I can see the performance metrics for the office flows.
- ◆ I can see that the only meetings being held are to set strategy and direction for business growth.

Understanding and visualizing what Operational Excellence looks like in the office is tough. It's easy to see streamlined flow in the manufacturing environment, where pieces of equipment are lined up next to each other or lines and squares are painted on the floor. However, in the office, it's different. Offices are spread throughout buildings, and information flows by e-mails on computer screens. No one can tell how everyone knows what to work on next. In order to help employees understand exactly what the office would look like, we want to provide answers that talk in terms of flow, normal flow, and abnormal flow, as these apply to any office or business process. Another key element is to have answers that we can teach. Think how easy it would be to teach the answers on the second list compared to teaching the typical answers on the first list. Think of how easy it would be to track whether or not we have achieved the answers on the second list as opposed to whether or not we have achieved the answers on the first list. The teaching element here is critical, as it provides a very practical way to know what the destination is and what it looks like when we get there.

14

The Eighth Question: What Would the Supply Chain Look Like if We Did Everything Right?

While our factory is a major part of the operation, we can work hard to create flow at the rate of customer demand, only to find that the flow frequently stops because a single part has not been delivered by a supplier. And as companies are finding more suppliers on a global level, the flow of information and material from and through the supply chain is becoming even more critical. We focus quite a bit of effort on "supply-chain management." We have layers of support people who constantly monitor, adjust, prioritize, oversee, and direct the supply chain each day just so that the needed parts show up at our factory before it's too late.

Rather than describe the supply chain in its entirety, we will look at three areas that partly make up the overall supply chain and tackle each one in turn: planning, where we flow information; the supplier's shipping deck, where we flow both information and material; and our receiving deck, where we flow both information and material. First, let us ask, "If we applied every continuous improvement tool to its fullest extent, what would our planning department look like?" We can think of the planning department here as the place where the needs and operational capability of the supply chain are planned and communicated to everyone. Some typical answers might include

- Planning is accurate and does not change the schedule once it has been issued.
- Planning is communicating with suppliers to make sure they are on time.
- Planning does not issue any "hot orders."
- Planning works with Production to ensure that it meets customer demand.
- Planning makes sure that all parts have arrived before issuing production orders.
- Fewer planning resources are required.

Now, let's take a look at how we would describe an exact destination for our planning department in terms of what we would or would not be able to see or observe. Again, think of the planning department as an area where we flow information.

- I can see preset times at which binary signals are sent to suppliers.
- I can see Planning scheduling production at preset times.
- I can see the single binary source that initiates these signals.
- I can see whether all our suppliers are on time.
- I can see the early warning system that lets us know that we might soon have a problem with one of our suppliers.
- I can see the standard work that is initiated when a supplier triggers our early warning system to tell us that there is a problem.
- I know the capability of each supplier in terms of mix and volume.
- I know that planners are loading suppliers to their capability so that the suppliers will never fail.
- I can see Planning receiving binary signals when a supplier's capability is exceeded and following preset standard work to ensure flow to the customer.

Let's move on to the supplier's shipping deck, where we flow both information and material. "If our supplier applied every continuous improvement tool to its fullest extent, what would its shipping deck look like?" Some typical answers would include

- ◆ Shipping is on time to customer demand.
- ◆ Shipments are ready prior to the arrival of carriers.
- ◆ The shipping capability matches the receiving plant's normal production schedule.
- ◆ Shipping uses small lot containers.
- ◆ Shipping is able to send mixed parts on the same pallet.

Now, let's think of describing the supplier's shipping deck in terms of what we would or would not be able to see or observe. Think of how the answers that follow could be used to establish an exact destination for what we want our supplier's shipping deck to look like.

- ◆ I can see preset times established that let the supplier know if they are going to be short or miss a shipment.
- ◆ I can see whether things are normal or abnormal at the supplier.
- ◆ I can see standard work for when things are not normal.
- ◆ I can tell when the next truck is leaving without asking.
- ◆ I can see whether problems with my production have affected the supplier.
- ◆ I can see finished goods being delivered to Shipping and placed into FIFO lanes at preset times.
- ◆ I can see if Shipping is on schedule prior to the arrival of the pickup time.
- ◆ I can see early warning triggers identifying potential late shipments and preset standard work being followed to make sure that shipments stay on time.

Finally, let's take a look at our receiving deck. "If we applied every continuous improvement tool to its fullest extent, what would our receiving deck look like?" In keeping with our format, let's take a look at some typical answers first:

◆ All paperwork is accurate.
◆ Parts are placed in the warehouse as soon as a truck is received.
◆ Everything is clean and organized.
◆ Shipments are received without checks or delays at the receiving deck.
◆ We are able to receive everything that arrives each day.

Now, let's try to describe our receiving deck in terms of what we would or would not be able to see or observe.

◆ I can see whether we have the right amount of inventory for today's production.
◆ I can see when the next supplier's truck will arrive.
◆ I can see what I need to work on next and know whether or not I am on schedule.
◆ I can see that Receiving has established guaranteed turn-around times that ensure that items are received at a certain rate and by a certain time under normal conditions.
◆ I can see Receiving getting binary signals when it is not capable of meeting the current workload and following preset standard work to be able to handle the increase.

The supply chain is a difficult area in which to understand how the principles of Operational Excellence would apply in a practical sense. Yet, that is exactly what we are trying to do here. We want to give the people who interface with the supply chain a glimpse of their future environment, how it would operate, and what they would see. We want to give them a sense of what it would look like when the supply chain is *in motion* each day. We want to give them an idea of what their exact destination is in practical terms so that they can identify with it and know how they can achieve it in their respective areas.

Describing the destination for each area is the key to this and the previous two questions. It enables each person to truly understand that the intent is to move the company forward to a specific destination, and that this destination looks like the things we described in each respective area. Hopefully, these questions will help drive the point home to everyone who works in these areas that the company is not just trying to continuously improve; it is trying to create an operation that works in this fashion, and it has a destination for all the effort it puts into continuous improvement. This leads us to our last and most difficult question of all.

CHAPTER

15

The Final Question: Where Will Our Continuous Improvement Journey Take Us?

As mentioned earlier, we have always been taught that continuous improvement is a journey without a destination. It's a journey without end, and the learning is in the journey itself. It's a never-ending journey of improvement and eliminating waste, a journey of improvement in all aspects of a company's operation. Creating a culture that improves each day is the key. Having been taught that, we never had to ask or answer questions such as: Where will this journey take us? What is our destination? What are we trying to accomplish in our operation? How will we know if we are going in the right direction? What are the signposts along the way? Without answers to these questions, we just seek to improve every day. We learn new tools that help us do things better. We read books and perhaps hire consultants. We try to do what we learn from them because we know that companies that have eliminated waste have performed better in terms of inventory reduction, lead time reduction, on-time delivery, and perhaps cost by doing so.

Although we may have performed better on the metrics previously mentioned, we have been fortunate that we have not had to answer the question, "Where will our continuous improvement journey take us?" as it is one of the toughest questions to answer for anyone who has embarked on a continuous improvement journey. It is not an easy question to answer, but how we answer it will have a dramatic impact on our company one way or another. When we answer this question, we will unveil what our executives, managers, and continuous improvement people think the continuous improvement program is about, and we may find their answers to be good but impractical. Their answers may make sense, but they may also reflect more of a dream state than a reality that we can actually achieve.

While our other questions help to enable people to see that there is a different approach to continuous improvement, this question is the key. The companies that answer this question correctly "jump," or shortcut their journey significantly. They save years of learning through experience, bypass years of evolution, skip years of pain as they struggle to improve the company, and eliminate years of trial and error on new initiatives and strategies as new leaders come and go. The right answer to this question separates companies that have a vision from companies that have an exact destination that each employee knows and works to get to in his specific area. Companies that answer this question correctly are able to jump faster than other companies for one simple reason: *they know exactly where they are going.*

Suppose we ask the question, "Where will our continuous improvement journey take us?" Some of the typical answers might be

- ◆ We would be a world-class company.
- ◆ We would be the best of the best.
- ◆ We would be competitive with any company globally.
- ◆ We would be a "waste-free" company.
- ◆ We would have no inventory.
- ◆ We would have 100 percent customer satisfaction.
- ◆ We would have the lowest possible cost.
- ◆ We would be on time, every time.
- ◆ We would be a world-class producer.
- ◆ We would be the supplier of choice.

These are good answers in terms of company performance and results. They are good motivations that can inspire people to perform. They are also good answers that help employees envision what their company could be like and that they can be a part of it. These answers lead employees and managers to believe that if they keep using continuous improvement tools, if they continuously seek out waste and eliminate it, if they target getting better each day, and if they are able to create a culture of continuous improvement, then they will achieve these results. Unfortunately, this is simply not true.

Applying continuous improvement tools over and over, and even creating a culture of continuous improvement, does not create this nirvana of business results. While these answers may sound good, there is no connection, road map, or pathway that ensures that the improvements in the operation will lead to these types of business results. Here, the improvements in the operation are targeted at making it more efficient and reducing cost, lead time, and inventory, but the answer we want to provide should be in terms of increasing business growth and market share. While there may be some implied relationship, there is no direct linkage or logic that ensures that we are improving the right things to grow the business if we simply seek out waste each day and eliminate it. After all, how could there be? Our business and our customers are constantly changing.

Therefore, we need to seek a more practical answer that can be applied at each level of the organization, an answer that is framed in a way that lets all the employees in the organization know what they can do to contribute to attaining the destination. And, of course, it must be an answer that is teachable. By now, you have probably figured out the answer we are about to give, and that is that our lean journey will take us to Operational Excellence, where "each and every employee can see the flow of value to the customer, and fix that flow before it breaks down." While we described Operational Excellence earlier in this book, let's continue to describe exactly what it is in more practical terms and further answer where our improvement journey will take us.

Self-healing flow is one of the key concepts in Operational Excellence, but in reality, can the operators who build the product really solve all the problems in flow? Perhaps they can, but initially there is a break-in period. The flow is set up in an area at a robust level, and set up so that both normal flow and abnormal flow are defined. For example, a FIFO lane has three green squares, one yellow square, and a red square. Inventory in the yellow square is a warning; inventory in the red square means that action is needed. When a situation occurs and flow becomes abnormal (there are parts in the red square), one of two things can happen. The operators can see the problem and address it among themselves, or they can seek help from the outside and contact supervisors, engineers, managers, or others. In order to create a self-healing value stream, we would track how often we make internal fixes rather than asking for external help. For the workers in the flow, when things start to become abnormal, it may be easier for them to think of the problem as either "we got it" or "we need help." Eventually, tracking the "we got its" and "we need helps" and understanding what causes the need for outside help will lead to more of the "we got its" and less of the "we need helps."

As discussed earlier, another key concept in Operational Excellence is having a practical acid test to let us know, whether out on the manufacturing floor or in the office, whether we have achieved Operational Excellence. This acid test was defined as having a visitor come into the operation, look at any process without asking any questions, and be able to know whether that process is on time to provide what the customer wants right now. While this test may seem a bit academic, and be a tall order to fill in real life, we can bring this concept into our operation and define the destination with clarity with a small refinement. We simply need to show the visitor exactly where she should stand to observe the process while she is walking through the operation.

The concept of pulse points in the operation does just this. Pulse points are areas in the operation where a visitor (or anyone in the operation) can observe what is happening and know whether the flow is on time to meet customer demand. Pulse points are specific areas that are identified where flow can be clearly observed. These may be even defined with circles on the floor, signs, and whatever is necessary to identify the observation point. From the pulse point, one can observe whether the operation is "in the green" or whether there is a problem. A pulse point can also be combined with relevant information from the history of problems, the "we got it" versus the "we need help" trends, and other information, as long as that information does not obstruct the view.

Pulse points apply in the office as well. An area of the office should be identified as a pulse point from which anyone can observe the offices and work areas. From this point, he can see the flow indicators that let him know whether the flow is normal or abnormal. In the office, we may have to put some timing around the pulse points in order for them to make practical sense. In other words, if people are coming together to flow information at 10:00 a.m. each day, then we may need to specify that the pulse point is active each day from 10:00 a.m. to 12:00 p.m. (we will discuss how to do this in the upcoming chapters).

With defined pulse points, any employee walking through the operation knows exactly where to go to observe the flow and understand the status of the flow. She can walk over to the specific area, look at what's happening, and understand whether things are going right or whether something is wrong, perhaps without even stopping her walk.

Finally, our answer to the question, "Where will our continuous improvement journey take us?" has to bridge the gap between continuous improvement and business growth. We have to make a direct connection between the continuous improvement activities that we carry out and the impact they have on growing the business.

Earlier, we described this as freeing up time to "work on offense." A more practical way to think of connecting continuous improvement to business growth is to think of it as *putting offense into flow*.

Putting offense into flow means identifying the specific activities that grow the business and putting them into flow so that we can see when this flow becomes abnormal and fix it before it stops. However, putting flow into offense activities is not as easy as putting flow into manufacturing or into the supporting business processes, as offense activities can take place at many different levels. Different activities are sometimes even performed by the same person. Therefore, it may be easier to think of the different activities in terms of their return on investment. For example, a sales call may result in the immediate return of a sale and cash coming into the company. An engineer working with a production person to review process capability and specifications for a product that is due to be launched in six months would not provide an immediate return in the form of cash coming into the business.

The reason we want to understand the offense activities in terms of return on investment is not to direct or steer people toward doing those activities that have a quicker return, but to balance these activities when we put them into flow. We would like to create an even distribution of short-term offense and long-term offense. If these activities were to use different shades of green (perhaps brighter based on how quickly we will see a return), then we should see an even distribution of the different shades as we balance the offense activities for the week. The result of this is a "pump" that moves offense activities forward at a preset rate that every employee can see, a pump that keeps the offense activities constantly happening at a preset rate without interruptions for maintenance or defense activities, as the employees that work in these flows have those activities covered. We will talk quite a bit more about using Operational Excellence to create offense and business growth later in this book. For now, the key message is that Operational Excellence is about applying a design to the way an operation functions in order to support business growth.

So, where exactly will our continuous improvement journey take us? The answer is to Operational Excellence, where "each and every employee can see the flow of value to the customer, and fix that flow before it breaks down."

PART
III

The Eight Principles of Operational Excellence

CHAPTER

16

▼

The New Operations "Engine Design" for Operational Excellence

Now that we have taken some time to explain exactly what Operational Excellence is and the understanding that is needed for a company to "jump" to Operational Excellence, we will move on to the actual "engine design" for Operational Excellence.

As we mentioned earlier, the redesign of the car engine of the 1970s was not magic. At some point in the history of carmaking, someone in Sales or Marketing, or perhaps the company owner himself, realized that it would be a significant business advantage if the engines in the company's cars started the first time, every time. Again, the intent was to grow the business by building a better product that consumers would want. Based on this desire, engineers were given the specific objective of creating an engine that would start every time, and from this they set their *design objective*. They discovered that in order to achieve their objective, a precise mixture of air and fuel would have to flow into the cylinders at exactly the right time, and the spark plug would have to fire at exactly the right time to ignite the mixture. In order to get the precise mixture, carburetors (devices that mixed air with fuel, then sent the mixture to the cylinders through a manifold) would have to be eliminated, since they did not allow the precise mixture to be delivered into each cylinder.

Instead, a precise fuel/air mixture would have to be injected into the cylinder at the right time. Hence, fuel injectors were created. In order for the spark plug to fire at exactly the right time and ignite the mixture, the mechanical distributors that moved at high speeds, developed fatigue as a result of vibration, and wore out over time had to be replaced with nonmechanical devices that could provide electricity to the spark plug at exactly the right time. Hence, solid-state circuits and electronic ignitions were created. The advent of these changes, along with the way the engine was designed to interface with these systems, made starting the engine a very predictable, dependable, repeatable, and reliable process.

When we turn the key, a binary signal is sent to the engine control that signals the electronic ignition, which sequences the correct timing of the spark plug and the fuel injector through a circuit board. The timing is precise, and our engine starts every time. If, down the road, our engine does seem to be having trouble, we simply plug it into a diagnostic system that tells us what link in the process has failed. We can diagnose the failure easily, which means that we can also further improve the process of starting the engine. Again, the reason the modern car engine starts every time is that it was designed that way. In order for our operations to start every time, we will have to design them to do this as well.

THE NEW OPERATIONS DESIGN

Just as an engineer uses the laws of physics to design an aircraft, a bridge, or a car engine, we will follow some principles, too. Within each principle, there will be an objective, a set of design guidelines to follow, and a "what you would see" section to describe the behavior of the operation once the principle has been successfully applied. The principles we use will also create a process that we can use to achieve Operational Excellence in many areas of the company and throughout entire divisions. The same process that can be used on the production floor can also be used in Sales and Marketing, Accounting, Finance, Engineering, and every other area of an organization. This process provides a step-by-step teaching methodology that we can share with everyone in our business, no matter what position in the company she holds.

There are eight principles in total that we will use. You will probably find that all of the continuous improvement efforts that you have done in the past fit somewhere within these principles. There should not be a change of direction for any improvement efforts. Most likely, the result will be more of a realignment, or a new road map for your improvement efforts, in order to jump to Operational Excellence.

The principles of Operational Excellence are

1. Design lean value streams.
2. Make lean value streams flow.
3. Make flow visual.
4. Create standard work for flow.
5. Make abnormal flow visual.
6. Create standard work for abnormal flow.
7. Have employees in the flow improve the flow.
8. Perform offense activities.

There is a lot of material to cover for each of these principles; therefore, I will dedicate a chapter to each. We also will examine each principle in a practical manner so that we can see the application of each one and what it would look like in action. Let's get started with one of the most popular topics ever to hit manufacturing: lean value streams.

17

The First Principle: Design Lean Value Streams

OBJECTIVE: Design on paper an end-to-end lean value stream flow, starting from the time we receive an order from the customer or request for a service until the time we deliver the product or service.

———

The concept of value stream flow started in 1996 with the book *Lean Thinking*.[1] In 1998 the book *Learning to See*[2] took value stream flow from concept to reality by providing a practical approach to mapping value stream flow. The focus was on manufacturing, and a simplified case study was used to teach the basic concepts of value streams and the process for designing a lean value stream. The case study involved an automotive supplier that was producing two products through processes that were dedicated to those products, and a stamping press that was shared with other product families. Customer demand held constant, with little variation. Again, the emphasis was on teaching the concept of seeing end-to-end value stream flow using a simplified case study. We learned that the five basic steps in mapping value stream flow were identifying product families, mapping the current state of flow, applying seven lean guidelines to create value stream flow, mapping a future state of flow, then developing an implementation plan (see Figure 17.1).

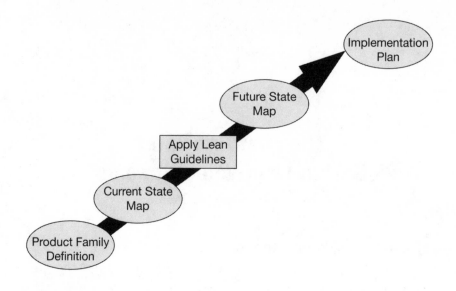

Figure 17.1 *Five Steps for Value Stream Design*

The book was brilliant, as it taught anyone in the company how to map the flow of information and material from raw material to the customer, then create a future state in which much of the waste was eliminated from these flows. However, many practitioners and consultants focused on the mapping tool, not on the seven guidelines for creating flow. In other words, they focused on creating a map of the current state, "brainstorming" a future state of what could be done (sometimes with the help of a consultant or facilitator), then creating a future state with less waste. The future state does look better after noting the improvements and the potential impact on lead time reduction, but this is *not* the process for designing a lean value stream. This is the process of brainstorming waste elimination, and it will limit us to the staircase of continuous improvement that we discussed in Chapter 2.

This point is brought up here with good reason. Value stream flow designed by facilitation and brainstorming *will not create or support Operational Excellence*. This type of value stream design will always be dependent on management and key people having good ideas at the right moment, and eventually the people and the management will change and the value stream will regress, leaving the need for strong leadership to hold it all together. The correct method for designing value stream flow is quite detailed and quite deep. However, this level of knowledge and application is necessary in order to create and support Operational Excellence, just as we have to design an aircraft for flight.

The overall process for designing lean value streams works like this:

1. *Determine product families.* Rough in or estimate what you think the current product families are, based on the processing steps that products go through. This will be refined in later steps.

2. *Design an end-to-end lean value stream for a family based on eight basic design guidelines.* These eight basic design guidelines are used to establish the types of connections that will be needed between the processes and with some of the major suppliers as well. They will also establish how information will flow in the lean value stream.

3. *Perform a deep dive on the numbers using the concepts of mixed-model flow.* The focus here is on the "pacemaker," or the single process to which we issue a schedule in the value stream. There are 10 design guidelines for creating mixed-model flow. These will establish the capability of our pacemaker in terms of volume and mix, which is key, as it will allow us to know whether a load that has been placed on the pacemaker is within the capability of the design, or whether something abnormal has happened right in the beginning. Mixed-model flow will help us establish the method for scheduling. Again, this is key, as it allows us to have standard work to schedule value stream flow.

4. *Once we have applied mixed-model concepts to the pace-maker, we design the flow at the rest of the processes, including shared resources.* Shared resources are processes that produce components for many different product families. They could also be monument equipment through which every family must flow. There are six design guidelines for dealing with shared resources, some of which require a host of calculations to be performed. One of the keys to creating flow through shared resources is to determine the interval at which the shared resources can cycle through a mix of parts it produces. The guidelines contain a process for doing this.

5. *Of course, none of this works without the flow of information that is needed from our business processes.* Therefore, we design value stream flow using nine design guidelines for information flow. It is important that we design the flow of information along with where we will capture knowledge in the office in order to supply information throughout the operation at the right time and rate.

6. *Once we have designed the flow within our four walls, we hook into our suppliers so that they can deliver parts in flow as well.* There are seven design guidelines for designing supply-chain connections. Once the connections are defined, the next step is to identify a connection type for each part with the supplier. Through this connection, a binary send/don't send signal can be established with the supplier at a preset time.

We could also extend value streams into Sales and Marketing, Finance, Research and Development, and other areas of the business and apply the concepts to each of these as well. However, for our focus, we will stick to the application of value streams in operations, where we take the orders and produce the product for the customer.

There have been many books written on the subject of lean value streams, and there is quite a bit of knowledge in the public domain as well. Therefore, I will not try to provide the complete book of value stream design; rather, I will highlight the design principles behind lean value streams in order to create Operational Excellence. It is important that we understand these principles and their appropriate use, just as an engineer understands the laws of physics and aerodynamics in order to design an airplane for flight. Again, understanding the principles behind the design will allow us to provide a checklist for the performance of the design once it is implemented. It will also help us avoid the temptation to brainstorm a design that will allow for only incremental gain and will not provide a foundation for Operational Excellence.

CASE IN POINT: GKN PLC

GKN plc is a publicly traded company with headquarters in Redditch, U.K., that has a 250-year history of dedication to continuous improvement and creating flow. The organization produces a wide range of products for the automotive, powdered metallurgy, land systems, and aerospace industries. Equally strong is its commitment to developing the capability of its people, which for more than eight years has provided the company with a solid foundation for growth by way of continuous improvement. In fact, every plant manager throughout the organization's 140 sites around the world receives a mandatory suite of education. Peter Watkins, the global lean enterprise & business excellence director for GKN, explained:

> *GKN sees that a continuous improvement culture can be sustained only if all the leaders act as teachers and coaches in Operational Excellence. This is very hard to do if the leaders have not been exposed to the detailed concepts involved. Having a standard method for teaching the application of the guidelines and detailed principles of flow and learning by doing*

are no doubt the best approach. All of our executives have been educated using this method for value stream design, as well as mixed-model, shared resource, business process, and supply-chain flow. It is three weeks of training, and it has been well worthwhile to our organization, as it allowed our company to progress along the road map to achieving Operational Excellence.

Throughout GKN, there are many examples of formal education in action. Practically every site has future-state value stream maps that have created flow through a countless number of complicated machining and assembly processes, and through business processes as well. While there are many examples of GKN facilities using the Operational Excellence approach to drive business results, I will provide a few here, as each of these has resulted in a positive impact on the customer:

◆ *In 2010, a GKN Aerospace division reduced the hours required on one key program by 31 percent, lead time by 70 percent, and inventory by 35 percent, and quadrupled the number of deliveries to customers.*

◆ *By applying the principles of flow to a business process, GKN Driveline Japan reduced costs for nonproductive stock by 32 percent, reduced purchasing cost by 15 percent, and decreased lead time by 37 percent. All of these improvements gave the division significant operational advantages, allowing it to be more competitive in the marketplace.*

◆ *GKN Land Systems's Woodridge plant applied the principles of value stream design in its new part approval process in order to reduce the time it takes to put new products into production. By applying this formal process, the plant not only reduced the time it took to put new products into production by 50 percent and significantly reduced costs but also considerably improved its ability to meet changing customer needs, strengthening its position in the marketplace.*

GETTING STARTED

Before we can apply the principles of detailed value stream design, we first have to select the product family to work on and map its current state. The formal process for creating product families is to use a product family matrix. The product family matrix can be a very involved tool, as it lists the processes that the operation has along one axis and the parts produced on another. The purpose is to find the parts that go through similar processing steps; this is done by placing an "X" in the appropriate process for each part, then grouping the "X" patterns together.[3] See Figure 17.2 for a simple example of a product family matrix.

Process

Products	Injection Mold	Stamp	Welding	Mech. Assembly	Electrical Assembly	Final Assembly	Configure & Test
Housing Interconnect	X	X	X	X	X	X	X
Connector Rod Assembly	X	X	X	X	X	X	X
Tie Rod Assembly	X	X	X	X	X	X	X
Drive Assembly		X		X			X
Motor Housing	X					X	X
Cover Plate Assembly	X				X	X	X

Figure 17.2 *Product Family Matrix*

Once we have selected our product family, we then create a current-state map of flow for this family. This end-to-end flow begins with the customer, traces the information flow from the customer to the main suppliers, then moves on to the production floor. Information flow enables us to know how we take customer demand and let each process know what to work on next. The current-state map will also show material flow and how material is moved from suppliers to the customer. The current state of flow is evaluated through a lead-time ladder, which compares process time to lead time. We can interpret the results of this ladder by saying, "The customer wants to buy about 180 minutes of work from us (this is the process time), and it takes us 24 days (the lead time) to deliver 180 minutes worth of work." See Figure 17.3 for a basic example of a current-state map.

THE BASIC EIGHT OF VALUE STREAM DESIGN

Once our current-state map is complete, we can design a door-to-door flow from our receiving deck to our shipping deck that we can teach to others. In order to do this, we will initially rough in a design by following eight design guidelines. Seven of these guidelines originated in the book *Learning to See*. To help prepare for the more

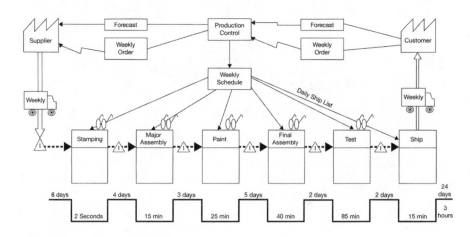

Figure 17.3 *Current-State Map*

detailed design that will follow, we've added a guideline on first-in, first-out, or FIFO, as it is a powerful method for connecting processes (even in the office), and this will be critical as we continue the design. These eight guidelines tell us how to create a value stream on paper that will show the flow of material and information from the receiving deck to the shipping deck. The guidelines are listed as questions to help ensure that they are applied by answering them. The eight design guidelines are

1. *What is the* **takt** *time?* *Takt* time is the calculated customer demand rate, usually expressed in time units per piece. For example, a part needs to be produced every 15 minutes in order to meet customer demand.

2. *What finished goods strategy will we use?* A finished goods strategy means a set system that has been established for determining how the factory will know what to build next for this value stream. For example, we might build to order; replenish inventory taken from a supermarket or pull system; or use a hybrid of the two. This guideline keeps us from letting Sales, the materials manager, or any other person determine or guess what inventory levels he thinks are needed, and instead determines this through a systematic method based on filling customer demand.

3. *Where can we use continuous flow?* To determine the answer to this question, we would interrogate the current value stream and determine every possible place that we can dedicate equipment, move machines and people close together, and move work into a one-piece flow, or a make-one, move-one process.

4. *Where can we apply FIFO?* In the places where we cannot create one-piece flow, the next choice is to connect processes with FIFO. FIFO not only sequences products but also controls inventory between the processes and allows downstream processes to know what to work on next without a schedule or a priority list.

5. *Where can we apply pull?* When we cannot apply either one-piece flow or FIFO, then and *only* then would we look to implement a pull or *kanban* system. Such a system is usually used when a supplying process is shared and unreliable, since reliable processes, even though they are shared, can be candidates for FIFO. Pull is also typically used as a connection with suppliers, but other options are available, as we will see.

6. *At what single point will we schedule?* Of all the processes involved in making the product, only one gets a schedule. The others know what to build next based on their connection to the processes upstream or downstream of them. The point at which we schedule is called the *pacemaker*. It is the key process in the value stream, as it sets the pace at which the value stream produces.

7. *What interval can we establish?* By setting an interval, we establish the pacemaker's ability to cycle through the mix of products in the product family that flows through it. For example, if there are 50 products in the family, the interval would determine how long it would take to produce some quantity of each product. This is sometimes referred to as EPEI, or every part every interval. Setting an interval allows us to schedule the appropriate mix for which the value stream was designed, or, in other words, understand the maximum normal load that the value stream can handle in terms of mix. This concept is covered in more depth in the mixed-model section.

8. *What will be the pitch at the pacemaker?* Creating a pitch means designing a physical method to know whether the value stream flow at the pacemaker is on time. We make this physical activity happen at preset time frames, usually calculated as the *takt* time multiplied by a case or pack quantity. The result is that the material handler should pick up a box or tote every 30 minutes (for example). If this does not happen, we know that we are not meeting *takt*.

The intent of these design principles is to design a future state that has a connected flow of information and material. As on an electric circuit board, where electricity flows through wires, soldered pathways, resistors, switches, and other devices, there are no openings or dead ends for the flow. As on the electrical schematic, we should be able to trace the flow of information synchronized with the flow of material from the initial order from the customer to the delivery to the customer, and we should be able to do this physically on our future-state map. On the information side, information is given to only one process in the value stream, or one point. All other processes know what to do next because the information will flow with the product through the connections created from that one point. The key here is that each process is connected to the next, and material moves only when the next process needs it. After constructing the future-state map (see Figure 17.4), we should view our improvement in terms of the customer by now stating: "It used to take us 24 days to deliver 180 minutes' worth of work. In our future state, we can reduce the work to 150 minutes and deliver that work in 5 days. This will give us a competitive advantage in the marketplace."

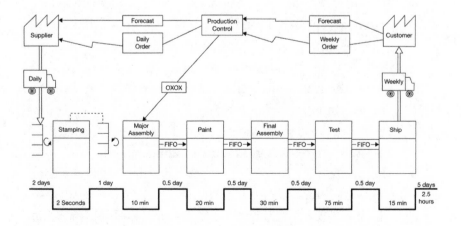

Figure 17.4 *Future-State Map*

At this point, the future-state map is a rough design that allows us to see how processes are connected and how information will flow from the customer to each process. It also allows us to build a rough implementation plan to put this design into action.

What You Would See

At the completion of this part of the design process, most likely you would walk into a war room or conference room in which poster-sized sheets of paper are hanging on the wall. If the process has been followed correctly, the following items should be posted on the wall:

- ◆ A current-state map.
- ◆ A list of the eight design guidelines, with the application of these guidelines explained.
- ◆ A future-state map.
- ◆ An implementation plan.

A few important notes that will ensure that the employees who did the work understood and followed the correct process are as follows:

- ◆ The current-state map has a lead-time ladder, which is a graphical representation of the total amount of time it takes to deliver the product compared with the total amount of work that it actually takes to build the product. In other words, the lead-time ladder shows the ratio of lead time to process time.
- ◆ The list of the eight guidelines should have an explanation of how and where each guideline is being applied.
- ◆ The future-state map should not have any inventory triangles, which represent uncontrolled inventory, or eyeglasses, which means that management oversees and sets priorities,

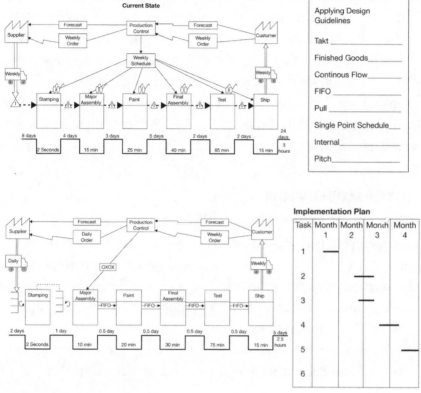

Figure 17.5 *Value Stream Design—What You Would See*

and should have a schedule sent to only one process. We also should be able to trace the total flow of material and information in a closed loop, as mentioned earlier.

◆ The implementation plan should be developed by implementing flow closest to the customer, then working back upstream. In the upstream processes, work can be done in parallel or concurrently, but the actual connection of the processes must take place in sequence, starting from the customer and then working upstream.

One final note on value stream maps: these maps are usually done with sticky notes or hand-drawn, as they should be put together by a team, not by an engineer sitting at a computer. Computer maps are fine as long as they are cleaned-up documentation of what a team originally produced, which should be a current-state map and a future-state map. For more information on value stream mapping, the book *Learning to See* is highly recommended and an excellent resource.

MIXED-MODEL FLOW

After we have roughed in our design using the eight guidelines, the next step is to perform a deep dive into the pacemaker process (see Figure 17.6) to truly design how it will perform in real life, where demand changes every day, cycle times are different, and there are more technicalities involved with product mix, setup times, uptime, yield, and other such factors.

To perform this deep dive, we will apply the 10 design guidelines that are needed to design a mixed-model pacemaker. Again,

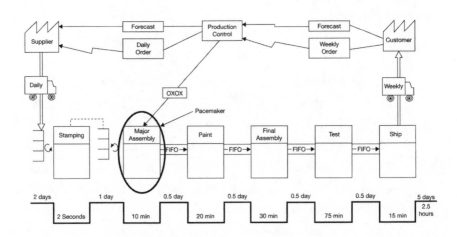

Figure 17.6 *Mixed-Model Pacemaker*

the guidelines are given as questions to help ensure that they are applied. The 10 design guidelines for a mixed-model pacemaker are

1. *Do we have the right product families?* To determine true product families that can flow through similar processes, we need to use a more advanced product family matrix. The product family matrix is an involved tool that allows us to do what-ifs with various hypothetical product family configurations. The end result should be that a product family is a group of products that have similar total work content time (roughly within 30 percent) and greater than 80 percent similarity in processing steps.

2. *What is the* **takt** *time at the pacemaker?* To determine the *takt* time at the pacemaker, we take a much more detailed look at customer demand for the family defined in Question 1. Demand profiles are created, the variation in total demand for the family is calculated, multiple "*takt* capabilities" (which we'll talk about later) are established, and different scenarios are developed to determine the limits of the level at which the value stream needs to perform, in terms of mix and volume, to satisfy real-life changing customer demand.

3. *Can the equipment at the pacemaker support the* **takt** *time?* Any equipment involved in the pacemaker process has to be analyzed in terms of the load that changing customer demand and a changing product mix will place on that equipment. The number of machines needed is calculated using factors such as uptime in order to determine the correct equipment needs for each *takt* capability.

4. *What is the interval?* If there is any equipment in the pacemaker process, we have to determine how many products this equipment can cycle through over what period of time, thereby establishing an interval for product mix.

5. ***What are the balance charts for the products?*** Since there will be a mix of products with varying work content, a detailed balance chart needs to be created for each product in the family. Balance charts tell us exactly how much work each operator will perform before he passes the work along to the next operator. If there are hundreds of products, this can be simplified by grouping products that are similar in build steps and build time and making one balance chart for them.

6. ***How will we balance flow for the mix?*** Variations in work content, mix changes, and volume changes all affect the manner in which we schedule the pacemaker. A detailed review of finished goods inventory strategy and part type (make to order, make to stock, custom part, and so on) is needed to determine the correct method for balancing the flow along with resources.

7. ***How will we create standard work for the mix?*** When there are several products running through the pacemaker, we have to create a way for operators to know how to build each product without reading. Pictures and graphics are ideal here.

8. ***How will we create pitch at the pacemaker?*** A mix of products with different build times and different pack quantities makes creating pitch very challenging. In some way, we have to make a preset time to issue the schedule for the next product in order to build and move material for a high-mix environment. Concepts such as floating pitch (where it can change every day) and inverse pitch (used where *takt* time is greater than a day) can help achieve this.

9. ***How do we schedule the mix at the pacemaker?*** We will need a method for taking daily demand from the customers and leveling it to match the balanced flow and inventory strategies. Logic charts, which provide standard work for production leveling, need to be created in order to achieve this.

10. ***How do we deal with changes in customer demand?*** Some
    changes in customer demand can be handled by buffering
    inventory. However, knowing the limits of the value stream
    is key. We may need to create multiple "modes" of the value
    stream to handle customer demand changes that go beyond
    the existing design limits of our pacemaker. This may in-
    volve creating two or three additional future-state value
    streams and recalculating the answers to Questions 1 to 10
    here, starting with a demand that exceeds what the current
    design can achieve.

Mixed-model calculations are more than roughed-in numbers.
They require good data along with some spreadsheet work. Tem-
plates should be set up, as things will change in the future, and several what-if scenarios have to be created to ensure that our pacemaker
can meet the customers' demands.

WHAT YOU WOULD SEE

Once the mixed-model calculations have been performed, there is
more information on or near the future-state map (see Figure 17.7).
This includes

- A large product family matrix with the products grouped
  into families.
- A depiction of the pacemaker that contains graphic information such as:

  - The number of stations.
  - The number of operators.
  - The exact equipment identified.
  - The machine load on the equipment.
  - The interval that the equipment can support.

Processes

Products	PCB Assembly	Wire Harness Assembly	Spot Weld	Electrical Assembly	Mechanical Assembly	Burn In	Test	Ship	
Housing Interconnect	X	X	X	X	X	X	X	X	Attachments Family
Connector Rod Assembly		X	X	X	X	X	X	X	
Tie Rod Assembly	X	X	X	X	X	X	X	X	
Drive Assembly		X		X				X	Drive Family
Motor Housing	X						X	X	Housing Family
Cover Plate Assembly	X					X	X	X	

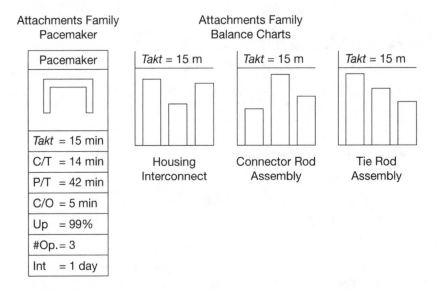

Attachments Family
Pacemaker

Pacemaker
Takt = 15 min
C/T = 14 min
P/T = 42 min
C/O = 5 min
Up = 99%
#Op.= 3
Int = 1 day

Attachments Family
Balance Charts

Takt = 15 m   Takt = 15 m   Takt = 15 m

Housing
Interconnect

Connector Rod
Assembly

Tie Rod
Assembly

Figure 17.7 *Mixed-Model Pacemaker*

◆ Balance charts for the active products produced.

◆ A graphical layout of the balancing methods that will be used for flow.

◆ A detailed layout for finished goods inventory and an inventory strategy for build-to-order products.

◆ Illustrations of how pitch will be created.

◆ A sample logic chart for scheduling the pacemaker.

◆ An analysis of customer demand vs. *takt* capability and a display of additional future states with different *takt* capabilities if needed.

A final note on mixed-model analysis: mixed-model analysis is a detailed subject, and we are covering only the highlights here. The information is presented in detail in the book *Creating Mixed Model Value Streams*.[4]

SHARED RESOURCES

Once we have designed our pacemaker for mixed-model flow, we would next review the other processes in the value stream, in particular any shared resources that may exist (see Figure 17.8). Shared resources are most common in machine shop environments, where it seems that every machine can be used to make any part as long as we make the right tooling changes. Therefore, a spaghetti flow tends to exist. Creating flow through shared resources is another subject that requires a deep dive, but there are six design guidelines that can help us break apart the spaghetti flow and create product and process families. When we are dealing with shared resources, we should first try to dedicate as many of the shared resources as possible to create an uninterrupted flow. First, we should check to see whether we can extend the product family farther upstream by dedicating some of the equipment to the product family. If we cannot do this, then we try to create process families by assigning a group of parts to always run on the same equipment, no matter what product family they are

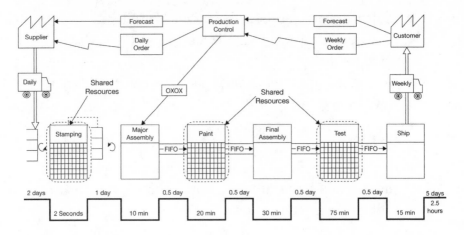

Figure 17.8 *Shared Resources*

in. If we cannot create product or process families, then we have a true shared resource that will involve such things as sequenced FIFO and offset scheduling.

Unlike our earlier analyses, where we answered the design guideline questions in sequence, this time we will answer the first three questions with a yes or a no, and as soon as we get a yes answer, jump directly to Question 4 and continue the process from there. Here are the six design guideline questions for creating flow through shared resources:

1. ***Can we extend the product families?*** The first step is to determine whether it is possible to dedicate the parts in a product family to the shared resource. This is done by considering the parts that go across the shared resource and performing a load analysis. Many options have to be taken into account, such as using an alternative machine or retooling an older machine to produce parts outside the family. If we can rearrange which parts go across a shared resource and extend the product family, we can go directly to Question 4.

2. ***Can we create process families with dedicated equipment?*** If we cannot extend the product family, the next step is to review the processing steps and the parts produced to see whether we can create a process family. When we create a process family, a group of machines that have been shared previously will now be dedicated to a group of parts that can be used by different product families. This group dedication means that a group of parts is tied to a group of machines, no matter where those parts are used in the operation. It also means that we can create flow within this group of machines, too. An analysis of machine loading, tooling, *takt* time, and other factors goes into determining process families. Again, if we can create a process family, we can go directly to Question 4.

3. ***Can we create flow through true shared resources?*** If we cannot extend the family and we cannot create a process family, then we know that we have a true shared resource. In handling a shared resource, the concept of the interval is critical, which tells us how long it will take to cycle through the mix of products that go through the shared resource. Another way to think of this is as our ability to handle a mix of parts across the shared resource. Once this is established, we then create a guaranteed turnaround time (GTT), or throughput time. This time guarantees to the other processes that if a product is at the shared resource (most likely in a FIFO lane) by a certain time, it will be delivered to the next process by a certain time.

4. ***Can we balance to create continuous flow?*** Once we have determined whether we can extend the family, create a process family, or treat the process like a true shared resource, we now have to balance the work done within the shared resource in order to create flow. This means using balance charts to create machine cells, where we determine how many people are

needed to run the machines at the rate required to satisfy *takt* for the product families they support.

5. ***How will the shared resource know what to make next?*** Shared resources are usually a high point of contention when it comes to scheduling. The answer here is to eliminate the scheduling through the use of different types of FIFO, such as sequenced FIFO, in which multiple lanes are sequenced through the shared resource in a set order, and offset scheduling, where the shared resource works through a sequence list when a spot in the FIFO lane opens up.

6. ***How will we manage the shared resource?*** Shared resources are valuable and are usually heavily managed to optimize their efficiency. Here, we want to determine how *not* to manage them, and instead let flow do the work. If there are technical needs that require technical managers, then we must ensure that the managers focus not only on the technical side of the equipment but also on the flow side. Besides the technical performance, a useful measurement in this case might be the number of interruptions to flow, to the product families as well as to the customer.

Creating flow through shared resources is challenging. The set of guidelines given here provides a process for addressing these challenges. It is important to note that after these guidelines have been followed, things will change. New products will be introduced, technical requirements will change, and new tooling will be procured. These and other changes will mean that the guidelines will need to be followed again and the numbers rerun. It is important that a process is set up to handle these changes, as they will become a way of life. It is also important that we address shared resources in terms of flow. When purchasing a new piece of machinery, while the technical specifications matter, the impact on flow should be the overarching principle that drives our decision.

WHAT YOU WOULD SEE

Back in the war room, we would see our future-state map with the shared resources identified. For each shared resource, there should be a separate piece of paper with the answers to each of the guideline questions. Along with these answers, a set of four graphs should be attached (see Figure 17.9). These charts graphically show

- The future-state load against the shared resource.
- The interval for the shared resource.
- The branch *takt* vs. weighted cycle time.
- The connection type—FIFO, sequenced FIFO, offset scheduling, supermarket, hybrid, or something else—that the shared resource will use.

Additional data, such as the parts list for the new process families, the tooling changes needed, where the parts that were removed from the resource will now be produced, improvements needed in uptime and setup time, and more, will also need to be listed. Dealing with shared resources is a deeply technical part of designing flow. The key is to be able to teach the design of flow not just to the managers to get approval for the changes, but to everyone, so that everyone will know how to operate the shared resource in a flow environment, thereby creating a normal designed flow that will allow us to see when abnormal flow begins to happen.

THE OFFICE

Once we have designed the detailed flow for the value streams within our manufacturing operation, the next step is to design the flow of information in our office environments in order to support seamless flow on the production floor and to our customers. While we do not necessarily build product in the office, our business processes are there to perform a service. The service can be to another area of flow,

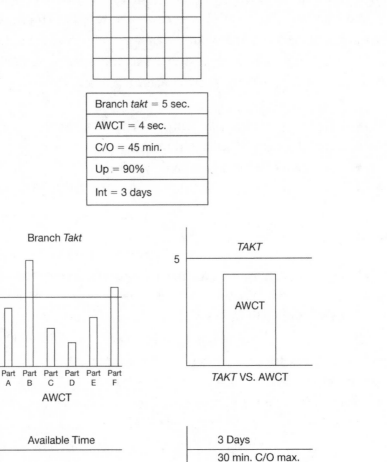

Figure 17.9 *Shared Resources—What You Would See*

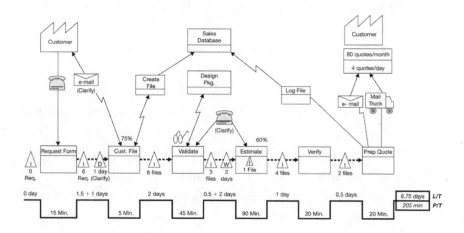

Figure 17.10 *Quoting Process—Current State*

or to the customer. For example, a current-state map for the quoting process is shown in Figure 17.10.

The office is also a place where we should formally capture knowledge. We do not want to be reworking information; we want to be formally capturing it for future use. Although there have been many brainstorming sessions in the office to improve how work flows, as we have mentioned earlier, a robust flow that creates Operational Excellence in the office is not created by brainstorming. It is created by following design guidelines for business processes. There are nine of these guidelines that will teach us how to connect processes, establish pathways for flow, and set timing for the flow, and will allow us to know whether the flow is normal or abnormal.

The concepts presented here have been published in a story format in the book *The Office That Grows your Business: Achieving Operational Excellence in Your Business Processes.*[5] Again, the guidelines are given as questions to help ensure they are applied. The nine design guidelines for business processes are

1. ***What is the* takt *or* takt *capability for the service needed?*** *Takt* time can be a difficult concept in the office, where we tend to do things as needed. However, it is important to set a rate at which the service should happen so that we can create a flow that supports this rate. If we do not know how often the customer will want the service, then we should set a capability for what we can do. As with our pacemaker on the production floor, capability is expressed in terms of mix and volume. For example, in processing quotes, not only would we set a capability of performing five quotes per day but we would also know that we could do only one complex quote within that five per day.

2. ***Where can we apply continuous flow?*** The office is not like the production flow, and creating cells in which people process information in one-piece flow all day does not seem likely. However, we can bring people together at a preset time each day or each week as needed, based on *takt* capability, in order to process information in a one-piece flow format. Hence, we can create processing cells. A good example of a processing cell would be to have the people who need to sign approvals meet each week at a preset time. Then, in a one-piece flow manner, they would review and sign the approvals. By establishing a set time for the processing cell to meet, we eliminate the endless chasing of information, since we know when the approvals are supposed to happen.

3. ***Where can we apply FIFO?*** Once processing cells are established, we have to ensure that the cell knows what to work on next without a manager setting priorities. FIFO is a method of doing this. FIFO can involve physical folders that are hanging where the processing cells meet, or it can use an electronic inbox. Whatever the method, the key is to have only one choice of what to do next.

4. ***Where can we apply workflow cycles?*** Workflow cycles are defined as having information follow a preset physical pathway at preset times. Having a physical pathway means creating a physical route, be it folders or an electronic format, that has a starting and an ending point. Preset times means that information will follow this pathway at certain times and only at those times, similar to the way trains run down a track: the physical pathway is the track, and the trains run only at certain times. Workflow cycles are a key design principle in the office, as they set up a GTT similar to that for our shared resource flow. This eliminates endless e-mails, voice mails, and meetings, as everyone knows when the workflow cycle happens, and therefore knows when the information will flow.

5. ***Where will we need to apply integration events?*** Integration events are used to move large blocks of information from one area of the company to another. These events do not take place on a daily basis. If they did, we would use workflow cycles. These are events that happen only every few weeks or even less frequently. Think about closing the books or turning over information on a new product from Engineering to Production. Integration events match outputs to inputs and are also ways to capture knowledge that is created as information flows to different areas of the company.

6. ***How can we create standard work?*** As in manufacturing, we need to create not only standard work for how things are done in the office but also standard work for the *flow* in the office. This tends to be more difficult, since office personnel seem to develop their own methods not only for how to do something but also for when to do it.

7. ***At what single point will we initialize the work?*** In manufacturing, we schedule a single process called the pacemaker and let flow and pull do the rest. In the office, we should try to

apply this as much as possible. We may not be able to have only one process get a schedule that determines everything else that is done in the office, but we can probably set an initialization point for each type of flow, such as quoting, engineering changes, invoicing, and so on. This single point will set the sequence in which the work flows through these value streams, while the workflow cycles will set the timing and path of the flow.

8 *How will we create pitch?* Pitch lets us know whether the flow is on time. We strive to create this by having a physical activity happen at the rate of *takt* or *takt* capability. At the end of a workflow cycle, information should move, and this may be a good place to create pitch, as it can be binary: either the work has been completed during the cycle, or it has not. Again, it is important that we make this a very visual indication of flow and not leave it up to someone to report. For example, at the end of the workflow cycle, a green flag or indicator should be posted so that everyone can see that the flow is on time.

9. *How will we deal with changes in demand?* Demand for the types of work done in the office will always be variable. Knowing the limits of the design is key, as we can then see whether things are within the limits or not. We will also need an established "Plan B" for when demand exceeds our limits. This could include running workflow cycles more often, extending the time for the processing cell, or diverting work to other cross-trained staff members.

By using these guidelines, we can design a flow for the office in which everyone knows what to work on next based on the process flow, not management. Processing cells, FIFO, and workflow cycles set up physical pathways and timing for the information to flow. The end result of these are guaranteed turnaround times that inform everyone in the office exactly when information will flow, eliminating

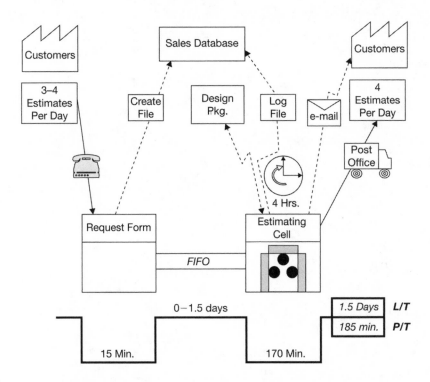

Figure 17.11 *Quoting Process—Future State*

the endless searching for information and interruptions that derail employees from performing their work at a steady rate. Figure 17.11 shows the future-state map for the quoting process.

WHAT YOU WOULD SEE

Back to our war room, where we have created the design for business process flow. On the walls, there should be poster-sized sheets of paper showing a current-state map, the answers to the nine design questions, a future-state map, and an implementation plan (see Figure 17.12). Again, these are hand-drawn maps made using sticky

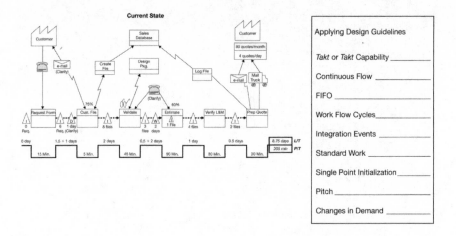

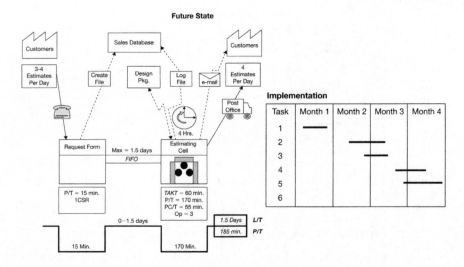

Figure 17.12 *Office—What You Would See*

notes. They should have been put together by people working as a group, not by one person sitting in front of a computer. As with a value stream map in manufacturing, we should see

◆ A current-state map showing the business process steps and the queues of work between them. The current-state map should also have a lead-time ladder, which is a graphical representation of the total amount of time it takes to deliver the service compared with the total amount of time it actually takes to process the information. The lead-time ladder shows the ratio of lead time to process time.

◆ The list of the nine guidelines, with an explanation of how and where each guideline is being applied.

◆ A future-state map. The future-state map should not have any wait or delay symbols or any eyeglasses, which mean that management oversees the process and sets priorities. Workflow cycles should have a dotted line that indicates the starting processes and the ending processes that involve the workflow cycle, along with the timing of the cycle. We also should be able to trace the total flow of information in a closed loop, as mentioned earlier.

◆ An implementation plan that has been developed by implementing flow closest to the customer, starting with the processing cells, then FIFO, then workflow cycles, then working upstream. Work in the upstream processes can be done in parallel or concurrently, but the actual connection of the processes must take place in sequence, starting from the customer and then working upstream.

A final note on business processes: there can be quite a bit of variation in the day-to-day workload in the office. Applying the guidelines may seem difficult in these situations, so we may need to develop multiple *takt* capabilities, as we did in manufacturing. It is also important to note that the variety of tasks handled by the people in the office and changing demand for different tasks may seem to make it impossible for people to work in flow. If this is the case, then we might not be able to work in flow 100 percent of the time. However, we would target working in flow at some points in time on a regular basis. If demand is down on a given day, a processing cell may be canceled for that day. If demand is up, we run the cell more often. Understanding the true process families and what should go through the workflow cycles and FIFO lanes that we create (and what should not) will help with this.

THE SUPPLY CHAIN

Along with designing a robust flow that creates Operational Excellence in manufacturing and the office, we also need to design flow in the supply chain as well (see Figure 17.13).

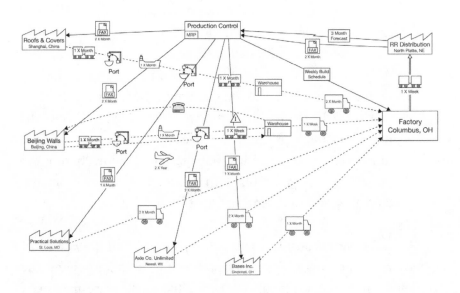

Figure 17.13 *Supply Chain Current-State Map*

Again, we can develop great flow in our facilities, but that flow will frequently fail if one part is missing because of the supply chain. In the supply chain, it's not just about working with suppliers on their production floor to ensure that we know that they are applying continuous improvement in terms of quality, delivery, and cost. It is about educating the suppliers on the design that we have put into our own operation and teaching them how this design applies to them. Our goal is to build a formal, robust connection with the suppliers, similar to the connections that we built between our own processes on our manufacturing floor and in our office. However, before we can successfully build this connection with the suppliers, *the suppliers have to apply the guidelines of flow within their facilities.*

There are several types of connections that can be built with a supplier. These connections are binary, meaning that they have a single source from which they originate and a single receiver to which they are sent, and they have standard work on both ends in order to ensure that the supplier knows what to send and when to send it. These connections let us know if there's a problem and can tell us before it's too late that the supplier will be unable to meet a delivery.

The following design guidelines allow us to create these binary connections and signals and pathways, the sum of which helps us to create a supply chain that never fails. Again, the guidelines are listed as questions to help ensure that they are applied. The seven design guidelines for flow through the supply chain are

1. *What type of supply chain do you have?* The first step is to take an overall look at the type of supply chain you would like to establish. Is the philosophy in your operation one of vertical integration, where you purchase raw material, such as bar stock, pellets, or sheet steel, and perform fabrication and assembly steps to build the complete product and ship it to the customer? Or is your philosophy to buy components or modules from the supply chain and just perform final

assembly and testing operations? Deciding which type of supply chain you have will help you make decisions on how to design for flow.

2. *How will the supplier know what to build next?* It is important that we have a single signal and only one signal that tells the supplier what to build next. The signal should be generated from only one source. The signal must be binary, and there should be standard work on how to send it and on what the supplier should do when they receive the signal.

3. *How will the material flow from the supplier?* We should try to establish a physical pathway through which the material flows from the supplier to our facility. This includes the pathway for the signal once it reaches the supplier to the supplier's production floor, the pathway for the material being produced on the production floor to the shipping deck, the pickup of the material, the vehicle for transportation, the route, and the receiving, all to the point of final consumption.

4. *What type of connection will we use?* A signal and a pathway create the connection. However, there are different types of connections. Sequenced FIFO, single supermarket pull systems, dual supermarket pull systems, and rolling *kanbans* are all different types of connections that we might use. The key is to understand which type of part gets which type of connection. A matrix of supplier distance, reliability, part cost, demand variation, and other variables can set up standard work for the type of connection that we should use for each part.

5. *How will we determine a supplier's capability?* This involves much more than just the supplier's capacity. For each supplier, we should have an established capability in terms of mix and volume for the parts it supplies. The supplier should have established a pacemaker for the flow of each product

family within its facility, and then identify that capability to its respective customers.

6. ***How will we level load the supplier?*** Once we know the supplier's capability in terms of mix and volume, we will always know whether we have exceeded this capability when planning or placing orders. It will also let us know long before the product is due when a supply chain has the potential to fail.

7. ***How do we know that a supplier will never fail?*** Once we have established robust connections based on the design guidelines inside the supplier's four walls and between the supplier and our operation, an early warning system can be put in, as things will happen in real life. The supplier can initiate a signal to the customer when there has been a problem with its flow. The signal should have standard work on whom it is to be sent to, how to send it, and what information to include, and we should also have standard work on what to do when we receive the signal.

Creating flow in the supply chain is a difficult task. One of the difficulties is that we tend to think of how we are going to *manage* the supply chain, when in fact a supply chain that has good flow requires little or no management. How we view the supply chain will affect our ability to create robust flow. If we view it as the supplier's responsibility to provide the parts using whatever means it has, then we will always be dependent upon the supplier's knowledge when it comes to designing flow. If we educate the supplier, share how our operation has been designed for flow, and view the supplier as an integral part of this, then we may be more successful in designing flow in the supply chain and ensuring that the supplier never fails (see Figure 17.14).

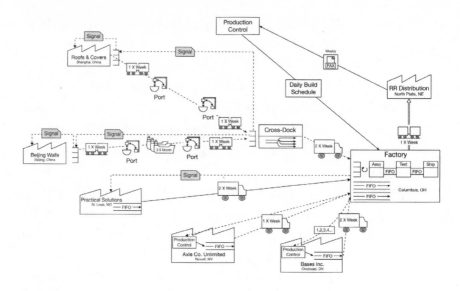

Figure 17.14 *Supply Chain Future-State Map*

WHAT YOU WOULD SEE

Let's go back to our war room. Here, we should see the main suppliers depicted on a future-state map along with the type of connection that we plan to establish with each of them. A few extra sheets of paper should contain some details on how we will build each connection with each supplier (see Figure 17.15 on pages 162 and 163). This includes

- ◆ A connection matrix.
- ◆ A lead-time Pareto for part numbers.
- ◆ A current-state map of the supply chain.
- ◆ A future-state map of the supply chain.
- ◆ An implementation plan.
- ◆ How the signal will be sent to each supplier.
- ◆ Where the signal specifically originates from.

- ◆ Whom the signal gets sent to.
- ◆ How often the signal gets sent.
- ◆ How the material will be delivered (truck, rail, or another method).
- ◆ What containers it will be placed in (pallets, rolls, barrels, or another container).
- ◆ How often it will be delivered.
- ◆ How we will know before it affects us if there is a breakdown in flow from the supplier.
- ◆ What actions have to be performed with the supplier to ensure that it is working in flow in its operation.

Again, the intent here is to teach the design, especially to those in the supply chain, as there will be many questions and many different thoughts on how to "manage" it. Each supplier is also different, so it may be a good idea to start with the ones that have progressed with a formal continuous improvement program. Perhaps have them join in an educational session, tour your site, and have them visit your war room. With the supply chain, the key to creating flow and Operational Excellence is not negotiation but education. With this education, the suppliers will realize that this design will help them grow their business as well, a good win/win for all parties involved.

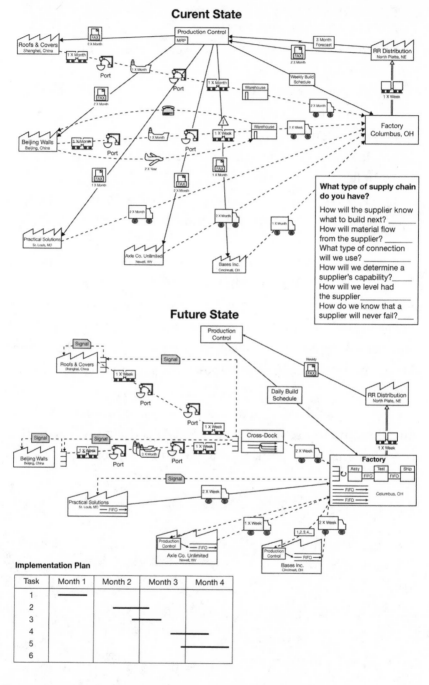

Figure 17.15 *Supply Chain—What You Would See (continued)*

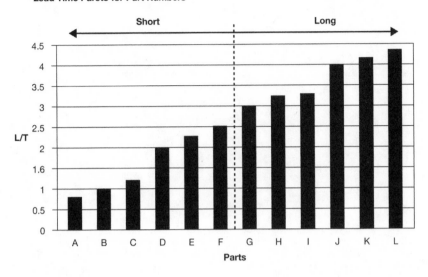

Lead Time Pareto for Part Numbers

Connection Matrix

Connection	Lead-Time		Demand Part Usage			Part Cost			Reliability	
	Long	Short	Runner	Repeater	Stranger	High	Medium	Low	Good	Fair
Sequence FIFO		X	X	X		X			X	
Single Supermarket		X	X	X		X	X	X	X	
Dual Supermarket	X		X	X			X	X		X
Rolling Kanban	X		X				X	X	X	X
VMI		X	X	X	X			X	X	X
Spot P.O.	X				X	X	X		X	X

Figure 17.15 *(continued)*

The Second Principle: Make Lean Value Streams Flow

Once we have designed a true lean value stream using the design principles discussed in the previous chapter, the next step is to bring the design to life. Think of this principle as the beginning of "from paper to performance," taking our design from the paper in our war room, our future-state value stream map and implementation plan, and achieving the design out in the real world of our operation. There is quite a bit of information that can be found on the subject of implementing lean flow, and many good tools are available. We won't be exploring these tools in detail, as the focus here is not on how to implement a lean value stream but on how to implement a lean value stream in a manner that creates Operational Excellence. In other words, while we created a detailed design of the flow in our future-state value stream, we are not looking just to put in a lean flow. We are looking to implement a self-healing flow that eliminates the need for management. It is also important that we set up a formal process to present the concepts and process to the employees who are working in the flow so that they know the company's destination and know what it would look like when it is achieved, thus enabling them to contribute to achieving the destination. And to be successful, all of this involves formal education.

The first step in going from paper to performance is to provide formal classroom and hands-on education. While we have a nice war room full of information to share, this is not the place to start. In fact, bringing workers into the room and showing them the design would be more like giving them a presentation that could seem like just another management initiative. Since the workers know the current products and processes well, we could easily slip back into suggestions and brainstorming on how to improve specific areas. Again, these may be good suggestions for specific areas, but our goal is to implement a complete design for Operational Excellence throughout the organization.

In the Classroom

The initial classroom educational session should set the objectives and be very clear about the intended outcome of the design. It is very important that the employees who build the product know that this process is about much more than continuous improvement, where we try to eliminate waste or to improve productivity, efficiency, or quality. Let's be very clear: the objective of our design is to have self-healing flow and flow without management. Each employee must know exactly where we are going with the new design and know that it *does* have the expected result of having the employees be able to see flow and fix it before it breaks down. This will add a new dimension, as workers will now be challenged in an area where they have not been challenged before.

In order to accomplish this, we should start with academic training on continuous improvement and how it traditionally works. Then, there should be an exercise that includes the nine questions for Operational Excellence. The employees who are being trained should be broken up into groups and asked to answer each question on a flipchart, then present their answers. Show them the number of different answers that the various groups have developed, then provide the single one-sentence answers that we provided in Chapters 7 to 15.

After the questions have been answered, next we would review the process used to design the flow. This includes

◆ An overview of a current-state value stream map, with emphasis on the lead-time ladder, the information flows (and how many there are), and the eyeglasses, which represent the amount of management oversight and reprioritization involved in production.

◆ An overview of the eight guidelines for flow, with a practical explanation of each principle.

◆ An academic example of applying these guidelines.

◆ An interactive simulation or exercise.

◆ An application of applying these guidelines to the targeted value stream.

◆ A review of the implementation plan.

◆ At the end of the session, a walk out to the targeted area and a discussion of the design and how it applies to the actual manufacturing of the product.

A formal classroom session could last from one to three days, depending upon the detail needed and the processes and products involved. It would probably be a good idea to hold off on the more technical guidelines for mixed-model and shared resource flow until the basics are well understood. Perhaps save these sessions for a few weeks later, after the initial training has been applied.

ON THE SHOP FLOOR

Immediately after the classroom training, the actual application out on the shop floor should start. During this application, we use the standard lean tools, such as cell design, balance charts, *kanban* design, poka-yoke, and SMED. Other tools can be taught and applied as needed, all to achieve the designed future state. Once the details have been worked out on paper, the next step is a "cardboard city," or a cardboard-and-duct-tape mockup of the new design. This is sometimes referred to as 3P (production, preparation, process), and it can be used when new products are introduced into an existing value stream as well as when an existing process is being redesigned. Building full-scale mockups allows the operators to see a life-size representation of the applied tools that are being used to achieve each guideline, such as a one-piece flow cell connecting to a FIFO. With this mockup, operators can figure out exactly where material will be placed, how it will be presented, where tooling will be placed, where the next setup will be stored, and much more.

Once the mockup has been created and all the details have been worked out, the equipment can be placed in accordance with the mockup, and production using the new design can begin. It is important that we implement the new design starting from the customer and then moving upstream to raw material. Our implementation plan should reflect this, and it needs to be followed in that order. Flow could break down quite often if we were to start from the raw material end or in the middle in a specific "targeted area for improvement" without having established a steady flow at the customer end first.

WHAT YOU WOULD SEE ON THE SHOP FLOOR

Once we have educated the workers on the design objectives, the process of the design, and the implementation of the design, and have created mockups or put actual machinery in place with lean tools, we are set to "flip the switch" and allow value stream flow to begin in the implemented areas. Again, while we may have worked on many areas in accordance with our plan to stabilize them and prep them for flow, the "switch" connecting these areas should be flipped from the customer back to the receiving deck.

Once the switch has been flipped and value stream flow has begun, a walk on the shop floor should reveal several things:

- We should see one-piece flow cells in which operators perform work in a make-one, move-one fashion. These are usually found in assembly areas, but they can be found in machining and fabrication areas as well.

- We should see different potential configurations for these cells based on demand, standard work for building the product, a skills matrix with the different skills required, tool presentation and good 5S, and set places where inventory can be placed between the operators, with room enough for only one piece being optimal.

- We should also see formal standards for material presentation, operator flowcharts that show which positions operators should take for different demand configurations, standard work for building the product, and standard times.

- We may also see processes that are connected by physical FIFO lanes, which can be identified by markings on the floor or on shelves, constructed with conveyors, or created using many other different methods.

- If applicable, we may see processes that are connected by *kanban* or supermarket systems, usually shared resources or supplier connections. This could involve a card system or color-coded zones, or perhaps be done electronically.

- If we have done well with the implementation, we should see a *heijunka*, or load-level schedule box that contains what the value stream should produce next. This should have timing along the top that tells when the schedule should be delivered to the schedule point or pacemaker.

WHAT YOU WOULD SEE IN THE OFFICE

While we have discussed the classroom and shop floor implementation of flow, the same process applies in the office as well. We would perform the classroom education, followed by application in the office. When this is completed, we would see physical changes happening. These would include

- ◆ Areas identified as processing cells, with the equipment each worker needs to perform the work in the cell, such as computers, printers, and books.
- ◆ The processing cells meeting at preset times to flow information.
- ◆ Workflow cycles established to move information to and from the processing cells.
- ◆ Physical FIFO lanes that hold folders of work marked ingoing and outgoing.
- ◆ A method for seeing that pitch has been established.

Now that we have taken the design from paper and physically created the framework for flow in our shop floor and in our office, the next step is to make flow visual. Companies that use continuous improvement tools spend quite a bit of time creating flow through their processes by using cells with one-piece flow, FIFO, *kanban*, and other such techniques. However, in order to create Operational Excellence, we have to make that flow visual so that each employee can see how the processes are connected to one another and to the customer.

19

The Third Principle: Make Flow Visual

Physical changes have been made, machines have been moved, cells have been formed, and standard work has been put in place. People have been trained, and the operation has begun producing products in the new future-state design. In the office, *takt* capability has been established, processing cells have been set up, workflow cycles have been created, and the people in the office now understand how information should flow. At this point, we are about to enter the performance stage, where we try to get the value stream to flow the way it was designed. It is also the point where we begin to apply the first part of exactly what Operational Excellence is, "When each and every employee can see the flow of value to the customer."

While it is often thought that the visual factory is one in which each area, such as the painting department, the toolroom, Accounting, and others, or each location for items, such as tools or parts, is clearly identified by a visual indicator, this is not the true purpose of a visual factory in a design that supports Operational Excellence. Plainly stated, in Operational Excellence, *visuals are for flow*. This means that just about any visual indicator in the operation should have something to do with the flow or the progression of the flow of product to the customer. This means not only on the production floor, but also in the office, where we flow information to the customer and also flow information that supports the operation. Although this is not specifically stated in our definition, it also means creating visuals for flow in nonproduction or non-customer-related processes. In Finance, we require information from many different areas of the company in order to pay taxes. In Human Resources, we hire people and administer benefits. At the executive level, we review potential acquisitions that are strategic to growth. All these activities and more can and should be performed in flow, and that flow should be made visual.

The visuals for flow that we are discussing here are broken into two categories to reflect and support the two types of designs for the operation: *static* visuals and *dynamic* visuals. As a reminder, static is the design at rest, and dynamic is the design when the operation is in motion. Visuals that support the static design are indicators of how flow should work normally, based on the design from our future-state map. Dynamic indicators let us know the current status of flow as we are observing it, or how we are performing to the design as we observe it happening.

STATIC VISUALS

One of the basic static visuals is a map of the flow that shows each person who is working in the flow exactly where he is in it and the processes that connect him all the way to the customer. In other words, it shows the employees the design of the end-to-end flow and where each of them is located with regard to that flow. This can be done by posting the value stream map at each process. A drawing of the facility layout should also be posted, showing the physical pathway that the product travels through the factory along with the time it takes to do so. On both the value stream map and the facility layout, a "you are here" identification should be shown so that everyone can tell where this process is in the flow to the customer. Figure 19.1 shows an example of such a map.

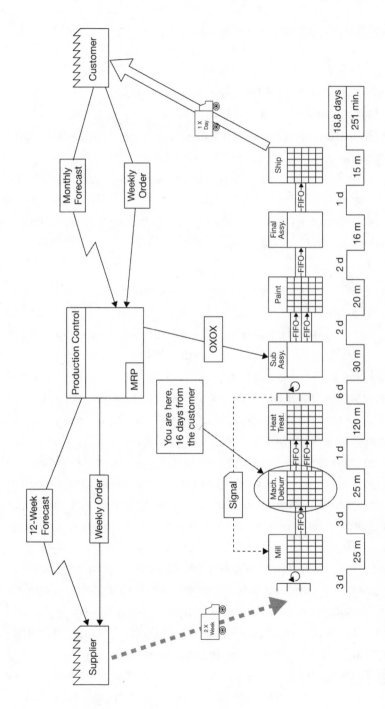

Figure 19.1 *Identifying a process in flow.*

From this visual, employees who work in the flow should be able to tell

- ◆ The overall design for the end-to-end flow.
- ◆ Where they are located in the flow.
- ◆ How they are connected to the processes before them and after them.
- ◆ How many processes there are between them and the customer.
- ◆ How much time it will take the product to get from where they are to the customer.

Along with the overall map of flow, another static visual would be a fixed area that is clearly labeled for the input and output for each process. This indicator should state the inputs and outputs of the process in terms of where parts come from and where they go. It should also state when the parts should move to the next process based on the design of the flow. Note that the indicator may have to be flexible (a post with a sign that can be changed, for example), as the size and location of parts may change.

Supermarkets and *kanban* systems are good examples of static visuals. Having green, yellow, and red zones that match the designed inventory levels lets employees know the right amount of inventory for flow. Other static visuals include outlines or spaces that identify how much inventory should be kept between the processes. This could be on a tabletop between stations in a cell or in a supermarket of inventory that connects a supplier to a process. It could also be a sign on the shipping deck stating when the next customer truck will arrive or when the next truck will leave. Static visuals show the framework of how the flow has been designed and how the flow is supposed to work. A good test for the static visuals at each process is that they should answer the following five questions concerning flow *visually*:

◆ How do I know what to work on next?
◆ Where do I get my work from?
◆ How long will it take me to complete the work?
◆ Where do I send the work?
◆ When do I send the work?

If a static visual at each process can answer these questions with a single binary answer, not "it depends" or "see your supervisor," then you probably have good visuals that will support Operational Excellence.

DYNAMIC VISUALS

If we are standing at a process, not only do we want to see how the flow is designed to work but we also want to know whether the flow is on time relative to our customer demand. The visuals that indicate this are dynamic visuals. They enable the employees who are in the flow and everyone else to know the performance of the flow as it happens. "As it happens" does not mean that at each minute or each second each employee can tell if she is exactly on time to the customer. It means that as the flow is happening there are set times at which each employee can tell whether she is on time or not. In the book *Learning to See*, this is referred to as a "management time-frame" or "pitch."[1] It's the same concept in Operational Excellence, except that it is not for management; it's for the employees who are working in the flow. An example of pitch is that a finished case holding 12 products should be completed every 24 minutes; hence the *takt* time for each product is two minutes. Therefore, we will tell the material handler to go to that process every 24 minutes and move the product to the next process. If the material handler shows up and the case of product is ready to go, then the flow is on time. If the case has not been completed, then there is something wrong, and the flow is not performing as designed. Other dynamic visuals can measure potential part shortages before they affect flow. A look at a supermarket system that shows cards in the red zone will alert us if a potential part will not show up when needed and thus affect the flow.

VISUALS FOR THE OFFICE

In an office, it is typically difficult to see whether there is an end-to-end design for the flow of information. It is even more difficult to tell whether that design is working and performing as it should. The only way we really know whether end-to-end flow is on time is through management. Management does try to create flow by making schedules, establishing due dates, setting priorities, and other similar activities. But this is done in the individual segments of the flow by the manager who is responsible for each segment. In order to connect the flow of information to different areas or try to get the right information to flow through different areas when needed, we hold a meeting.

In the office, it is difficult to think about a design for end-to-end flow. Even if we design it correctly, we have a tendency to tinker with it every day. People in the office usually want to make their own decisions concerning what to work on next, and if these decisions are in line with their manager's priorities, everything is fine. If they are not, the manager sets new priorities for them. It is very easy to go off course in the office, very easy for the design of flow to erode quickly and slip back into prioritizing, expediting, and meetings. Therefore, it is critical that we establish static and dynamic visuals to keep us on course in the office. Think of it this way: if the design of flow provides the road to follow to achieve Operational Excellence in the office, then the visuals are the guardrails.

Creating static and dynamic visuals for the office may seem difficult, since information flows by various means. Physical information flows through e-mail, fax, paperwork, pictures, blueprints, and spreadsheets, while other nonphysical information flows through communication by voice mail, formal meetings, and informal meetings at the water cooler, in the coffee area, in hallways, and in other places. The flow of information is not consistent, as people frequently travel out of the office and are not available. The design guidelines for information flow in the office are intended to take the nonphysical information that flows through communication and synchronize it with the physical flow of information, which is why we use processing cells and workflow cycles that establish times when informal information will meet formal, physical information. Our static visuals in the office need to reflect this. Static visuals indicate when processing cells will meet, when a workflow cycle will be completed, the guaranteed turnaround time for an area of information flow, when the next integration event will happen, and what point in the flow initializes the sequence of work. All of this should be identified visually.

As in manufacturing, the dynamic design enables us to know how the designed flow is performing. If we know when the processing cell should meet, we also know when information should flow, and we can make this visual as well. For example, quotes are processed in a processing cell at 10:00 a.m. each day, then they go to Sales at 3:00 p.m. so that Sales can call the customer at 4:00 p.m. The dynamic indicator could be a small green flag that is put up at 3:00 p.m. to indicate that all quotes have been completed in the preceding cell and sent to Sales. Another dynamic indicator could be a flag in the Sales area that shows that all quotes have been given to the customer on time. A simple walk through the area at the appropriate time would reveal whether the flow of information in the office has been on time or not without having to ask any questions, hold any meetings, or request any reports.

It All Adds Up

In many cases, companies have set up tracking centers or areas of information so that employees can review the performance of the operation. However, these can eventually become "management wallpaper" to the employees. While the information presented at the tracking center is trying to show whether the operation is performing in accordance with the goals or objectives set by management, it usually has little or no connection to the design of flow or the relationship of the performance to the design. Understanding the static and dynamic visuals and their respective uses is key in resolving this conflict, as visuals for flow fill exactly this gap. The static visuals let the people working in the flow know exactly how the flow is designed in order to get the performance desired, and the dynamic visuals let them know whether the flow is performing as designed while it is happening. The sum of the two should add up to the performance measured in a tracking center. A walk around the floor should tell us whether the design for flow is working as intended. In addition, instead of reviewing performance weeks later or reviewing trends, a walk around the floor can tell the employees in the flow, management, and even a visitor the current performance of the operation relative to customer demand right as he walks by.

What You Would See

After establishing static and dynamic visuals for value stream flow, a walk on the shop floor would reveal

- How the end-to-end flow is designed.
- The product families identified with the flow of each value stream.
- How each process is identified in terms of where it is in the flow.
- How each process is visually connected to the next process.
- Equipment that is shared by multiple product families identified as shared resources.
- The amount of space required for each process, including space for incoming and outgoing material, clearly identified.

◆ The amount of inventory between stations and between processes, clearly identified in terms of the normal level of inventory that should be there.

◆ All inventory storage locations, identified in terms of the normal level of inventory and the minimum and maximum amount of that type of inventory.

◆ Signs that indicate where product flows to and comes from, and when the movement of material will happen.

◆ Visual indicators that let anyone know whether the flow is on time relative to customer demand.

After establishing visuals for flow in the office, a walk through the office would reveal

◆ How end-to-end flow is designed.

◆ Each process identified in terms of where it is in the flow.

◆ How each process is visually connected to the next process.

◆ Clear identification of areas established for processing cells.

◆ Signs that indicate the scope and times of workflow cycles.

◆ Signaling systems such as small flags on desks or cubicles that indicate whether each person is on time in terms of her specific workflow cycle.

◆ Folders located in FIFO lanes that identify the normal amount of work.

◆ The current work waiting or queued to be processed.

When it comes to the visual factory or the visual office, it is crucial that these visuals provide the static and dynamic design for flow. They should show how processes are connected, allow the employees to know how product flows from raw material to the customer through these connections, and indicate the part that each employee plays in creating and maintaining this flow. They should also let the employees who work in the flow know whether the flow is on time.

Our visuals should allow us to know whether we will meet the performance objectives. If the performance objectives are not met, then a diagnostic process can be put in place to determine why the operation is not performing to the design. Management can teach this diagnostic process to the employees in the flow so that they can later perform it themselves. If all is going well but the performance metrics are not being met and the visuals have not made this apparent, then something in the visuals may be wrong. It should also be noted that we may find that the visuals are correct but the performance goals were unrealistic with regard to the design. In either case, the alignment of the visuals for flow with the performance metrics is key. Above all, remember that the way to tell whether the visuals are effective is simple: the visuals should make flow so visible that a visitor could walk in, give himself a tour, and tell you whether your flow is on time without asking any questions or talking to anyone.

CHAPTER

20

:
↓

The Fourth Principle: Create Standard Work for Flow

Once we've created a good visual lean flow that lets employees see how the flow should normally work and the present condition of the flow, our next step is to apply the concept of standard work to that flow. Think of this principle as raising the guardrails and narrowing the road to keep us on course.

Standard work is a fundamental tool in continuous improvement. It is usually applied at the process level to ensure that operators can perform a specific amount of work in a preset amount of time by following a prescribed method. Standard work is usually posted at the process in the form of a sketch, drawing, computer-generated model, or some other visual means in order to supply the operator with specific instructions on how to build the product. This is done to ensure that the operators produce high-quality, consistent output. While the typical application is to apply standard work at the processes, which we did in the second principle, in this principle, we will establish standard work *between the processes.* By applying standard work both at the processes and between the processes, we stabilize the complete end-to-end flow. The intent is to reduce variation and create *normalcy* for the entire flow. First, we stabilize the flow (Principle 2), then we make it visual (Principle 3), and then we set standard work for it so that the visual flow is repeatable.

When we apply standard work between the processes, we are specifically targeting the connections that have been established between them. Since processes are defined as areas of one-piece flow, such as a single operator processing parts or a cell that moves parts through several operators in one-piece flow, the connection at the process level or within the process is a single piece of inventory. The standard work for flow within the process is usually covered by the standard work document that tells the operator how to build the product. In establishing standard work between the processes, there are basically two types of connections: first-in, first-out (FIFO) systems and supermarket systems. There are different methods for setting up and using these connections, but for our purposes, a discussion of standard work for these connections should cover most areas on the shop floor. In the office, it is different. Connections are made through workflow cycles, and we will cover these as well.

SHOP FLOOR CONNECTIONS

Out on the shop floor, if we have processes that are separated, we learned through the design guidelines that our first choice is to connect them using FIFO. FIFO is not a new concept, but how we view FIFO is an indicator of how far we can go toward achieving Operational Excellence. While most companies use FIFO to set the sequence of work, here we are setting standard work for the normal flow of work. The normal flow of work means that the FIFO lane indicates to the process that is feeding it when to send work and when to stop sending work. These "instructions" have *the same authority* that a supervisor, manager, or even the president of the company providing them would have. One way to visualize how these instructions work on the shop floor is to think of FIFO as tunnels that connect processes. An open space at the beginning of the tunnel is an instruction to the process that is feeding it to put the next product in sequence into the open space. If the tunnel is full, then the instruction to the process that is feeding it is to stop producing, since there is nowhere to put the product. Once products are in the tunnel, no one can rearrange them or change the sequence, since no one can physically get at the product. Of course, the secret to a good FIFO lane is to have the time interval during which product will sit in the tunnel be very short. The longer our FIFO lanes are, the more temptation we will have to rearrange the priorities in those lanes.

Standard work is also established in supermarkets to make sure that they are controlled. Floors that are taped or shelving that is identified to show the exact space needed for supermarkets should be evident. The product families that the inventory supports should be evident as well. As with our tunnel, finding ways of not allowing people to move cards or set priorities is important. However, we do not want to set up cages that lock up inventory; we want to do this through education, by teaching the impact of such actions on the customer and on our business. The check for good standard work at a supermarket is a simple one. Just ask the operator who runs the process that is filling the supermarket, "How do you know what to work on next?" If the answer is, "I look at the inventory level in the supermarket, then I check my priority list," that's not the right answer, as the operator has two ways of knowing, and there should only be one. It's time to update the standard work.

Supermarkets also need to be resized periodically, as customer demand and replenishment times change. Therefore, we want to make sure that our standard work for flow is adaptable. We may want to avoid painting lines and shelves and instead think more about how we will identify the supermarket as its size and the products within it change.

NORMALCY AT THE PACEMAKER

Although we have been talking about creating standard work for flow between the processes, we also need to talk about creating standard work for flow at one particular process, and that is the pacemaker. The pacemaker is the only point in the value stream that receives a schedule, and it sets the pace for the whole value stream. The pacemaker is also the single point in the value stream where information flow and material flow are initially joined, where the information is "welded" to the product. Strong standard work is needed not only for how to build the mix of products but even more for the flow of information and material into and out of the pacemaker. This standard work for flow includes how the schedule is delivered, how we ensure that the schedule is delivered on time, how we make sure that the pacemaker is on time, and how product flows from the pacemaker to the next downstream process. It is imperative that the pacemaker perform as designed in order to establish normal conditions at the point where the material and the information flows are joined. If it does not perform as designed, we can introduce a high amount of variation into the value stream.

IN THE OFFICE

In the office, creating standard work for flow may seem more challenging. It's not that the task of setting standard work for flow is more difficult, but rather that people in the office are used to making decisions right down to what they work on next. Standard work for flow takes away their ability to make decisions, and that's usually not something that people in the office are used to. For this reason, education on the design of flow and the impact on company growth is key.

In our design of flow for the office, processes have been connected through workflow cycles. These cycles let people know the physical pathway along which information flows and the timing of that pathway. Therefore, our target is to set standard work for the pathway and timing of each workflow cycle.

The first step in the office is to set standard work for flow for each individual in the flow. A detailed review of this would have been performed when we created the processing cells and workflow cycles in Principles 1 and 2. This would have included how the individuals do their work, what tools they use, where they get their information from, how they process that information, what decisions they are making, and so on. In this principle, we are creating standard work not for *how* the individuals perform their work but for *when* they perform the work and *where* it goes when they have completed it. Since each person in the flow will have to complete tasks by a certain time in order to achieve the workflow cycle, this is the first place to establish normal flow. This includes creating set times during the day that are allocated for doing the work. For example, our daily calendar might show that each day at 9:00 a.m. we book time to review requests that have come in through e-mail last night. There are no other interruptions during this time. There is no answering the phone, checking e-mail, or booking meetings. The calendar is blocked off as if you were traveling and unreachable for 30 minutes. This might seem difficult given the number of random events that occur in the office, but if everyone knows that you are unavailable from 9:00 a.m. to 9:30 a.m., then people will not expect an answer during that time. More important, if we line up these work times so that each individual in the flow uses similar time frames, then most people will be performing work and not interrupting others.

Once the timing for the activity of each individual is set, the next element of standard work for flow is determining when the processing cells will meet. This is a balancing act that involves reviewing the demand for the service provided, aligning the times for each individual to do the work, and then setting a time for the team members to come together and process the information. Since there are many tasks that an individual can perform in the office, we have to allow time for the other tasks to be performed and for the variation that will occur.

Since the office is the place where each individual is charged with making decisions, setting times for activities to occur may seem like a rigid system that requires high discipline and something that might be more suited to the shop floor. However, it is simply a different way to work, and it must be taught that way. In total, the amount of work that is performed will probably be less, as we are eliminating many phone calls and e-mails simply by letting everyone know *when* information will flow. There's no more chasing information. We have also reviewed how the work is done and the number of clarifications needed, and eliminated those as well. In effect, we have reduced the workload on the individual by setting the structure for flow. The key for this structure to work, as on the shop floor, is to have the events on each individual's daily calendar provide the instructions for what to work on at a specific time. Remember, just as in our shop floor connections, these instructions have to carry enough weight or have the same authority as if a manager or the president were standing there giving them.

WHAT YOU WOULD SEE

At this stage, we should have established flow and set standard work for how normal flow should operate based on the design guidelines. After applying this principle on the shop floor and in the office, we would see the following:

- ◆ Each process is connected to the next process through a formal connection.
- ◆ Each process has standard work for the flow of material and product into and out of that process.
- ◆ Every process other than the pacemaker knows what to work on next through the standard work for the connection it has to the other processes.
- ◆ Every employee in the flow knows what to build and when to build it from the standard work for flow, not from a supervisor or an expedite list.
- ◆ In the office, set times are established for when and where processing cells will meet to process information.

- In the office, workflow cycles are established and posted to let employees know when information must flow in order to provide information to the processing cells.
- Each employee in the office has preset allocated time on his calendar to perform the tasks needed within the workflow cycles that have been established.

Standard work for flow is needed to avoid the erosion of the design for flow that we have implemented. By having standard work for flow, we can deter and perhaps even prevent managers and supervisors from moving parts within FIFO lanes or making decisions on what to work on next. This is key if we are to achieve Operational Excellence, because if we allow independent decisions to override the rules of flow at one place in the value stream, this will have an impact somewhere else in the value stream. It will lead to more decisions being made over and over again until there is no longer any standard work for flow. A good test for good standard work is the ability to tell whether normalcy has been established. This is evident by not having any expedites, priority lists, or verbal instructions from supervisors on what to build next.

Normalcy also means that we are not in a reactive environment. It means that the normal environment in which we work day to day is uneventful. The customer gives us orders, we build the product, and we ship the order. Just as the airline captain who flies a large jet airliner overseas a few times per week once said, "I take off, fly the plane overseas, and land the plane. My flights are pretty uneventful, *just the way I like them.*"

CHAPTER

21

↓

The Fifth Principle: Make Abnormal Flow Visual

Once we have established flow, created visuals for the flow, and set standard work for the flow, we have effectively created the guardrails that keep us on course to Operational Excellence. The previous principle, setting standard work for the flow, has raised these guardrails and narrowed the road to keep us tight within the course. Since our guardrails are now keeping us tight within the course, we will begin to collide with them more often. However, rather than hiding the dents we make when we collide, having management take care of them, or even applying continuous improvement tools to try to repair them once they happen, in Operational Excellence, we would strive to create the ability to allow every employee to see each collision by making the collisions visual. This way, we can learn not just how to correct them but also how to prevent them from occurring in the future without management. The premise here is that if we rigidly define what normal flow is (as we have done in the first four principles), then we should be able to see the "dents" when or before abnormal flow happens, and it will happen.

Before jumping into how to make abnormal flow visual, let's examine a good practical application of seeing abnormal flow. Let's imagine that we are walking through a hospital. During our walk, we see gurneys in the corridors with patients waiting on them. Many of us who have been through hospitals know that this is a common occurrence. Doctors and nurses walk by them; visitors walk by them; just about everyone can walk by them. They do not seem to be anything unusual. People who work there just walk by and accept (or ignore) the current condition of patient flow. Why? Because in this hospital, we have not determined whether a patient on a gurney out in the hallway represents normal or abnormal flow. And if we have not determined this and made abnormal flow visual, then it will just be ignored and left for management to deal with. The same will happen in our operations with the flow of product to the customer. The state of flow will be ignored, and abnormal flow will be business as usual. Responding to the customer will again be management's responsibility, and that's where it will spend its time. Therefore, the credibility of our normal flow visuals and the robustness of our abnormal flow visuals are among the keys to achieving Operational Excellence.

When we are defining exactly what abnormal flow is and how we will see it, we should think back to how we developed normal flow and made it visual. We did this by using design guidelines to design the flow, then set static visuals so that we could see the design, then set dynamic visuals so that we could see how the design was performing. It is important to note that the static visuals show us only how the flow has been designed to work normally; they do not show us abnormal flow. We may have to tune in or adjust what normal flow is as we implement, but once we set the visuals for normal flow, these must have credibility. If they don't, then the visuals of normal flow will always be subject to management or workers overriding them, and seeing abnormal flow will always be in question, as will fixing it.

Once we have established that the static visuals are robust and have credibility, we look to the dynamic visuals to show abnormal flow. The dynamic visuals show us how the flow is performing, and we want to make the condition of the flow stand out for each employee (or a visitor) to see. The point here is that the static visuals are intended to show only the design of flow; *it's the dynamic visuals that should show abnormal flow.*

THE VISUAL CHECKLIST

Another way to think about seeing abnormal flow is to think back to our aircraft designed for flight. The dynamic design of the airplane tells us how the aircraft should perform once it is in flight. To check its performance, the pilot goes through a structured checklist, and that is exactly what we are trying to do in our operations: set a design for flow, teach the employees working in the flow how to use a structured process to see how the flow is performing, and then teach them to initiate corrective action when the flow starts to become abnormal.

A good way to create a visual checklist to reveal abnormal flow is through the use of material movement, or the flow of material to the customer. This method is robust, as it provides a *physical method* rather than production counts on a whiteboard or a schedule attainment monitoring system. Not only is it physical, but it is easy to see, anticipated (employees know when the physical activity will happen), and binary. We can create a strong visual checklist by using material flow. The first step is to divide material flow into two areas:

1. Material quantities at a process and in a connection.
2. Material movement through the value stream.

MATERIAL QUANTITIES

Strong visual indicators should let us know whether the amount of material that is present *at a process* or *in a connection* is normal or abnormal. Spaces outlined within the process, such as squares on a tabletop, a cart with an outline on it, or a space on the floor, that are identified as holding only so much material are a good start. Physically limiting the space to only what should be there is even better. Either way, in some form, we need an indication of the normal amount of material that should be present. The space required for normal flow can be identified as "green zones." When material is in the green zone, flow is normal. Every green zone should have an accompanying "red zone," or whatever color you choose to use to show abnormal flow. When material is in the red zone, flow is abnormal. In some cases, a "yellow zone," or warning track, can be used to indicate that something is about to become abnormal.

Simply by color-coding the material at the process or the material in a connection, we can teach each worker in the flow what normal flow and abnormal flow look like. If parts are in the green zone, it means that flow at this location is normal. If parts have backed up to the yellow zone, flow is starting to become abnormal, and if parts have backed up to the red zone, flow *is* abnormal. There are many other methods as well. Simply seeing parts in an area without a location identified for them should be considered abnormal flow. Again, the best abnormal flow indicators for material quantities are the ones that are physical. For example, we may set up a small roller conveyor as a FIFO lane. The conveyor is long enough to hold 10 trays of product. Therefore, a quantity of 10 trays is defined as the normal flow. However, if a worker sees the conveyor full and begins stacking trays two or three high when the part numbers match, is this abnormal flow? No matter what the answer actually is, it will become debatable, and flow will begin to erode. A better indicator of abnormal flow would be a conveyor with a bar over it that prevents trays from being stacked more than two high (if two high is the normal flow).

MATERIAL MOVEMENT

Once we establish how to see whether flow at a process or in a connection is abnormal, the second part of our checklist for flow is done through the use of material movement. In our design of flow, material should move from a process to a connection or from a connection to a process at a preset time. At the pacemaker process, the amount of work we schedule should match the time at which we move the completed work. Let's say, for example, that we schedule an hour's worth of work. If we do so, then we would plan to move the material from the pacemaker every hour. As mentioned earlier, this is called pitch. The idea is that we set specific times for material to move, and if the material is not moved at one of those preset times, we know that abnormal flow has occurred. By applying this concept initially at the pacemaker process, we set a rate that should match customer demand to feed or pull product through the rest of the value stream.

When we think of moving material at preset times, we should think of the material movers as trains in a subway station and the product as people trying to get on the trains. First, we ensure that the trains are running at the right times, then we check to see whether all the people got on at the right stops. It works the same way with our visual checklist. First, we set times for material handlers to move material, then we walk a preset route and check to see whether all the product has gotten picked up at each stop. If either condition is not met, we should be able to see it visually and know that the flow is abnormal.

PULSE POINTS

Once we have created the first part of our visual checklist using material flow, the next step is to create a method of navigation through the checklist. As mentioned earlier, pulse points in the operation are areas in the operation where anyone can simply observe what is happening and know whether the flow is on time relative to customer demand. Pulse points are also navigation points that let us know specifically where to go to use our visual checklist. Pulse points should be set up at places where material movement is set to happen at preset times, with the pacemaker being one of the key processes where this should happen. At each pulse point, we should know where we are in the total flow of product to the customer and whether the process itself has the right amount of material, and we should easily be able to see the times at which material should move and the quantity that should move. A map or illustration of other pulse points should be listed. Figure 21.1 is an example of such a map.

By setting up a map of pulse points and material flow to determine abnormal flow, we have created our visual checklist for

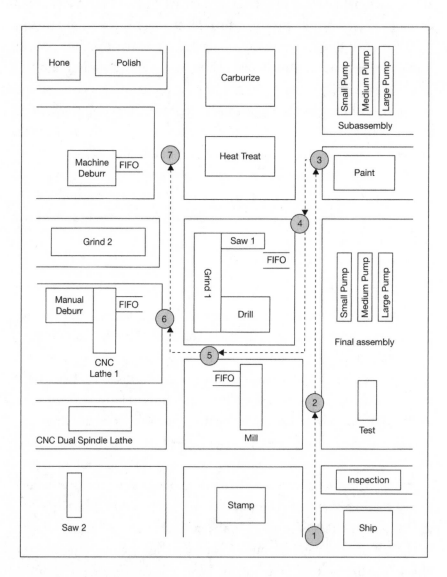

Figure 21.1 *Map of Pulse Points*

abnormal conditions. This checklist also provides standard work to tell whether the flow of product to the customer is on time. Remember, this status of flow is not information for management. It is information that the employees who work in the flow can see and respond to. Since we have created such a robust flow and a visual checklist to ensure that flow is on time, there may be other advantages as well. For example, imagine a salesperson walking through the shop floor with a customer. During the tour, the salesperson asks, "Can you tell whether your order is on time?" When the customer answers, "Yes," the salesman can reply, "So can everyone else in our operation, and they know what to do if it's not on time without having to call management." Perhaps after seeing and hearing this, the customer would not want to do business with anyone else.

ABNORMAL FLOW IN THE OFFICE

In the office, we don't move material, but we do move information. Here, we have to create the ability to see whether information is flowing on time. It will be harder to create a visual checklist to show whether the right amount of information is at a process or in a connection, so we will have to focus our checklist on the timing of the flow. Processing cells are set up to meet at certain times and to take only so long, then to move information to the next step. The processing cell is a good place to set up a pulse point in the office. A visual indicator at the end of the processing cell's allotted time can be a simple binary method to let everyone know whether all the information that was required to flow through the processing cell actually got processed. It could be as simple as a movable pointer placed on a pie chart. When the allotted time for the processing cell has expired, an employee in the cell moves the pointer to green, meaning that everything has been completed, or red, meaning that not everything has been completed. With this method, everyone in the office will know whether the flow is on time during the preset, established times, and in the preset, established places.

Workflow cycles are also designed to move information from many different areas to the processing cells or further along in the business processes. Since workflow cycles are made up of activities that happen at the process level (an employee working at her desk in the office), it is hard to see whether abnormal flow has occurred. Different employees also might not be working on activities that need to be done within the workflow cycle at the same time, so trying to set up visuals for what is happening each hour might not allow us to see abnormal flow, as it will be normal for some employees not to complete their work at the same time as other employees. But as long as everyone completes his work by the time designated by the workflow cycle, flow to the customer is normal.

One of the better methods for seeing abnormal flow is to have a preset alert prior to the end of the workflow cycle. Perhaps there is a "two-hour ticker" that lets everyone know that the workflow cycle will end and information must move to the processing cells in two hours. At this time, the employees will present their visuals, letting everyone know that the information either is on time or is not. Workflow cycle alerts and confirmations can be done through e-mail for information flows that must travel across distances where the employees cannot physically see one another. However, these alerts and confirmations are intended for the employees that work in the flow. It is key that these alerts *not* be sent to management. If they are, prioritizing, expedites, meetings, and negotiations will begin, and none of these activities are time well spent on growing the business.

WHAT YOU WOULD SEE

Once we have established our visual checklist to see abnormal flow, a walk through the operation would reveal the following:

- When you enter the manufacturing floor, there is an area where the map of flow is posted. This map shows the pulse points and the route to follow for the visual checklist.
- At the pulse points, you can see the visual indicator that shows at what time material should move from one process to the next.
- At any process, you can see whether there is or will be a problem by looking at the amount of empty space for material.
- In any connection between the processes, you can tell whether an abnormal condition exists that will affect the next process through red zones being exposed.
- On the shipping deck, you can see whether the flow of product to customers is behind schedule.
- In the office, you can see whether all pending work has been processed in the processing cell on time.
- You can see by way of visual indicators whether the next workflow cycle will be met before the end of the cycle.
- There are visual indicators outside the conference rooms that let us know that the people inside are meeting to try to correct abnormal flow somewhere in the organization.
- Outside the conference rooms, there is a summary of the number of times the room has been used for a meeting to fix flow.

The ability to see abnormal flow is created by the checklist for our design of flow to achieve Operational Excellence. It provides a simple process that anyone can follow in order to see the status of the operation in response to customer demand. Creating the ability to see abnormal flow with a simple glance at the operation is also essential. Remember, it is important that we do not dilute our visuals, especially in the office. The intent is for a visitor to know by simply walking through the operation how the operation is performing. And, as we know, if a visitor can tell, anyone can tell.

A final thought on seeing abnormal flow: let's go back to the hospital example at the beginning of the chapter and apply this concept. It is normal for a hospital to experience demand changes for patient care and variations in treatment times. This situation requires that patients be placed on gurneys in corridors when work "overflows." If this is the case, then we can tape down green lines or put a green sign on the wall that indicates the parking spaces for these gurneys. Gurneys that are in these spaces are still considered to be in normal flow. If we put down green lines or signs that indicate parking spaces for normal flow, we should also put down red lines (or lines of whatever color we choose to use) or signs that indicate abnormal flow. Though the hospital may still have gurneys in the hallways with patients on them, every doctor, nurse, technician, security guard, and visitor would know whether the patient flow is normal or abnormal.

Having a robust system of visuals that have the authority to designate normal and abnormal flow sets up the framework for our next step, which is crucial, as it separates companies that seek to continuously improve by eliminating waste from the companies that seek to achieve Operational Excellence. It's important that we do everything we can to get this next step right, or we will fall into the trap that will forever limit how much offense and business growth we can deliver, and that trap is *management dependency*.

CHAPTER

22

The Sixth Principle: Create Standard Work for Abnormal Flow

Physical changes have been made, and people have started working in the newly designed flow. We have established robust visuals for this flow that have the authority to let each employee know what to work on next, when to produce, and when to stop producing. These visuals have effectively replaced the traditional management activities of scheduling, prioritizing, expediting, and telling people where and when to work along with what to work on next. These visuals also allow us to see normal and abnormal flow. They let us know whether the operation is performing in accordance with customer demand, and whether things are going right and we are keeping customers happy or things are going wrong.

Even though operators have been taught how to adjust the flow in order to maintain it and keep it from catastrophic failure or breakage, the flow will still sometimes break down. That's the reality. Eventually, the flow will break down. What counts is what we do when that happens. If a part doesn't show up when it was supposed to or when a machine breaks down, if our response is to have a meeting, that's not the answer. The key in the design is to understand a course of action that an operator would take or a diagnostic that he would use before calling a supervisor. Also key is having standard work established to get the flow back on track. At key points in our processes, whether they are business processes or out on the shop floor, we have to ask questions about our operational design: What happens when this FIFO lane gets empty? What are we going to do? What happens when we have a critical process but the process that it's feeding breaks down? Should we stop the critical process as well? What if we can sell every product that's produced on it? Answering questions like these before the problem occurs alleviates the need for management to make decisions to correct the flow. It also allows us to enter the stage of Operational Excellence in which the flow evolves into a self-healing flow. This is a critical point, as it is where we can fall into the trap that prevents us from achieving Operational Excellence, and as mentioned at the end of the last chapter, that trap is *management dependency*.

As we begin to work in this new environment, management is striving to reap the benefits of the investment, just as it should. It is looking for improvements in productivity, efficiency, quality, and on-time delivery, along with a reduction in inventory, lead time, and working capital. To ensure that these objectives are attained, management monitors and measures performance in order to provide guidance. Performance review meetings are held because management wants to know the issues involved so that it can help clear roadblocks and solve those issues. Managers want to help. Their intentions are good. They offer, or perhaps just begin, to solve problems, improve flow, and eventually become the go-to people when things go wrong. They may also step in, let us know what we are doing wrong, and suggest ways to fix the problem. These fixes may even go against the design guidelines that we used in designing our flow. Eventually, the unspoken rule of flow becomes: *workers follow the standard work for flow, but management is allowed to break it.* At this point, a dependence on management is created and embedded in the system, and management will forever be needed just to sustain the flow of product to the customer. It will always be there, embedded in the everyday life in the operation. As one operations manager of a very large facility put it, "I wouldn't know what to do if I didn't solve problems and set direction all day." This is an easy trap to fall into, and most companies do so, even if they have come this far. And when this occurs, we never will achieve Operational Excellence.

One way to avoid this trap is to be clear with management about exactly what its role is and where the managers should be spending their time. While this sounds simple, it is definitely not. Management has always been a part of continuous improvement. In fact, it is designed into the process of continuous improvement itself. Managers may form steering committees, select target areas, put teams together, schedule events, provide tools, set priorities for improvements, review progress, and be actively involved in "managing" the improvement process. In their traditional role, operations managers feel that this is what they must do to improve performance.

This is where the difficulty or paradox lies: *to achieve Operational Excellence, management has to coach, guide, teach, and instill the concept of getting rid of the use of management in supporting the flow of product to the customer.* This is not an easy task, and it's one of the main reasons why many companies have not achieved Operational Excellence. To be successful at this difficult task, it may help to think of management's role as one of providing *guidance to create self-healing flow*, not achieving performance objectives (just yet). To do this, management should focus on the process for creating standard work not only for normal flow but also for abnormal flow. Its focus is on taking managers out of the role of ensuring the flow of product to the customer and into a new role of creating offense, which we will examine in the upcoming chapters.

RED EQUALS REACTION

In many cases company operations may be organized by set locations for everything. We may even have green, yellow, and red zones everywhere material is located. We also might have established pitch, with material handlers moving parts at preset times. There might be day-by-hour boards that let us know the status of production each hour. There might be television screens that let us know whether we are ahead or behind, or any number of other methods to show us where we stand. Having a nice visual operation with many indicators of flow may seem to be the epitome of a visual factory, but in fact it's not.

When there are a large number of indicators of flow, how do we know which ones to react to? When does the standard work for abnormal flow kick in? In order to get management out of the habit of fixing flow, one of the first things to teach each employee is *when* management needs to step in. What causes managers to react, and what should they react to? The answer is to have a specific standard that does just this: it lets people know when management will usually jump in, and then makes this event highly visible. This can be taught as *red equals reaction*. Red equals reaction means that while there may be many colored visuals that indicate the status of flow in our factory or in our office, it is only when a visual indicator goes into the red that we should react. In addition, when this reaction takes place, everyone should know that the red condition has been acted upon. In other words, we have made it clear that a red condition existed and that a reaction has taken place. In the flow of product, red zones should be assigned only when a reaction is needed. Thus, we define what is too much inventory in the FIFO lane. We define when a supermarket is going empty and will not be replenished in time, and what type of flow stoppage in a cell will affect shipments to customers. All of these will need a reaction that is simple, clear, and unambiguous.

The same concept applies elsewhere in the operation. Support groups can use this concept to make the reaction visible so we know that the issue is being addressed. For example, Maintenance may have two or three machines in the red, meaning that these machines have broken down. In the maintenance area and at each machine, there should be an indicator in the red, along with something that informs everyone who is working on it, what the problem is once it has been diagnosed and the anticipated time when the machine will be functional again.

REACTION IN THE OFFICE

Although we apply it differently, red equals reaction is used in the office as well. We can establish visuals that set a binary boundary. One side is green, and one side is red. This boundary allows us to see where we need a reaction. For example, in the quoting process, we can define exactly what a late quote is. Once we put engineering change orders into the flow, we can define when a reaction is needed to deal with the abnormal flow (see Figure 22.1). In all cases in the office, the key is to establish the boundaries of normal flow and then establish a binary boundary for abnormal flow that requires a reaction. The boundary is visible for everyone in the office to see, allowing the people in the office who work in the flow to know when they need to react.

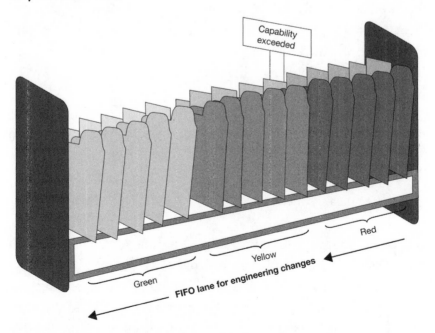

Figure 22.1 *Red Equals Reaction—Office*

CREATING THE RIGHT REACTION

When the flow of material or information hits our red zone, there is a seemingly infinite number of reactions that can take place. When an employee has a question for a supervisor, how many different responses can that supervisor give? Trying to develop standard work for an infinite number of responses is an impossible feat, no matter how logical we try to make the sequence. Instead of trying to create standard work for an infinite number of responses, we should first look at why we need an infinite number of responses in the first place.

As discussed earlier, in a traditional operation, each manager is trying to make her department or the areas within her span of control efficient and cost-effective while responding to the customer. She is constantly making business decisions, setting priorities, and adjusting workloads. These decisions spawn more decisions; we approach infinity. However, in our new design of flow, we have put in place principles and guidelines for how flow should work. By doing this, we have effectively stripped away the need for many management decisions. The only decisions that management will still want to make involve directing people when things go wrong. To counteract this, we can follow this process:

- ◆ Record the types of abnormal flow that have occurred and management's responses to them (think of this as the top 10 list of things we do when abnormal flow occurs).
- ◆ Assign the responses to the types of abnormal flow that occur.
- ◆ Create a *visual response*.

For example, a testing operation could be a trouble spot, with supervision always seeming to be present. The supervisor is constantly monitoring the operation and setting priorities, and he provides direction whenever anything abnormal comes up. In this case, we would interview the supervisor and find out what his "top 10" responses are, such as, "Have the relief operator cover lunch breaks," or, "I'll see if I can call in the second shift early." From these responses, we would find out which types of abnormal flow yield which types of response. For example, the supervisor might tell us, "If it is after 1:00 p.m. and work has backed up to a point where I think we won't recover, then I'll call in the second shift early."

Through further discussion, we get agreement on where the point at which we will not recover is located (at least as a starting point). Then, we make this point and the reaction visual out on the shop floor. The end result might be a different lane for each product family entering the test area (see Figure 22.2). The lanes have tick marks for green, yellow, and red zones. When work backs up into the yellow zone in the morning, this means a relief operator will continue to work through lunch to catch up. When work backs up into the yellow zone in the afternoon, a second operator assists. When

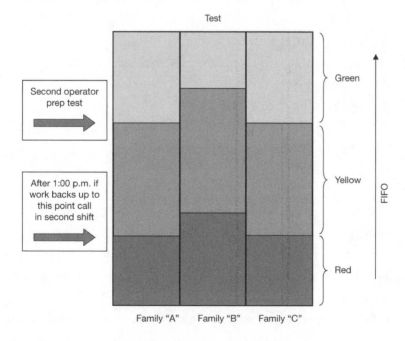

Figure 22.2 *Visual Standard Work*

works back up into the red zone in the afternoon, the second shift is called in early.

Another method is to take the top 10 management responses and from this create a *menu of responses*. This method can be used where there are more than a few responses and the responses may have further "if-then" actions. Let's say the tester in the previous example finds a product failure, which will also back up the flow. The supervisor would want to review each failure to ensure that it is actually a failure, and also to see whether the product is salvageable. He would also want to know if there were any issues in the assembly areas that we should immediately correct for future units. After a detailed review with the supervisor, we can develop the top 10 responses to a failure:

1. Retest the part.
2. Send a signal to the engineer.
3. Place the part in a holding location. Pull the next job from FIFO.
4. Change fittings for the retest.
5. Disassemble and inspect. Reassemble and retest.
6. Recalibrate the tester.
7. Replace the check valve.
8. Tag with the reason for rejection, and perform diagnostics.
9. Check with the lead tester to confirm.
10. Check the torque seals on all bolts.

From this, we can work with the supervisor further and with Engineering to create a menu of responses (see Table 22.1).

All of these responses are done without asking a supervisor or having a meeting run by management. The people who are in the flow take these actions automatically, which means that the visuals for flow have enough authority that an operator who is building the product can call another operator and have her come in to work overtime without seeking the approval of a supervisor or manager.

TABLE 22.1
MENU OF RESPONSES, TEST FAILURE

CAUSE	ACTION
Pressure failure	1. Retest. 2. Check torque. 3. Change fitting. 4. Replace check valve.
Vibrator failure	1. Check with lead tester to confirm. 2. Disassemble and inspect. Reassemble and retest. 3. Send signal to engineer.
Voltage failure	1. Recalibrate the tester and retest. 2. Send signal to engineer.
After 5 minutes	1. Put in quality hold location. 2. Pull the next job from FIFO. 3. Tag with reason for rejection and perform diagnostics. 4. Send e-mail to technician.

She can also contact Engineering directly, without going through her supervisor. The visuals provide the approval, and the operator simply takes the right course of action to maintain the flow of product to the customer.

RED-CONDITION RESPONSE CHART

When a menu of responses does not apply, as in a case where there are many situations and circumstances to consider, another method is to use a red-condition response chart (see Figure 22.3). This is

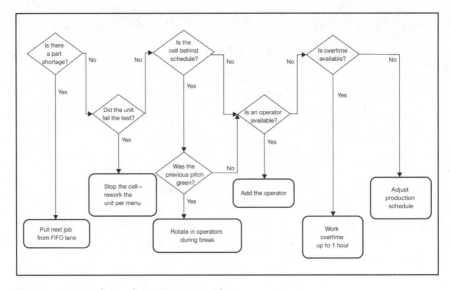

Figure 22.3 *Red-Condition Response Chart*

a decision tree flowchart that employees can follow to guide them to their course of action. If a red condition exists, they follow the logic chart through a series of yes/no questions that eventually lead them to a course of action. This ensures that employees always make the right decision and that the decision is consistent no matter who they are, what shift they are on, or what knowledge and experience they have. If the decision reached does not seem to provide the best course of action, we simply update the red-condition response chart.

THE EMERGENCY CHECKLIST

We have created a visual checklist that teaches us how to see abnormal flow on the manufacturing floor. We have applied this concept to the office as well. Just as for an aircraft in flight, these checklists show whether flow is normal or abnormal. But what happens when flow *does* become abnormal? We know that flow *will* break down, no matter how good our processes are. No matter how robust our flow is, in real life, this is going to happen, and events will happen that affect flow. *What counts is what we do when things start to go wrong.*

Once again, let's go back to our example of an aircraft in flight. While the plane is flying, the pilot reviews a checklist to make sure that everything is normal. However, things may happen that cause the conditions to become abnormal. A landing gear indicator light tells the pilot that the landing gear is down and locked into position. Without this indicator, the pilot knows that there may be a failure in the landing gear. This lack of indication refers the pilot to a step-by-step process to follow to ensure that the landing gear gets deployed and locked into position. Amazingly enough, the first step in the standard work might be to check the lightbulb behind the green indicator to ensure that the reading is not false.

If conditions deteriorate to the point where the flight is in danger, there is also an emergency checklist for the pilot to follow. Even though the pilot may have a great deal of experience, he does not deviate from the emergency checklist. He is trained to follow the checklist and use his extensive experience to carry out the steps in the process. Even with this emergency checklist, the pilot still needs to make decisions and execute actions in an expedited manner, and even at this level, pilots are trained heavily in aeronautical decision making so that they can make the right decision in a short amount of time. The concept here is to have standard work for when things go wrong at all levels, from a slight abnormality to a life-threatening emergency situation, in order to enable the pilot to make the right decision quickly while under pressure. When things go wrong, we want standard work to be applied by the people who are performing the value-added service for the customer. We will create the equivalent of this in our operation.

In most operations, we are not seeking to create emergency checklists, as lives are not in danger. However, we will seek to create an abnormal flow checklist that will let the employees know what to do when flow begins to break down, which will allow them to perform these activities without the need for management. In each operation, there will be many options, methods, and alternatives for creating standard work for abnormal conditions. It is doubtful that there will ever be one best method that covers all conditions. Therefore, we will put the emphasis on the process that creates standard work for abnormal conditions. A good process for this is the *Plan-Do-Check-Act cycle*; however, we are going to use it a little differently from the way it is traditionally used.

The Plan-Do-Check-Act cycle is a common tool for continuous improvement. It is most often used at a process in order to improve quality, uptime, efficiency, or another aspect of the process. We *make* a plan for how we are going to improve the process. We *do* the improvement, we *check* the improvement, and then we *act* as needed to correct problems or make adjustments. The cycle is repeated over and over again in order to gain more improvement. Typically, management sets objectives and teaches workers how to apply the Plan-Do-Check-Act cycle in order to try to achieve those objectives. Using the Plan-Do-Check-Act cycle is a good practice; however, using it to achieve a management objective *without providing a process for meeting this objective* makes us susceptible to falling into the trap of management dependency.

The proper use of a Plan-Do-Check-Act cycle, the one that helps us achieve Operational Excellence, is to teach workers how to apply it as a process for creating a flow that self-heals. Root-cause problem solving is a big part of this as well, but it too is applied differently from the traditional approach. When we look for the root cause of the problem, we do it within the design parameters of how the flow has been developed. We also solve problems by working within the design for flow and not allowing creativity to override the design for flow. When pilots are trained, they are not told to "brainstorm" or to "be creative" when a warning light comes on. They are taught to use a checklist to come up with the right response given the situation at hand. In the event of an emergency, they are trained to use an emergency checklist as well as aeronautical decision making to come up with the right decision in a life-threatening situation. However, one emergency checklist does not fit all aircraft. It changes as new technologies emerge and aircraft designs are updated. The point is that the checklist matches the intended design and that we create our standard work for abnormal conditions by working within that design.

For example, in an assembly operation, let's say that we have established material movement or pitch of 30 minutes. This means that a carton of finished product is supposed to be picked up at the assembly area by the material handler every 30 minutes and moved to the shipping area. The material handler shows up at the designated point in the assembly area, yet there is no carton to move. What action should be taken? There are several possibilities. One may be to have the material handler alert the area supervisor. However, this is not the standard work we are looking for, since it works outside the design of having self-healing flow without management.

Most likely, there are many other good answers. Which one is the best answer? We don't know. However, instead of trying to find the best answer, we would apply the Plan-Do-Check-Act cycle as follows: We *plan* to have the material handler wait up to five minutes if a carton is not present. We *do* implement this procedure and instruct the material handler to follow it. We *check* and find out that the material handler waits five minutes most of the time and still leaves without the carton. We then *act* to develop new standard work to correct the reason why the product is being delayed in Assembly. In other words, we use the standard work for abnormal flow to help us direct root-cause problem solving within the design of flow.

WHAT YOU WOULD SEE

Now that we have applied the principle of standard work for abnormal flow, a walk through our operation would reveal the following:

- ◆ A posted menu of responses or a red-condition response chart for a red condition at the pacemaker or at other key processes, such as shared resources.
- ◆ Employees referring to the posted standard work or using small laminated cards to direct them to take appropriate action when abnormal flow exists.
- ◆ At any process, the use of a red visual indicator to show that there is a problem, and also to show whether a reaction has been initiated.
- ◆ Active use of the Plan-Do-Check-Act cycle for improving standard work for abnormal flow.
- ◆ A list of open abnormal flow items that need standard work created.
- ◆ In the office, red-condition response charts posted in the areas where the processing cells take place.
- ◆ In the office, management working with employees to create standard work for abnormal flow.

In the first five principles, we have created an environment that lets each employee know whether the flow is normal and everything is all right or whether the flow is starting to become abnormal and things are starting to go wrong. When things start to go wrong and flow becomes abnormal, we want to avoid reverting to the old practices of finding the supervisor, finding the manager, or having a meeting. We have created flow through a set of guidelines and principles, and we want to troubleshoot these guidelines and principles to find out where our process has begun to break down and our flow has begun to erode.

When we see flow begin to erode, we should strive to have the people who are working in the flow correct it without any management intervention. In order to do this, we have to create standard work for those situations when abnormal flow occurs by first determining when management has to jump in. Then, we record the top 10 list of responses that management usually gives. From this, a menu of responses is created. If more detail is needed, a red-condition response chart can provide a path of logic to follow to determine the right reaction.

Determining the appropriate response for different situations will be a way of life in Operational Excellence, and it is something that we will always be addressing. There can be many reactions to abnormal flow, and we may not be able to cover them all. Therefore, we will need a process to address it. That process is the Plan-Do-Check-Act cycle. Along with *kaizen* events to create new standard work, this is where we focus our continuous improvement efforts. Finally, all of these efforts will probably not completely eliminate the need for management to get involved and make a decision from time to time. However, by addressing the majority of the abnormal flow conditions with standard work, we free up significant time for management to work on offense, or business growth.

23

The Seventh Principle: Have Employees in the Flow Improve the Flow

By now, we have come a long way. Both on the manufacturing floor and in the office, we have designed our flow on paper, using specific design guidelines. We have implemented that flow through a formal implementation process. We have set standard work for the flow between the processes so that each employee who is working in the flow knows specifically how he is connected to the next process and to the customer. We have made the normal flow so visual that a visitor who has never been to our operation before can see it. We have also made abnormal flow so visual that every employee can see when the flow of product or information to the customer is beginning to be in jeopardy. We have created standard work for abnormal flow by determining when and how employees who are in the flow should react. We have completed and implemented the dynamic design for our business in motion. As with a plane in flight, there is a design for it to fly, a checklist to let us know how it is performing, and a checklist telling us what to do if the performance begins to deteriorate. The result of our actions is a "smooth flight" from the time the customer gives us an order until the time we deliver that order. We have learned to do this without the need for management to be involved with the flow of product and information to the customer. Like the airline company that has turned over the actual flight—*the part that delivers value to the customer*—to the pilot and crew of the aircraft, we have turned over the delivery of product—*the part that delivers value to the customer*—to the employees who work in the flow. It's in their hands. The question is now, what do they do with it?

A New Use of Old Tools

At this point, we have implemented the design by which the employees who work in the flow continuously build a product from raw material to the customer. However, as with any design, we are always seeking to improve it as time passes, and we will always continue to do this. In fact, if there is any part of Operational Excellence that is considered an ongoing journey, this is it. However, this is not an endless journey of eliminating waste; this is about the operations side of the business attaining a level of performance *that affects business growth* and then maintaining and improving that performance in order to support further growth. We will get to exactly how this is done along with case studies of companies that have done it in the following chapter and Part IV.

One of the easiest ways to continuously improve the performance of our design is by using some of the proven continuous improvement tools. However, we will not be using them in the same way that we used them in the past. We will have to teach our employees to use these tools differently. We will have to give them a different focus. We have to apply the tools to support the design of flow and improve what we have achieved. To put it plainly, we don't want to arm each employee with tools, then tell her to find problems and fix them. This would be very destructive to the implemented design of flow, and we would soon be back in the trap of management dependency. Therefore, we have to teach our employees the correct application of these tools in order to support and improve the design of flow and achieve business growth. The correct application of these tools in an environment of Operational Excellence is to have them prevent abnormal flow from happening, and that's where we place the focus. Exactly how do we do this? Some hints are provided here.

5S FOR FLOW

The first basic tool of continuous improvement is 5S. It's based on five words (originally in Japanese) that begin with the letter S that teach us how to organize the workplace. In English, we commonly use Sort, Set in order, Shine, Standardize, and Sustain. We typically use this tool at the process level to teach operators how to develop a highly organized workplace in which there is a place for everything and everything is in its place. To achieve Operational Excellence, 5S is a foundational tool that is needed, and we probably used it at the very beginning of implementing our design. To focus this tool on creating self-healing flow and supporting business growth, however, we want to change the focus of this tool to just that. In other words, instead of a 5S program, we want our employees to think of it as "5S for flow." This means that we will apply the concept of 5S not just at the process level but also at the flow level. We want employees who work in the flow (including newly hired employees) to know that in order to have uninterrupted flow to the customer we need to have impeccable 5S for that flow. Interruptions caused by the need to look for tools and material will affect our flow and cause an abnormal condition. Therefore, we will teach the tool of 5S not with the intention of cleaning up and organizing the workplace but as a tool that supports flow and the improvement of flow to the customer, and that also prevents abnormal conditions.

SETUP REDUCTION TO INCREASE CAPABILITY

Setup reduction is often done by having management set a "stretch goal" of reducing the changeover time at a process. For example, a CNC machine may have a 2-hour changeover. In order to improve this, a team is created and a *kaizen* event is scheduled. Management sets a goal for the team of reducing the changeover time to 20 minutes. The team follows the principles of SMED and improves the changeover time from the existing 2 hours down to 40 minutes.

Management is happy, as even though the stretch goal of 20 minutes has not been achieved, the changeover time has been reduced by 1 hour and 20 minutes. This is viewed as a great success, and the achievement is celebrated, as the workers have improved the process and management has created more production time.

In our new environment in which the design for self-healing flow has been implemented, we will teach the tool of setup reduction quite differently. First, we need to understand the role of setup times as they relate to our capability to produce a "mix" of products. The smaller the setup time, the larger the mix of products we can produce. When the flow was designed, a capability was established using the amount of mix that we could produce over a certain period of time. We want to increase the mix of products that we can produce (which means increasing our capability) as new products are designed, new customers with small orders come on board, and customers change their ordering patterns. Having the capability to produce a larger mix of products to satisfy more customers will affect our business growth, and we will teach setup reduction for this purpose. To do this, we will illustrate the "cause and effect for business growth." For example, the current setup time of 2 hours allows us to produce 10 part numbers per week. If we reduce this time to 30 minutes, we will be able to produce 40 part numbers per week. This will allow Sales to attract new customers who want smaller quantities with shorter lead times than our competitors can offer. As we progress, we will continue to apply setup reduction to the right processes to produce a higher mix of parts and to support breaking into new markets with new customers.

TOTAL PRODUCTIVE MAINTENANCE FOR FLOW

When we develop total productive maintenance (TPM) programs, we typically are trying to improve the performance of a machine. This could be through a reduction in downtime, improved performance to cycle time, or producing better quality. A combined measurement of these three factors is referred to as overall equipment effectiveness, or OEE. Again, the typical goal is to eliminate waste and become more efficient and productive by having a formal maintenance program that prevents breakdowns.

In our new design of flow, this becomes another useful tool if it is taught differently than the old design. We have designed a robust flow, and employees in the flow have standard work for abnormal flow. Although we have standard work for abnormal flow, we want to place a high emphasis on preventing abnormal flow from happening in the first place, and this is where TPM comes in. It's not about reducing machine breakdowns; it's about reducing flow breakdowns. As we did with 5S, we want employees who work in the flow to understand that in order to have uninterrupted flow to the customer, we need to have the machines perform reliably. If they do not, it will affect our flow and cause an abnormal condition. Just as the airline industry needs highly reliable aircraft if it is to have a business, we should teach our employees that the role of TPM is to maintain the equipment to the reliability of our design levels or better in order to grow the business. Once again, we want to educate the employees that the activities they do now have a direct effect on business growth.

KAIZEN

One of the most popular continuous improvement tools ever, *kaizen*, or rapid improvement events, also has a place in improving our self-healing flow and affecting business growth. In using *kaizen* events, we typically target a specific problem or an area of poor performance, put a team together with a charter, and seclude the team for a few days or perhaps a week to fix the problem or improve the performance. During the event, we may teach the team other improvement tools as needed. The overall intent is rapid improvement by focusing resources, providing training, and letting those involved apply the training or their knowledge to make the improvement, all in a week or less.

In our new world of Operational Excellence, we have designed our end-to-end flow along with standard work for what to do when the flow becomes abnormal. While we may have used *kaizen* to implement the design for our flow during the implementation phase (and that is a good use of *kaizen*), we now do not want to assign teams to brainstorm improvements in specific areas, as the end-to-end flow has been designed as a whole. Remember, at this point, flow is self-healing, with checklists and standard work, and this is what fixes problem areas.

In our new world of Operational Excellence, there is a much more powerful use of *kaizen*, and that is *to create and improve the standard work for abnormal flow*. This is the area where we want teams and management to come together and decide when a reaction is needed and what that reaction should be. We also want to review and improve the standard work for reactions, as this will constantly evolve. While we have offered some options on what standard work for abnormal flow looks like, this is an area in which we can be creative for each application. This applies in the office as well as on the shop floor. As abnormal conditions occur, we review these occurrences, then set up a *kaizen* event on how to create standard work when these events or similar events happen. Yes, we still do root-cause problem solving to find out why flow became abnormal, and that may be part of the reaction. However, we know that no matter how robust we make our flow, it will still break down. And what we do when this happens counts. Therefore, a good use of *kaizen* in Operational Excellence is to *relentlessly create and update our standard work for abnormal conditions*.

One final note on the use of *kaizen*. Perhaps it's best if we think of the right use of *kaizen* in Operational Excellence as *using kaizen to eliminate the need for management in the flow of product to the customer*.

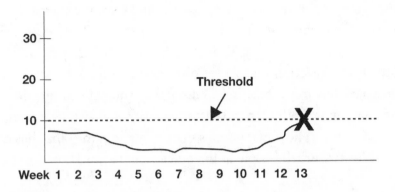

Figure 23.1 *Graduation Criterion—Management Interventions*

GRADUATION CRITERIA

All of the tools mentioned here enable us to sustain and improve the flow to the customer, with the intent of creating business growth. While we do want to measure performance so that each employee knows whether the system is working well over time or whether it has slid backward, we can do this by tracking our performance in terms of establishing "graduation criteria" and tracking performance relative to these criteria (see Figure 23.1).

Graduation criteria are different from a management goal or objective. They are based on the system design for flow, while a management goal could be just that: a goal that management created. The criteria themselves are focused on the behavior of the flow more than on the results or output of the flow. For example, the purpose for designing a self-healing flow is to reduce the need for management intervention, or to create flow without management. Therefore, one of our graduation criteria would be establishing a maximum number of management interventions per day or per week. We would then track or measure how many times management has to come to the rescue to correct the flow against this criterion. In the office, we would like employees to work on offense and grow the business (and we will discuss how they do this in the next chapter). Therefore, we would set a graduation criterion for the number of meetings needed to fix flow. This criterion focuses on how many times people in the office have had to get together to discuss a problem with the flow of information or product to the customer. We could also set a graduation criterion on how many times management in the office has had to reprioritize or tell people in the office what to do.

WHAT YOU WOULD SEE

At this point, we have established our flow, or our engine that starts every time. Now, we are placing our focus on continuously improving that flow. Therefore, we should see activities that do this in our operation. A walk through our operation would reveal

- Employees in the flow are reviewing pulse point information, including graduation criteria, at a regular preset time. (*Note*: since the operation is running smoothly, this is not a daily activity.)
- The next scheduled *kaizen* event is posted; it has the intended purpose of creating new standard work for abnormal conditions or improving the existing standard work. This was initiated based on the graduation criteria because too many management interventions occurred last month.
- Some connections, such as FIFO lanes and supermarkets, have "test markers" in them, which means that employees are adjusting the size of the connection to improve flow.
- Employees in the flow are comparing setup times to the mix interval required to meet customer demand. Setup reduction events are planned to increase the capability to meet future mix needs.
- Employees in the flow are accompanying management to visit suppliers to integrate the delivery of material into the flow.

Improving the flow is the stage of Operational Excellence where we can apply the traditional tools of continuous improvement. However, we will use these tools differently. We will provide a new approach to these tools that supports flow and that in turn supports Operational Excellence. By doing so, we align our continuous improvement efforts with business growth out on the shop floor or in the office. We create a highly educated workforce that knows how the improvements it makes have a direct impact on the ability to grow the business. The employees understand the design of flow and its linkage to business growth. They also understand how to make the right improvements to improve the flow in order to grow the business.

This is a self-perpetuating system. The employees in the flow improve the flow, providing Sales with the ability to sell a higher mix of products and enter new markets. Sales brings in even more new business, and Operations again has to improve the flow in order to maintain that business, and improve it even more in order to capture more business. The cycle continues, allowing sustained business growth to become a reality.

THE FIRST SEVEN: THE LOOK AND FEEL

We have just covered the first seven principles of Operational Excellence. There is one more to come, but before we cover it, it is important to understand the collective impact of the first seven principles on our shop floor and in our office. More than just what you would see, think of this as the look and feel of the operation after these principles have been applied, also providing a sense of what the culture will be like. It is important that we understand the behavior of the operation and ensure that this behavior has been achieved *before* we move on to the last principle. If we don't, we will be setting up management for failure by providing them with the conflicting roles of running the day-to-day operation while trying to remove themselves from the operation to work on business growth.

Once we have completed the first seven principles, our operation should exhibit the following behaviors.

ON THE SHOP FLOOR

1. Each employee should know the flow of value to the customer in manufacturing, from the receiving deck to the shipping deck. Each employee should also be able to teach the flow to a visitor as the two go through the factory. The employee should be able to explain how the flow is designed, what principles have been used, and how those principles have been applied.

2. Each employee at each process should know whether the flow is normal or abnormal. Upon inquiry, each employee should be able to provide this information at any time.

3. Visuals in the factory are viewed as the authority to perform work or to stop performing work. They also provide information on what to work on next. Only one process has a schedule, and that process is the pacemaker. No priority lists or expedite lists exist in the operation.

4. Material moves at a preset pace. You can feel the "pulse" of the operation when this happens.

5. Management uses a visual checklist and walks a preset route to pulse points to know how the operation is performing. Employees in the flow do this as well.

6. A visitor should be able to give a tour of the operation without any assistance. The visitor should also be able to tell the status of his orders as he tours the operation.

7. Almost no management interventions occur on a daily basis. These interventions spawn decisions, and decisions create rework, interrupt flow, and often break the standard work we've established for the operation.

8. Red really means reaction. If something is in the red zone, you can see that an action has been taken and that the problem is being addressed by people in the flow.

IN THE OFFICE

1. Our office should have a clock speed, like that of a computer processor. A processor cycles through a set of instructions at a preset rate called the clock speed. This means that a processor with a speed of 2.2 gigahertz can cycle through instructions at a rate of 2.2 billion cycles per second. In a way, our office is a processor of information as well, and it too should have a clock speed. We should be able to sense that clock speed in our office.

2. We should have a preset time to let us know whether things are going right or whether they are going wrong. This lets us know if our clock speed is being met.

3. There should be no daily meetings and perhaps not even weekly management meetings to review status. Very few meetings should take place in order to fix flow, maybe one or two per month.

4. There should be very few e-mails or voice mails to clarify information. The e-mail traffic that does exist should be focused on offense.

5. Employees in the office have set times at which to perform tasks. Each employee knows that performing these tasks on time ensures that the workflow cycles move information on time. This results in timely responses to the customer, which leads to business growth.

Now that you have a good idea of what the application of the first seven principles of Operational Excellence will look and feel like, let's move on to the eighth principle, in which we will see the true impact Operational Excellence can have on our business.

CHAPTER

24

The Eighth Principle: Perform Offense Activities

Imagine that you are the operations manager for a midsize business. You show up for work at 7:00 a.m., settle in, and check your calendar. It's pretty full. There's the standard 8:00 a.m. meeting with Operations personnel to review the status of second-shift production, key orders, quality issues, schedule attainment, forecasts, and any other issues. At 8:30 a.m., a conference call is scheduled with a supplier to discuss the expediting of key parts. The purchasing manager will stay after the call to discuss how the problem arose and what corrective action is required. At 9:15 a.m., a walk down to Accounting is in order. The numbers from last month looked unusually high. Probably a prepayment was made and accounted for incorrectly. It has happened before, and you may have to shake a few trees on this one.

At 10:00 a.m., there is a sales meeting. In other words, Sales will give us the list of orders that need to be expedited in order to keep key customers happy. The list seems to change daily. At 11:30 a.m., you are meeting with the marketing vice president. She wants to have a pre-meeting to discuss priorities before the noon meeting with Engineering. Then, of course, it's the noontime meeting on new products. This is a two-hour working lunch where you will have to put on your striped shirt and get out your whistle in order to play referee between R&D, Marketing, and Engineering. At 2:00 p.m., if the meeting ends then (and it never does), the first window exists to make phone calls and start to catch up on e-mails. The window is small, though, as at 3:00 p.m. the vice president of finance wants to review a presentation for Corporate. He's good with numbers, but he's not good at presenting, so it's going to take a bit of coaching. It's your last appointment of the day, but it's going to take some time. You take a deep breath, put your plan together, collect your thoughts, and the day begins.

By the time you leave to go home, you feel that it has been a good day. The second shift did well, almost ran to schedule, and you were able to get the supplier to commit to a shipment tomorrow. The sales meeting wasn't bad; it produced almost the same list that you were working on. You were actually able to keep the peace in the new product meeting by having each person write a priority list and build consensus. Then, after an hour and a half of negotiating and coaching, you were able to simplify the finance presentation to about ten slides and five key points. The vice president of finance should do okay. You feel good; it has been a good, productive day. Or so you think.

While you were spending your time giving guidance to subordinates, building consensus on issues, solving problems, making decisions, and moving people in the right direction, what weren't you spending time on? *Offense, or the activities that are directly related to growing the business.* In this example, it wasn't just the top person who didn't work on offense. What about the directors, managers, and other subordinates who were involved? Most likely, they spent their time preparing for the meetings, gathering information to show their point of view, or creating PowerPoint presentations, with other people assisting as well. They most likely placed phone calls and e-mails to discuss the subject in question with others. When they were not doing this, they were most likely solving problems and handling other issues that arose during the day. How much time did they spend on offense?

As mentioned throughout this book, *Operational Excellence is about business growth.* It gives us the ability to take time away from running the operation and put it into growing the business. This is done by reducing or perhaps even eliminating the activities that operations management performs when delivering the product to the customer. While I have talked quite a bit about the design of an operation that allows this, I have not talked about the management side—in other words, how we will change the role of operations management in order to create Operational Excellence and focus on business growth.

At the beginning of this book, I stated that this is the design book, or the blueprint book. We have taken this approach for one simple reason: the first step in changing the role of operations management is to let the managers know what the role of Operations in the business will be and the plan to migrate to that new role. We will share with them the design process and the design for Operations that establishes this role. Education is the key. In order to get managers to want to get out of their current role of getting product to customers and into a new role of leveraging operations for business growth, we have to teach them the approach to growing the business and what their specific role will be.

The nine questions for Operational Excellence are a good start for this, as they allow the managers to think about what their operation would look like in the world of Operational Excellence. These questions show the need for alignment. Once that need is established, it opens the door for formal education on the design of operations. Following a process creates alignment as well. A key element is that we do not let management brainstorm what Operational Excellence is or how to achieve it. It is critical that we teach managers the process to follow, as during this process they will realize their roles will change.

Eventually, they will discover the objective of reducing management intervention in the flow of product to the customer, and the need for them to remove themselves from this role. We will know that the operations managers really buy into this concept when they find that it is important for them to measure how much involvement they have in getting a product to a customer. When they have this amount of interest, then we will know that they fully understand the design and believe in it as well.

Finally, if the people at the executive level of the organization know that it is key for operations management to work on offense, then those executives should also pay attention to this measurement. The executives would want to keep track of where the operations managers are spending their time. They would want to ask the operations managers how the operation is running in terms of management intervention. They would want to know whether our flow of product to the customer is self-healing. They would want to know whether the employees who are in the flow fix the flow when it breaks down. The executives would want to drive this behavior by educating and asking the right questions. All of this is key, because in order for the design for Operational Excellence to work, the managers have to want to get out of intervening in the flow. It may not be natural for them, but it does support a formal process that grows the business.

OFFENSE—PRIMING THE PUMP

The customers gave us orders, we built the product, and we shipped the orders. The process was uneventful. The engine of our operation started and ran smoothly. There were no meetings, no expedites, no managing people. Our self-healing flow worked, and in the operation, it was just another day. It was uneventful. Uneventful is good. Uneventful is what we are striving for. Uneventful means that our engine is working smoothly. It starts every time, and it delivers the product. It's a well-oiled machine. Now the question is: what do we do with it?

The first step in leveraging our operation for growth is to connect Sales to the engine. We need to teach the sales force "how to feed the engine." The engine is designed to have a certain amount of capability, and we want to educate Sales on how to sell to that capability. This specifically means that Sales should clearly understand the concept of the "mix intervals" to which we level the volume and mix of products. By knowing this, Sales can leverage small-quantity orders, quick delivery, and of course high quality and perfect on-time delivery. It can use this information to break into new markets that it has historically passed over. Sales should also be an active part of determining the capability needed for each product family. It might even request that the operation have different capabilities established to meet different seasonal demands. Finally, Sales should have a preset interface with Operations as part of the work in a workflow cycle to provide information to Operations in a standard format at a regulated interval. Of course, this allows us to see whether the flow of information from Sales is normal or abnormal.

In order to have a robust interface with Operations, the next step is to put the activities that Sales and Marketing perform into flow. Just as we created flow for the information in the office that supports Operations, we would apply the same process to these offense groups as well. We would create workflow cycles to move information on sales leads, set up processing cells to review customer requests and approvals, and develop a preset time and process for Sales to perform a formal and robust handoff to Operations. A formal and robust hand-off means that Operations receives the information in the format in which it wants it, and Sales presents it in this format. It also means that there are never any phone calls, voice mails, e-mails, or meetings to clarify information once it has been handed over to Operations.

Again, the first step is to educate the Sales and Marketing group on the design of the engine, then synchronize its activities to feed the engine in the flow. The pump is primed; the engine is ready to turn and deliver product to the customer. We just need to get the orders.

OFFENSE IN THE MARKETPLACE

We have primed the pump by building a reliable engine that delivers products dependably. We have now educated Sales and set up a formal process by which sales information can flow into the operation. The sales force is ready to leverage this competitive advantage in the market and entice more customers. This is only the very beginning—only the start of what we can do when the operation has achieved Operational Excellence.

Now that we have built a solid reputation for delivering products to our customers when they want them, with good quality, and at the right price, we will reach a point where the customers will notice our performance. They may even be curious about it. Perhaps we can invite them to take a look at the operation, which can double as a powerful marketing tool. We are seeking to earn the respect of the customers, as we are about to enter a new stage in our relationship with them, the stage called *innovation,* and we want to make sure that our existing relationship with them is strong enough to allow us to do this. You will hear what is probably the best way to put this in one of the case studies that follow, as one operations manager states, "You have to earn the right to innovate with the customer." That's very well put and very true.

INNOVATION

The word *innovation* can encompass quite a bit. There are many texts and quite a bit of knowledge about the subject in the public domain. Here, we are not teaching the concept of innovation, or how your company can innovate. The focus here is on how Operations can become an integral part of innovation by achieving Operational Excellence. This becomes quite a powerful package when it is accomplished, as you will see in the upcoming case studies.

Now that the customers have respect for what we have done and are interested in talking with us about further opportunities, the next step is to bring in some key people for a meeting with a customer. Some key people to bring are the operations manager and perhaps some of the more technical people in our operation. During this meeting, we can conduct a review of the parts that we supply to that customer. There will be a specific interest during this conversation, as we will be looking for opportunities to innovate new products. There are many things to be considered when one is trying to innovate; we will provide a small list of questions to demonstrate some of the process here. When we are meeting with the customer concerning the product that we supply, here are a few questions that we may want to ask:

- ◆ How is the part used in terms of the end product function?
- ◆ What function do the parts that connect to our part perform?
- ◆ Of what material are the mating parts made?
- ◆ How many different types of connections are there?
- ◆ How could we "modularize" our product with the connecting parts to make a bolt-on application?
- ◆ What are the quality issues with the final product that are related to the function of our part and the systems with which it connects?
- ◆ What is the supply-chain performance in terms of delivering all of the components?

There are many things that we are trying to accomplish during this meeting. What we are trying to find out with these questions is whether we can redesign the existing part that we supply so that it performs more of the functions that the customer's end product does. Can we eliminate some of the other parts that the customer is buying by providing their functions within our part? Can we lower the cost or improve the performance of the customer's product by changing the design of our part? The basic underlying theme is, *can we make the customer more successful*?

Once we have generated some ideas on how to make the customer more successful, we can put these through a process. As you will read in the chapters ahead, this process may be referred to as innovation funnels. And Operations is heavily involved as ideas flow through these funnels. It's not just the operations manager; it's a cross-functional team, with some members coming from other divisions. Operations has to dedicate time to review different ideas, work with Engineering to review different designs for manufacturing capability with existing equipment, or review new equipment that may be required. Operations has to be involved with prototype development to ensure that if the customer likes the prototype, it can actually be produced with the quality required and at the cost quoted.

Once a concept has been developed, a prototype can be produced and presented to the customer. The customer, seeing the new product in action, along with the new cost (and new cost savings), goes through its approval process and begins purchasing the newly designed part from us, and most likely purchasing a reduced amount from other suppliers (and perhaps competitors).

But it does not end there. Once we have earned our customers' trust and respect, they are likely to come back for more. They will begin to offer other parts that they would like our ideas on and ask us to review the designs of parts that we may not even produce (just yet) for improvement. They will offer us market share if we can spend the time and effort to make them more successful. And with Operational Excellence achieved, we have that time and effort to spend, *at no additional cost to us.*

FROM PARTS SUPPLIER TO SOLUTION PROVIDER

Another evolution of offense is to change from being a parts supplier to being a solution provider. Again, the first step is to earn the respect and trust of our customers through Operational Excellence. Once we have earned this respect and trust, we can really spend time with our customers, learning more than how the part or product that we provide fits into their final product. We can do more than just understand the functional interface with mating components and offer a new type of interface. We can review the intended function of a customer's final product and perhaps improve the cost, quality, or functionality of that product by offering innovative solutions to a problem that the customer is trying to solve with its product. If it is a technical product, we may have to tap into several resources from several divisions in our own company. And if we don't have the right technologies in our existing company, this presents a good strategy for future acquisitions. Of course, these acquisitions would have to be already practicing the principles of Operational Excellence that we applied to our existing operations or at least be willing to adopt them.

Being a solution provider means that we are looking at much more than what our part or product does in the customer's product or system. We are looking at what problem the customer's product is trying to solve or what service it provides. Then, we leverage our resources of time and effort across multiple divisions to develop a product that makes the customer more successful. Of course, in doing this, our time and effort are rewarded with more business for all the divisions involved, and less for our competitors. But even more important, the customers have seen success by allowing us to work with them on their needs. And the next time a customer is thinking of a new product or service, who is it going to call to help it put that product or service together? The supplier that has put in the time and effort to make it successful. The supplier that has achieved Operational Excellence.

While many companies already have innovation funnels and work closely with their customers, the difference here is that Operations is now part of that process. It is involved up front, interfacing directly with the customer and developing the processes that lead to the solution. This takes quite an effort and is time-consuming, and it will be successful only if we have achieved Operational Excellence in our operation first, prior to promising innovative solutions to the customer.

WHAT YOU WOULD SEE

When we reach the point where Operations can focus its activities on offense and business growth, a walk through the operation would reveal the following:

- Every conference room has an offense meter posted, along with a tracking sheet that indicates how much time is spent on offense in the conference rooms.
- There are posted times for when the next innovation funnel interface will happen.
- There are posted times for the workflow cycles that feed the innovation funnel.
- Processing cells meet at preset times to review potential solution ideas for customers.
- The operations manager's office is empty, as he is at a customer with the sales manager.

When we achieve Operational Excellence, we are able to focus our time and efforts on offense. Offense creates business growth by first integrating Sales into the design of flow for the operation. Sales can then sell products at the appropriate capability for each product family. The result of consistently short lead times, 100 percent on-time delivery, and good quality is that we earn the respect and trust of our customers. Once we have earned that, we can now adapt our products to make the customer more successful. With this strong relationship with our customers, we can evolve from being a parts supplier to being a solution provider, and we can be the go-to supplier when our customer has new ideas for products and services.

All of this is possible only if we first achieve Operational Excellence. Without Operational Excellence, Sales would see the customer, brainstorm some ideas with the customer, then provide those ideas to our company. The ideas would be "thrown over the wall" to the operations manager. After this, the negotiation process would begin:

prioritization of resources, endless meetings, determination of which order is more important, and lots of management muscle to get products to the customer and at the same time find new ways to innovate for the customer. Of course, this process has a high probability of setbacks and failures. After all, if Sales provides ideas to the customer and gets the customer excited but fails to deliver even a prototype on time, we will lose the respect of the customer and have to start all over again.

PART
IV

Extended Case Studies

Introduction to Case Studies

In the pages that follow, we will look at three companies that have traveled down the road to achieving Operational Excellence and leveraged their operations to enable and drive top-line growth. We'll look at how IDEX and Parker Hannifin, both large, publicly traded corporations, were able to apply the design guidelines throughout their facilities on a global basis to create flow through a mixture of machining, fabrication, and assembly processes across a broad range of precision-engineered products. Once the flow had been installed, they leveraged their flow to work on offense. This offense came in the form of product development, new technology, and innovation programs in which Operations was a major part of delivering innovation. In some cases, the entire offense was funded through the savings and working capital freed up by applying the principles of Operational Excellence. And in both corporations, achieving Operational Excellence led to significant business growth.

In our final case study, we'll take a look at a privately owned company located in New Hampshire that has created a unique organization. Since the early 1990s, an organic evolution has taken place, as the leaders of the company believed early on that each employee should focus on the customer, then designed the facilities, including the offices, in a manner that would support this. They also believed that each employee should contribute to business growth and set up a program to reward each employee for doing just that. In fact, the leaders of the company maintain a steadfast commitment to offense, having structured the organization to eliminate management intervention in the flow so that managers can spend their time growing the business.

These three very interesting case studies center on applying the principles discussed in this text. We hope you enjoy reading about them as much as we did visiting them and writing about them. They are companies that have "walked the walk" in Operational Excellence.

CHAPTER
25

Parker Hannifin Corporation

Parker Hannifin is a publicly traded corporation that employs 55,000 people across 390 sites around the world, 304 of which are manufacturing locations. At the end of June 2010, when the company's fiscal year ended, it had net sales of $10 billion spread across eight product groups: Aerospace, Automation, Filtration, Hydraulics, Instrumentation, Fluid Connectors, Climate and Industrial Controls, and Seal. Parker Hannifin produces a wide range of products to serve its customers' needs in the demanding motion and control technologies market, offering a varied suite of products ranging from actuators to valves, hoses to vibration dampening equipment, and much, much more. The company was founded in 1918 by Arthur L. Parker in Cleveland, Ohio (where the company maintains its current headquarters), and has seen substantial organic and acquisitive growth over the past 90 years.

Since 2001, Parker Hannifin has had a strong continuous improvement program in all its divisions that has been created and supported by company leadership. The focus has been on lean and value stream flow, with a heavy emphasis on using processes and guidelines to drive results. "Establishing a standard, robust process for improvement was critical for an organization of our size and global reach," said Kathy Miller, vice president of lean enterprise and quality. "Goals are set across the company for each of the key metrics, and we provide the sites with a process and education on formal continuous improvement in order to achieve consistent results."

Like an aircraft that is designed to fly, Parker Hannifin believes in using the Parker Lean System for value stream flow. In fact, while Parker Hannifin uses outside consultants to assist it, those consultants first have to be approved by the company's leaders before they can enter one of the company's facilities. Consultants have to provide formal education that matches Parker's design for growth. While Parker believes in doing *kaizen* events, it ensures that it is running the *right kaizen* events by following the value stream maps in order to improve flow. This approach has been successful at Parker, as a tour through each division shows consistency in the site's continuous improvement boards and the value stream improvement boards. "Applying the process of improvement consistently is one of our strongest initiatives," said Miller. "When we visit a site, we take a hard look at how it is applying the process, no matter how good its performance may be."

While Parker Hannifin's companywide continuous improvement initiative has served it well, one group was an early adopter and has taken this initiative to another level. Located in the county of Devon, England, this group is part of the Instrumentation Products Division Europe (IPDE). Housed in a 220,000-square-foot facility with 220 employees, the group produces a wide variety of fittings, valves, and manifolds for the oil and gas industry and petrochemical markets. A good way to think of the function that the division's products serve is to imagine a gauge or testing application for a fluid or gas, and then the source from which that fluid or gas comes. Parker IPDE's products live in the space between these two areas, ensuring that the fluid or gas sample is delivered to the testing equipment "Faster, Cleaner, Smarter, and Safer."[1]

In 2001, Parker IPDE began to embrace the continuous improvement program that had been adopted by the company's leaders and focused almost exclusively on increasing operating efficiency through the use of tools such as SMED, 5S, and TPM. "They were doing great work," said the current innovation and technology manager for the division, who joined Parker IPDE back in 2001 as the technical manager. "But I felt they didn't really have a goal for why they were doing it. What was happening was that all of the efficiencies they were making were just helping them maintain the status quo."

In 2001, Parker IPDE was half its current size and was not realizing its growth or profit potential. Like all businesses, Parker IPDE wanted growth, but from where the technical manager sat, there was no clear plan for how the company was going to get it. More than 100 *kaizen* events were run within two years, and Parker IPDE even began working with value streams in 2002, but since there was no end destination for all the improvement initiatives that were taking place, it was unclear how those initiatives tied in with growth. "At that time, we were managing the business to make sure that things didn't get worse, as opposed to managing the business to make sure that they were getting better," said the innovation and technology manager.

The current general division manager of Parker IPDE has been with the company since 2001, but back then, he was running the logistics side of the business, while the technical manager worked by himself on new product and technology development. Working in their separate areas of the organization, the two would informally discuss various aspects of the business; one would discuss new products and innovation, while the other would discuss operations and logistics. They soon discovered the linkage between improving operations and increasing sales through innovation, a concept that they both agreed would provide the business with sustained growth. When the general division manager assumed his current role in early 2004, he was in a position to apply the concepts that he and the technical manager had discussed during their informal moments, and the formal link between improving operations and leveraging business growth began. As the GM remembers:

> We knew then that every improvement we made would be worthless unless it led to increased sales or business growth. As [the technical manager] and I had discussed many times, it's one

thing to use continuous improvement tools to create an efficient factory, but it's quite another to have the new products that customers want when they want them.

As Parker's companywide continuous improvement program evolved to include flow and value streams, the work at Parker IPDE evolved quickly. It began with a robust application of the guidelines and principles that the group had been taught. Since much of the other continuous improvement work (such as 5S, SMED, TPM, and so on) had been done previously, this provided an established foundation that enabled Parker IPDE to apply the new concepts of value stream flow rapidly.

With the foundation in place, the application of value stream flow guidelines occurred on the manufacturing floor. But Parker IPDE did not stop with implementing flow; it knew that each operator had to know the status of flow, or the state of delivery to the customer, in a way that didn't involve the resource-consuming management meetings that were usually needed to get the product to the customer. Given this requirement, Parker IPDE adopted visuals on the shop floor that let every employee know whether the flow was normal or abnormal, and then began to teach the employees what to do in each case. After experimenting and refining the process in accordance with the Parker Lean System, and adopting visuals for flow on the shop floor, the managers moved on to other areas of the operation, areas where few companies today have ventured to implement flow. These areas included the warehousing operations, including the establishment of customer *kanbans* through the distributors, the office, and the supply chain.

The warehouse is an area of the factory that often gets a heavy dose of 5S and perhaps some fixed inventory storage locations, but little attention is typically paid to creating flow in the warehouse or shipping areas, and even less to knowing whether the flow is on time. But in this facility, one look into the shipping area lets anyone know whether the flow is on time. In the receiving area, one quick look at the supplier *kanban* board lets anyone know if there is the right amount of inventory in the warehouse or if a part will become a problem. In the shipping area, the use of a FIFO lane that has been separated into green, yellow, and red zones allows anyone to see whether things are "in the green" or whether flow is becoming abnormal. The sizing of the FIFO lane has been set up according to the time it takes to process shipments. If product backs up into the yellow zone and is starting to become abnormal, the employees know that there might be a problem with the flow, and if product backs up into the red zone, the employees know that there *is* a problem with the flow, and action is taken to correct it.

The office at Parker IPDE has seen tremendous change, even from just a purely physical standpoint. Back in 2001 and 2002, when the GM was still the logistics manager, the office was filled from wall to wall with desks and personnel. After applying the guidelines of flow in the office, a new office layout was designed in order to facilitate that flow. With the new streamlined layout, extra space that had previously been needed for Customer Service, Engineering, and Quote Processing was transformed into an innovation room that is used for product and technology development. Robust flow has been established in the office to deliver quotes to customers. Each quote is assigned a level of difficulty based on the estimated time it will take to complete and the complexity of the elements involved. An experienced employee performs this triage activity and then sends the quote in continuous flow through the right value stream for processing, as seen in Figure 25.1.

In addition, every day, a *workflow cycle* happens at a preset time, bringing together quote personnel, buyers, the pricing analyst, and even the purchasing manager (if necessary) to ensure the flow of information by completing any outstanding items on quotes. Although technical support engineers are colocated with the other personnel involved in the workflow cycle, they spend most of their time

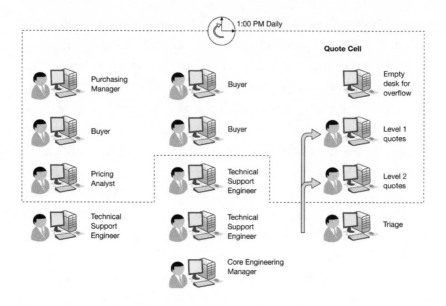

Figure 25.1 *Parker IPDE Office Layout*

working on other engineering activities such as technical inquiries and engineering drawings. In order to support the quoting process (which brings in new business and new customers), they "prebuild" time into their daily schedules to ensure the workflow cycle is met.

The result of the workflow cycle is a reduction in interruptions and variation during the workday, as these are now channeled to one preset time. Another result is that everyone knows when information will flow and when they will be able to get the information they need, which means they won't have to chase people for it. If someone from Quoting needs engineering help or another type of assistance, she can simply ask the right person present at the workflow cycle. The overall result of creating flow in the quoting process through the use of continuous flow and the workflow cycle is the reduction of lead time for quotes to customers, giving Parker IPDE a greater chance to win business.

Not only has Parker IPDE created flow in the office; it also has come up with a particularly novel way to maintain that flow when changes in customer demand occur that exceed *takt* capability. An empty desk is deliberately placed at the beginning of the Quoting process. When the number of quotes begins to exceed the preestablished *takt* capability, a visual indicator goes red. A worker sees this red condition and moves to the empty desk to assist in processing quotes. He will stay there assisting until the demand returns to "green," or normal. All of this happens without management setting priorities or giving direction; in fact, it happens with no management at all. This system is binary: a signal is sent, and a worker responds. And if someone is sitting at that desk, everyone knows that flow has become abnormal and is being corrected; if the desk is empty, everyone knows that flow is proceeding normally.

Quite often the question arises, "Where do they get the other worker who comes over and assists? Wasn't he working on something else?" As the GM explains, "The workers are here, and the customer needs are here. The signaling system ensures that the workers are working on the right things, and that ensures that customer needs are met without management supervising and overseeing the system." The sum of this system is that Parker IPDE has been able to set up a guaranteed turnaround time for quotes: in at this time, out by this time, guaranteed, all designed by the guidelines of flow. And with this system, not only can the employees tell whether their office is on time without asking any questions or requesting any reports but a visitor can do so as well, the true acid test. The results are there, too. Parker IPDE can process 30 percent more quotes in a day, with one less person, than it could before flow was established. The total processing time has been reduced by 75 percent, and Parker IPDE is achieving 23 percent more value from quoted items than it did prior to establishing flow.

Not only has Parker IPDE developed the ability to see abnormal flow in its facility but also it is one of the few factories that has developed the ability to see abnormal flow at its suppliers *as it occurs*.

In addition to educating its suppliers on the principles and guide-lines of manufacturing and strategically outsourcing certain types of components and product assemblies to them (we'll talk about this in more depth shortly), Parker IPDE has established an early warning system with its suppliers. Like many companies, Parker IPDE has a system of *andon* lights to alert everyone when there are problems with machines or processes. However, each *andon* light is linked to digital displays that show the status of the value streams in the fac-tory. If the process is in the green, everything is okay, but when an operator cannot resolve an issue, she activates the *andon* light, and the digital display for that process flashes red, alerting the relevant support groups that action is needed. When the corrective action is taken, the operator who initially activated the *andon* light shuts it off, not the support person who fixes the problem. These displays are found throughout the operation: on the shop floor, in the shipping area, in the office, and even in the engineering department.

When the shop floor, warehouse, and office had been addressed to create the flow that drives Operational Excellence, one tough area still remained: the supply chain. To address suppliers, Parker IPDE used the same system found inside its four walls at the suppliers. Not only was flow designed at the supplier, but the *andon* system that sits at the supplier's site and is controlled by the supplier shows up on the digital displays at Parker IPDE. When something goes wrong in a process at a supplier, an employee there activates the *andon*, which sends a signal back to Parker IPDE, informing it of the problem in real time. The digital display for the supplier's process keeps flashing red until the supplier has taken corrective action. In this way, Parker IPDE has set up a system that lets it know when its suppliers have abnormal flow developing and that also ensures that its suppliers will never fail. Presently, response time has been reduced from an aver-age of several days to a maximum of one hour, and the time it takes to actually resolve a problem has decreased from several days, if not weeks, to a maximum of half a day.

The result of Parker IPDE's transformation as an early adopter of the guidelines and principles of Operational Excellence has been profound. Previously, there were more than a thousand individual part numbers held as finished goods in the warehouse, each with its associated inventory level. Now, the flow is so robust that "there is no manufactured product held as finished goods in the facility. It's all made, goes in a box, and goes to the customer," said the GM. All Parker IPDE's effort is focused on growth. In fact, in five years of internal quarterly business reviews, the company has never talked about manufacturing or issues with production. It always leads with quarterly growth and potential growth opportunities for the future. "I don't have sleepless nights wondering about whether I'm going to deliver something," said the GM. "I just know it happens."

Parker IPDE's goal has been to leverage its operation in order to drive business growth. One person who is intimately involved in this growth is the EMEA (Europe, Middle East, and Africa) sales and marketing manager for Parker IPDE, who has an interesting history with Parker IPDE: he worked for the company for several years until 2000, then went to work for Parker at the corporate level, and then *returned* to Parker IPDE in 2005, giving him a unique vantage point on the company's progress over time:

> In 2000, when we got busy, the factory was a flurry of activity. There were people everywhere, and they all seemed to have a dozen things to do. There were management meetings, schedule changes, all the typical firefighting each day just to get the product to the customer. The contrast when I came back to Parker IPDE in 2005 was incredible. I can clearly remember the first week. I came down to the plant a second time, and I went and saw [the general manager] and asked: are we going out of business? It seemed like nobody was doing anything. The floor was quiet, there was no chaos, no management giving direction, and no meetings! I never believed it was possible to support any growth like that, and the fact that it's grown without adding people is simply incredible.

The factory used to be a problem for the sales manager, as he lacked confidence in it when he was providing delivery dates to his customers. It isn't a problem anymore, and now quick, consistent, on-time deliverability is part of what enables Parker IPDE to charge a premium price. It also enables Parker IPDE's customers to order from it in a way that better suits the needs of their business because the factory is flexible enough to deliver what the customers want, when they want it, in the mix they want it. "I spend my time, my energy, and my force out positioning our company to win customer business, and I know our factory will be behind me to meet whatever objective I need it to," said the sales manager.

By implementing flow and being able to fix it before it breaks down, Parker IPDE essentially made the operational side of its business neutral; it was no longer putting any "drag" on the rest of the organization—not on Sales, Quoting, or any other area. The operation was no longer in a position where it was slowing down or even had the *potential* to slow down the rest of the business. "We could have stopped right there and just kept plodding along," said the GM. "But instead, we saw the operation as something that could supply power to the rest of the business."

One of the ways in which Parker IPDE did this was by shifting people out of production roles that were no longer needed and moving them into roles that were more focused on offense. Part of this came from Parker IPDE's approach to the employee redundancy cycle. If someone's job is technically no longer needed, rather than let her go, Parker IPDE redeploys her in another area of the company to help grow the business. An employee who used to work in Production Control, for example, was redeployed as a pricing analyst to make sure that the company was winning business through its strategic pricing initiatives.

A more compelling example of how Parker IPDE has been able to leverage the operation to supply power to the rest of the business is what happened on the innovation side of the company. "Within one year, we launched three highly technical products. Our competitors took 10 years to do the same thing," said the innovation and technology manager. How was Parker IPDE able to move so quickly and produce products at a rate that was an order of magnitude faster than its competitors'? A big part of the equation was freeing up personnel from Operations and relocating them to other parts of the business where their existing skill sets made sense. In conjunction with natural attrition, where replacement workers have not been needed because of the gains seen as a result of Operational Excellence, Parker IPDE has been able to provide resources for and fund the innovation side of the business. The improvements made through Operational Excellence have driven the lack of need for replacement employees and enabled Parker IPDE to move people to different areas of the business and also fund the hiring of new employees to drive innovation. "We took them out of manufacturing, the people who weren't adding value there any more," said the GM. "We freed up employees, and I have invested in salespeople, customer support people, and even innovation engineers as a result."

In 2001, when Parker IPDE was focused on increasing operating efficiency with tools like 5S and SMED, the technical manager was the only person who was working on innovation and product development. But because of the improvements made by pursuing Operational Excellence, Parker IPDE had the ability to hire five employees for the TM's area to begin helping him develop a new line of manifolds with an eye toward their manufacturability. By integrating this skill set into the innovation process, Parker IPDE has been able to drastically reduce the time it takes to begin manufacturing new manifolds. Within one week of the beginning of production, on-time delivery was already at 90 percent. Since its initial implementation, sales for that particular manifold line have grown tenfold, and they even *have grown* during the economic downturn. "This made a tremendous difference to us as a company in terms of helping us emerge from the recession in the position we are in," said the GM.

Indeed, once the drag was removed from Operations and Parker IPDE was able to use Operations to power the business, an intense focus was put on manifolds, something that the company had never tried to produce before, partly because it hadn't occurred to it to do so, but also because it didn't have the innovation resources needed to pursue such an effort. Much of the company's new product design effort and iteration centered on improving the process connectivity experience for its customers, and it was able to spend its resources here because it had freed them up on the operational side of the business. Simplifying products for customers and reducing the component connections necessary to allow those products to achieve their functionality not only has enabled better process connectivity for Parker IPDE's customers, but also has made their experience safer. "Whenever you're taking something out of a process, that system has got to be safe. From the process to the gauge, it's got to be safe," said the sales manager. "If you have multiple connections, which was the old way, you've got inherent risk. Every connection is a risk. We talk about reducing the number of connections, and thus reducing the potential risk."

For example, one of the gases that pass through one of Parker IPDE's manifold systems is hydrogen sulfide, which is lethal at thirty parts per million, said the innovation and technology manager. Any type of process interconnection has an inherent emission risk, he explained, as we sat in a conference room that was perhaps 30 feet long by 20 feet wide, with 10-foot-high ceilings. One of the projects he was able to develop because of the resources that had been freed up from operations was a manifold that reduced the emission risk for customers. With gases like hydrogen sulfide, reducing this emission risk becomes critical:

> To give you some idea, a normal valve would have an emission level sufficient so that it would fill this room with hydrogen sulfide in a year. But with our low emission manifold product, to fill this room with hydrogen sulfide would take a hundred years.

2003 Sales Mix

☐ Fittings   ☐ Valves   ■ Other

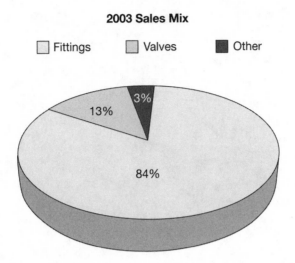

Figure 25.2 *Parker IPDE 2003 Sales*

As Parker IPDE's leaders spent more and more time on offense, they were able to devote more and more company resources to products that were increasingly complex, like manifolds. In fact, the product mix over the past 10 years has undergone quite a shift. In 2003, fittings made up 84 percent of Parker IPDE's products, valves made up 13 percent, and other miscellaneous products constituted the remaining 3 percent (see Figure 25.2).

By 2008, however, with a full focus on Operational Excellence and offense, Parker IPDE had expanded into the manifold market, which was an open playing field for them that held tremendous potential. While the total size of the sales "pie" has grown, the breakdown of the company's offerings has changed significantly, as can be seen in Figure 25.3.

In 2003, Parker IPDE did not have an effective manifold line to offer to its customers, but five years later, manifolds provided 28 percent of its total sales. In fact, the manifold line grew by 45 percent during the period between 2003 and 2008.

Parker IPDE also took an unusual step during these five years and turned what might be thought of as the standard outsourcing

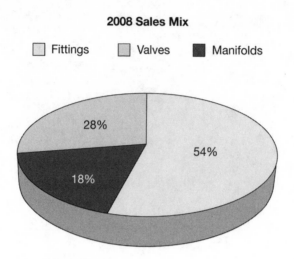

2008 Sales Mix

☐ Fittings   ☐ Valves   ■ Manifolds

Figure 25.3 *Parker IPDE 2008 Sales*

model on its head. It decided to keep in-house the products and components that were of low volume and high complexity, like some manifolds, and outsourced the comparatively easier products. This opened up capacity in the operation and enabled renewed dedication of both production and innovation resources. The suppliers that make the other products and components for Parker IPDE essentially run a Parker-like operation at their shops. In fact, in order to win the business from Parker IPDE, they have to adopt and use the same systems that are used at Parker IPDE to ensure that the products are manufactured the same way and on time. Parker IPDE's suppliers also have the same signaling systems and use the same manufacturing processes as Parker IPDE, enabling seamless integration of supplier and customer and guaranteeing quality and on-time delivery.

The reason that Parker IPDE outsourced some of its easier products and kept the harder ones like manifolds is that there were great growth opportunities in the manifold product line. In 2003, fittings made up 84 percent of Parker IPDE's sales, and other products constituted only 16 percent. But by 2008, even though more fittings were being sold than in 2003, they represented only 54 percent of Parker

IPDE's sales because its new products had grown more than fittings had over the same period. Had Parker IPDE not been able to invest in manifolds and other new products, its overall growth would not have been so dramatic. By outsourcing the time, labor, and resources necessary for low-complexity, high-volume products and components, and by pulling in resources from its own operation, Parker IPDE was able to increasingly shift its focus to manifolds, which offered great potential for customer integration. Currently, Parker IPDE has a 40 percent share of the process-to-instrument market sector of the oil and gas business in Europe, the Middle East, and Africa, up from an average of less than 10 percent, according to the sales manager.

Since 2000, the division has doubled in size, with growth continuing through the first bite of the recession. During these 10 years, Parker IPDE's workforce has shrunk by one-third, but there have been no layoffs. The majority of the workforce reduction has occurred as a result of natural attrition, with much of it taking place over the last six or seven years and not simply as a result of the recession. Operational Excellence improved the operation and innovation gave it growth, but because of the operational improvement, Parker IPDE didn't have to replace the employees that were lost to attrition. "We can't afford to shrink our way to greatness," said the GM. "Our long-term growth has been steady. We dipped a little during the recession, just like everyone else, but we've bounced back strong." While Parker IPDE's sales dipped during the recession, it fell less than what other divisions experienced. Indeed, not only were there no layoffs or reductions in employee time or pay during the recession, but "quarter after quarter, we actually paid improved profit-related pay," said the GM. Without the manifold line that had been developed using the resources that had been freed up on the manufacturing side of the business, Parker IPDE's experience during the recession could have been quite different.

Parker IPDE's ability to innovate increasingly desirable products for its key markets reflects a dedication to innovation and product development for which many companies strive. But it was the transformation that took place in Operations, eliminating those sleepless nights, that had the effect of not only reducing and ultimately eliminating the "drag" that Operations put on the rest of the business but also putting Operations in a position where it could drive growth in the rest of the company.

Looking forward to the future, Parker IPDE sees Operational Excellence as a driving force in its growth and a strategic weapon that gives it an advantage over the competition. According to the sales manager:

> The future for us is to project Operational Excellence forward to our customers. We had a debate around the one thing about our company that makes it great. It's Operational Excellence, and it will be Operational Excellence, and we're going to project that forward to our customers and use it to help them reduce cost and make them successful.

"By using the guidelines and principles of the Parker Lean System," said Miller, "each division has the opportunity to focus on future growth while still meeting the customer expectations of today."

CHAPTER

26

⋮
↓

IDEX Corporation

IDEX Corporation is a publicly traded company with headquarters in Lake Forest, Illinois, about 30 miles north of Chicago. IDEX manufactures engineered products, systems, and solutions that are marketed through four business segments: Fluid and Metering Technologies, Health and Science, Dispensing, and Fire and Safety. In the Fluid and Metering Technologies segment, IDEX offers products that move, measure, and dispense thousands of different types of fluids, ranging from chemicals and fuels to foods and pharmaceuticals. The Health and Science division produces "highly precise fluidics components and sub-assemblies used in analytical and diagnostic instruments,"[1] while the Dispensing business segment makes equipment that "specializes in point-of-use color formulation."[2] If you take a trip to the paint department of a major home improvement store, you will probably find one of IDEX's products custom-blending paints. On the Fire and Safety side of the business, products like firefighting pumps and consoles and rescue systems like the Jaws of Life® are made.

All of IDEX's business segments serve markets around the world, and the corporation has 42 individual sites scattered across the globe. In 2009, annual sales topped $1.3 billion from a mixture of both organic growth and acquisitions. The company employs more than 5,300 people, and in 2001 it began instituting a formal continuous improvement program based on Six Sigma throughout the organization. Like many other companies at this time, IDEX understood the need for strict process and quality control and the impact that this would have on the cost and quality of its products. It also understood that it could see even greater gains simply by putting these controlled processes into flow. With this in mind, in 2005, IDEX began to initialize a program of Operational Excellence across the organization. Operational Excellence was targeted to be implemented in every site in every business segment, from the largest company all the way down to the smallest. The organization pursued this path by educating its workforce on the principles of Operational Excellence. Model sites were chosen as the first facilities to implement Operational Excellence, and personnel from multiple sites attended the training to begin seeding the various plants with education on Operational Excellence.

Most of the operations in IDEX are a mix of vertical integration combined with a final assembly and test model. In other words, some components are fabricated on site, while others are purchased, and they are all then assembled into the final product. These realities meant that the company needed to do a deep dive into the principles of flow, including mixed-model and shared resource flow. And in order to ensure that the training was put to good use immediately after it concluded, IDEX did something novel to marry classroom education with shop floor implementation. In many companies, training is open enrollment, or "awareness" training, where everyone is brought in to receive the education. The IDEX approach was to assign employees the responsibility for implementing strategic areas of its Operational Excellence plan before the employee even knew what Operational Excellence was. As a result, the employees sought out the education and learned the material with the intent of applying it the very next week, which made them excellent students. This also ensured that the training and knowledge would be put to use right away, leaving little time for the knowledge to be lost or forgotten.

At the same time that IDEX was rolling out Operational Excellence across its 42 sites, a powerful focus was being placed on what the company calls Commercial Excellence, which it defines as

"Creating demand, enabling growth and delivering the value generated by way of Operational Excellence."[3] The point of IDEX's Commercial Excellence initiative is to "help [them] better partner with [their] customers to understand their spoken and unspoken needs and, ultimately, to drive growth."[4] The company began achieving Commercial Excellence with a formalized Voice of the Customer (VOC) process between 2006 and 2007. In every business segment and at every site, the VOC was designed to understand customers' problems in order to be able to better meet their needs, and it isn't done through brainstorming or people coming up with bright ideas on the spot. The entire process is tightly controlled and codified so that it can be taught and applied across the entire organization in a uniform manner. "That's the key linkage we have to the marketplace," said the vice president, group executive for IDEX. "It helps us understand what the customers' needs and problems are. Once we understand their problems, we can then take that information and develop solutions through new products and services."

IDEX has always been good at understanding sales and marketing and what it takes to meet customer needs, but at this point in the company's evolution, Operational Excellence and Commercial Excellence were essentially being worked on individually and separate from each other, as in the graphic shown in Figure 26.1.

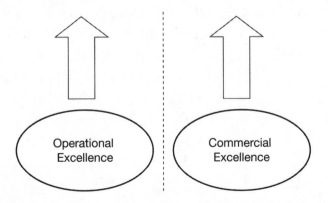

Figure 26.1 *Commercial Excellence and Operational Excellence Programs*

Operational Excellence and Commercial Excellence were being pursued along two parallel but separate tracks. At this point, there was no link between them, but that soon changed when the corporate leaders recognized the business growth that could be achieved by integrating the two initiatives. "IDEX thrives on innovation, and Operations is entrenched in that innovation," said Lawrence D. Kingsley, the CEO and chairman of the board for IDEX. "Both of these need to have the same objective of business growth and need to be linked together to create and deliver innovation."

The results of this marriage have been impressive, with IDEX growing organically at twice the rate of GDP from 2006 to 2008. In 2010, the most recent calendar performance available, the markets that IDEX serves grew about 7 percent, while IDEX grew 12 percent organically and 14 percent overall, a testament to the benefits of the marriage between Operational Excellence and Commercial Excellence. "While Commercial Excellence brought in new business to the factories, Operational Excellence supported this organic growth without adding to cost, square feet, or personnel," said IDEX's group executive.

As discussed earlier in the book, the acid test for Operational Excellence is one of its strongest attributes in that a visitor to the operation can literally see whether the flow is normal or abnormal. This was a great asset for the corporate leaders as they traveled from site to site around the world. With this yardstick, there was no guesswork involved when it came to determining whether a particular plant had achieved Operational Excellence; if the leaders could tell whether things were normal or abnormal just by walking through the operation, then they knew that the employees could see flow in their value streams as well. They also knew that the employees would fix that flow before it broke down, and both of these observations were good indicators that the site was well on its way to achieving Operational Excellence. If this was not the case, then there was still more work to do. As more and more sites reached Operational Excellence and jumped their operational performance, they used the newfound free time to focus on the VOC and using it to grow the business. "The benefit of a self-directed operational entity is that it frees up time to plan and identify growth strategies," said IDEX's group executive.

IDEX's corporate leadership soon harnessed the potential of its married Operational Excellence and Commercial Excellence initiatives. By applying the principles of Operational Excellence and freeing up employees' time to work on growing the business, IDEX's corporate leadership was able to unleash its managers to focus on offense by providing them with time to spend on growing the business through the VOC to attain Commercial Excellence.

While many companies under the IDEX umbrella have installed the principles of Operational Excellence through formal flow and self-healing value streams, we're going to look at two companies that serve as a microcosm of the application of these principles. We'll visit IDEX Health and Sciences, headquartered in Rohnert Park, California, and then take a trip to Micropump in Vancouver, Washington.

IDEX Health and Sciences

The manufacturing facility located in Rohnert Park, California, used to house an IDEX company called Rheodyne, which was acquired by IDEX in 2004 after having been in business since 1976. In January 2009, the Rheodyne brand was merged with three other IDEX brands to form a broader organization known as IDEX Health and Sciences (IH&S), which has its headquarters in Rohnert Park in the same building that was once Rheodyne's. While IDEX Health and Sciences has manufacturing operations in Oak Harbor, Washington; Middleboro, Massachusetts; and Bristol, Connecticut, the Rohnert Park operation is the lead facility for the organization and the one that we will be visiting.

IDEX Health and Sciences provides "advanced fluid-handling solutions for a wide range of analytical instrumentation and in vitro diagnostic systems."[5] The Rohnert Park operation employs about 110 people and has about 35,000 square feet of manufacturing floor space (75,000 square feet of total space). For much of its history, the Rohnert Park operation served as a manufacturer of the Rheodyne brand of rotary shear valves for the analytical instrumentation industry, producing highly engineered products with tight tolerances. Like any manufacturing business, it had to compete on price, quality, and delivery just to maintain its business and its position in the market.

To gain an edge in this arena, IH&S applied the principles of Operational Excellence to a wide variety of precision products at its four operating sites, including Rohnert Park. It created more than just normal flow through cells; it faced the challenge of flowing a broad mix of products down the same value streams and creating flow through its shared machining processes. As discussed earlier, there is a set of formal processes for handling both mixed-model and shared resource flow, and the Rohnert Park operation used formal education and applied these principles to strategically build Operational Excellence into its value streams. The results have been exactly what you would expect: significant lead-time reduction, reduced inventory, increased on-time delivery, improved quality, and more. However, of particular note is how much less time the supervisor needs to spend dealing with problems and issues in the flow. Where this would previously have required anywhere from three to four hours of her eight-hour day, today she estimates that only about thirty minutes of her day are spent dealing with problems in the flow. Two or three times per day she needs to fix flow problems, and sometimes one of those issues needs to be escalated to Engineering for help. She spends the rest of her time during the day working on offense, which in this case entails continuously improving the company's value streams and working with Engineering on the launch of new products.

In addition, the Rohnert Park operation's use of visual scheduling and standard material replenishment routes and runs has enabled it to significantly reduce its production control department to just two employees. More than 70 percent of all products are manufactured based on visual signals that come from the shop floor. There are far fewer schedules from the office, and there are no changing priorities. All of the chaos associated with daily scheduling is now gone, and the resources that are normally tied up in a traditional production control department have been freed up for use elsewhere.

On the shop floor at Rohnert Park, the division has what it calls a prototyping cell, where new products are assembled and tested and then sent back to the product development team, which can use the resulting data to further streamline the company's innovation initiative. By segregating the variation and unpredictability inherent in new product testing and not allowing this variation to enter the flow, the company is able to preserve the performance of the rest of its operation. This also ensures that new products have dedicated assembly and production time, which simplifies everything from scheduling to planning labor levels.

With Operational Excellence firmly in place on the production floor, Rohnert Park's leadership was no longer busy firefighting or chasing production and was able to use its free time to begin working on its formal VOC process. Through the VOC, the management team learned that its customers wanted solutions to their issues and problems. At this point, the Rohnert Park operation was simply supplying components, but the managers knew that they had the technical knowledge and expertise to provide the solutions that their customers were asking for if they could draw on the knowledge and expertise of some of the other IH&S brands at their individual operating sites and of Micropump, another IDEX business unit, located in Vancouver, Washington. See Figure 26.2.

In order to better meet customer needs as a solution provider, IDEX has pursued an aggressive acquisitions strategy to further strengthen IH&S's place in the solution provision market. Multiple businesses have been acquired to support Rohnert Park's efforts as a

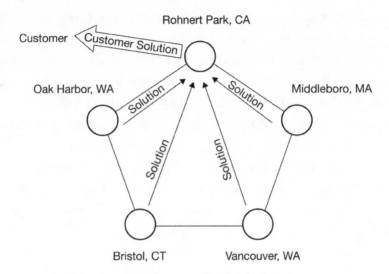

Management at each operation works together on offense.
Note: This model can work in any direction.

Figure 26.2 *IDEX Divisional Offense*

solution provider, and they are housed in the same building that was used to hold only its original manufacturing operation: there is more business, but there has been no increase in bricks and mortar. These newly acquired businesses are complementary to the needs of IH&S's customer base, and they give the organization a greater capability as a solution provider. For example, the Rohnert Park operation might work with multiple companies to make a solution come to life; that solution might include precision tubing and fittings from Oak Harbor, pumps from Middleboro, and a fluid manifold from Bristol. The results of this effort might be a completely new system for liquid chromatography instruments that its customers can simply plug into its product rather than designing it, sourcing components from various vendors, and then assembling it themselves.

But the reason that Rohnert Park is able to tap into the resources at all of these operating sites around the country is that Operational Excellence has been installed at each of them. The company could not leverage this capability across the organization if each operation did not run smoothly based on the principles of Operational Excellence, and this becomes a factor in two different ways. First, these other operating sites would not have had the time to devote to providing solutions if they had had to spend much of each day just making sure that product was shipped to customers. Second, in order for Rohnert Park to tap into these other operations effectively, it needed to effortlessly provide individual components without fail every time. Without Operational Excellence in place across IH&S, neither of these things would be guaranteed. After all, "It's one thing to be able to sell a solution to a customer in theory or concept in terms of what we are capable of doing," said the general manager of the Rohnert Park operation. "But it's quite another to actually deliver that solution in the form of a tangible product, when the customer wants it."

Today, when a customer has a problem or a need, that customer calls the Rohnert Park operation not for a component or a part, but rather for a solution to its problem, which benefits the company in several obvious ways and one perhaps not-so-obvious way. On the one hand, the Rohnert Park operation has now firmly endeared itself to its customer base. By providing reliable, effective solutions, the company has proved to its customers that it can meet their potential needs. With this approach and the increased integration of systems technology from multiple IH&S brands, Rohnert Park has now differentiated itself from its competition. With so many IDEX product offerings to draw on, and such a wide potential customer base, "one project seems to beget multiple projects," said the general manager.

The VOC process used by Rohnert Park and all the divisions under the IDEX umbrella is excellent when it comes to targeting each company to market opportunities, but the capability of the operation is what enables it to meet the requests of the VOC. In some sense, applying the principles of Operational Excellence freed up capacity throughout the Rohnert Park operation in terms of time, production capability, and personnel, but instead of simply using that extra capacity to produce more components, Rohnert Park grew into a solutions provider. Without developing this capability, "I think we would be growing at market rate at best," said the general manager, "and we'd be facing very tremendous headwinds." Without Operational Excellence, none of this would be possible, he said. "It's the price of admission nowadays."

SOME RESULTS

- ◆ Over the last year, the company grew at about three times the market average.
- ◆ Of the prior year's sales, 35 percent were generated from new systems and new products.
- ◆ R&D spending did not drop during the worst of the recession in 2009.
- ◆ Rohnert Park set three high-water marks for sales in 2010.
- ◆ The general manager spends about 60 to 70 percent of his time on offense.
- ◆ In 2010, Rohnert Park had twice as many products in development as it had compared to other years (and having more products means being able to provide more solutions to customers).

MICROPUMP

Micropump was acquired by IDEX in 1997 after having been in business since 1960. The division produces "seal-less, low-flow gear pumps" for "applications where precise fluid control is required."[6] It employs about 118 people and has about 60,000 square feet of manufacturing floor space, with two value streams operating on three shifts. Several years ago, the division operated according to what it called a "leaky bucket" approach. In other words, Micropump would design and manufacture pumps to handle one-off applications for customers' special needs. Like Rheodyne, it had to compete on price, quality, and delivery to hold it place in the market, and the operation had to be constantly managed to achieve these ends.

However, the president of Micropump knew from experience that there was a way to leverage Operational Excellence to drive business growth. While he was a member of the leadership team at BAND-IT, an IDEX company that produces "engineered band clamping and fastening solutions,"[7] he had successfully led the charge to reduce lead times from eight to twelve weeks down to one week to capture market share. Prior to joining Micropump, he had worked to implement flow in the operation at BAND-IT, so he was no stranger to the concepts when Micropump began applying the principles of Operational Excellence.

Like the Rohnert Park operation, Micropump had to deal with a broad mix of products and multiple shared resources, and it used formal principles and processes to create flow in these areas and to distinguish between normal and abnormal flow. The company worked hard to strategically implement Operational Excellence in its operation at the behest of the corporate leadership, and the operational results were similar to what we saw in the Rohnert Park operation. Micropump's leadership team was no longer firefighting or chasing production simply to ship product to the customer on time. As a result, Micropump's senior leaders took their newfound free time and turned their focus to offense.

But this is where the similarities between the Rohnert Park operation and Micropump end. The leadership team in Rohnert Park used its free time to grow into being a solutions provider, but Micropump did something different. Through the feedback gathered from the VOC, Micropump was led down an innovation pathway in which it examined the design of its pumps and compared them with its customers' needs, then created a new type of pump that would better meet those needs. For example, a customer's system might have valves, manifolds, and piping, but a new pump from

Micropump might have features integrated into it that eliminated these elements while still delivering the same functionality. In a real-life scenario, Micropump supplied a product that reduced the system cost for its customer by 40 percent. "While we needed to charge a slightly higher price, our customers are recognizing a 40 percent cost reduction, along with improved performance of their product, and we have differentiated ourselves from our competitors," said the president of Micropump. Throughout all this, Micropump is still able to supply the Rohnert Park operation with the individual components that it needs in order to enable its capability as a solution provider.

Currently, Micropump uses a formal system when it comes to determining where it should target its innovation efforts. This system, which the company calls its innovation funnel, informs it of where and how it should spend its time developing new solutions to meet customer needs. It is broken up into several phases that proceed chronologically. See Figure 26.3.

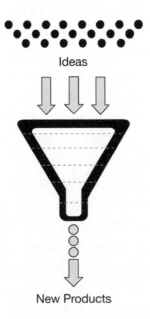

Ideas

New Products

Figure 26.3 *Innovation Funnel*

Roughly three to five ideas proceed through the innovation funnel each month, and Micropump has a formal process for determining what gets into the funnel and how far it goes, meaning whether it proceeds all the way to becoming an actual product or drops out at some point in the development stage. Micropump targets growth opportunities by researching what customers and potential customers might want in its products and also by looking at what its products (either those that it currently has or those that it is capable of making) might be able to do for a customer's existing system.

While many companies use some sort of iterative evaluation process when it comes to new product development, the key difference in this situation is that Micropump's manufacturing operation is heavily involved in its innovation process, improving the product commercialization process significantly. This is where the operations leaders now spend their free time, in the innovation funnel; this is what all the hard work of Operational Excellence has enabled them to do. Even support personnel like purchasing agents are using some of their time to evaluate strategic sourcing decisions for new products. Micropump describes this procedure as "earning the right to innovate," which means a few things, as the president of the business unit explains:

> One, you understand value and are viewed by the customer as a value-added supplier. You're making their life easy by consistently meeting quality and delivery expectations. That allows you to have the next conversation, which is: What's next? What else could we do for you? Would you allow us to come in and better understand your process and what you're trying to do? You have to earn that right first!

This trust and expectation of performance between customer and supplier is critical to opening the door for the customer to confide its problems in Micropump. Operational Excellence helps a great deal here, since it smooths out and improves the performance of the operation. Once this happens, then it's on to step two. The president of the business unit elaborates:

> *The second piece of earning the right to innovate is really about freeing up the resources to devote to innovation. We want to make our growth self-funding, and if you think about it, we actually have to fund it before it happens. You don't have the revenue coming in for the future project yet, so how do you fund it? With efficiency improvements, with cost reduction, by lowering warranty and scrap. Our Operation Excellence process took out significant dollars in 2009 and carried them over to 2010, and that funded some of the marketing resource that we use to run this innovation process.*

In other words, any resource that is to be reallocated to innovation, no matter whether it's time, money, or personnel, must first be freed up as a result of some savings elsewhere in the company. In terms of resource use, this is essentially a zero-sum game, and that is one of the reasons why the successful implementation of the principles of Operational Excellence is so critical. While Rheodyne's freed-up time went toward expanding and growing the business as a solution provider, Micropump went about designing new products and redesigning existing ones specifically to reduce a customer's overall system cost. "This all has to be supported by Operational Excellence," said the president of Micropump. "When I go to customers, they don't care what I have to offer if I'm not delivering on time, delivering good quality, and, in their eyes, delivering good value."

Some Results

- The company is growing at about four times the market average.
- Revenue from new products and markets increased 162 percent from 2009 to 2010.
- Top-line growth in 2010 more than doubled the retracement in 2009.

- ◆ Time spent on innovation increased 125 percent from 2009 to 2010.
- ◆ Dollars in the innovation funnel increased 240 percent from 2009 to 2010.

CONCLUSIONS

Here is the common thread between the Rohnert Park operation and Micropump, and indeed many of the companies that fall under the IDEX umbrella: First, the corporate leaders drove them to unleash their innovative powers within their company via its Commercial Excellence initiative. Then, IDEX installed Operational Excellence at each site and married it to the Commercial Excellence initiative to free up management time, which is used to target innovations in new markets that enable business growth. This happens throughout the corporation, including at sites like Lukas, located in Erlangen, Germany, a manufacturing site for rescue tool products such as the European equivalent of the U.S. Jaws of Life. This site has applied Operational Excellence and used the customer responses that it receives from the VOC to innovate new products such as hoseless, battery-operated rescue units (previous versions had to be plugged into a hydraulic source and used nonbattery electric power). The time spent on this innovation at Lukas and the ability to deliver it rapidly and consistently has affected its growth in a way similar to the effects at Rohnert Park and Micropump. "The process works in all of our divisions," said IDEX's group executive. "We have proved it over and over again."

The Rohnert Park operation, Micropump, and Lukas are specific examples of freeing up the time of plant and operational leaders and redeploying that time to VOC-generated initiatives, not by brainstorming or guesswork, but through a formal process. And linking Commercial Excellence and Operational Excellence has produced tremendous results for the organization. See Figure 26.4.

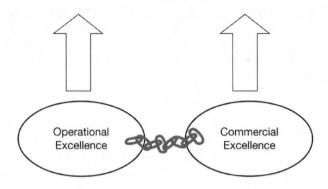

Figure 26.4 *IDEX Commercial Excellence and Operational Excellence Linked*

This linkage has also redefined the relationship between Commercial Excellence and Operational Excellence. Notice in Figure 26.4 that the two initiatives are joined with a chain. This is not coincidence, as a chain becomes taut when it reaches a certain length and will not stretch any farther without breaking. Such is the nature of the linkage now between Commercial Excellence and Operational Excellence. Because the two initiatives are so closely linked, one is able to progress only so far before being limited by the other. If one of them is outstripping the capability of the other, the chain pulls them back because of how closely linked they are.

"I have seen a significant change in how we go about making our customers successful," said Kingsley. "With Operational Excellence married to Commercial Excellence, not only can we innovate for the customer, but we can deliver that innovation to grow the business. The result is a formula for sustained business growth."

CHAPTER

27

↓

Hypertherm

Our last case study is a little different than the others. In contrast to public corporations that have applied the principles described in this text to achieve Operational Excellence and grow their business, this company is more of a natural at it. It is a privately held company whose founders early on saw the need for each associate to be involved with the growth of the business. Being engineers, they designed the operation to enable just this on its own, long before the writing of this book. As you will read in the pages ahead, the success of the design still holds today and is providing sustained business growth. Welcome to a company that applied the principles of Operational Excellence early on and has taken these concepts to a new level, one in which Operational Excellence is instilled in the hearts and minds of all of the company's more than 1,000 associates. Welcome to Hypertherm.

Hypertherm is located in Hanover, New Hampshire, about 120 miles northwest of Boston, and is one of the world's leading designers and manufacturers of advanced plasma[1] cutting systems. Hypertherm's mission statement is to provide its customers with the best thermal metal-cutting equipment in the world and to provide for the development and well-being of its associates. The company was founded in 1968 by Richard Couch, Jr., and Bob Dean in a converted garage not far from the company's current location and was born from an innovation that led to cleaner and faster cuts from plasma torches. Its highly technical products are fabricated and assembled primarily on its seven-site campus in Hanover and are offered in a wide variety of sizes for myriad cutting applications, from small, portable devices that weigh less than 20 pounds to units weighing nearly a ton, all of which are capable of producing temperatures nine times hotter than the sun.

Hypertherm is a unique organization. It behaves in accordance with its mission statement, with a strong dedication to its products and its associates (people who are employed at Hypertherm are referred to as "associates" in order to dispel thinking of the workplace culture in terms of a strict hierarchy). This dedication has been recognized on a local, state, and national level. Hypertherm has received an award naming it the best place to work in New Hampshire[2] and over the last 15 years, it has received several awards naming it one of the best medium-sized companies to work for *in the country*.[3] While Hypertherm's workplace is recognized as being one of the best, its culture is not a textbook "lean culture" per se but rather more of a culture in which the associates on the shop floor understand that they play a key role in delivering product to the customer and growing the business, and they do just this. The associates simply know that they don't need a lot of management in the day-to-day operation. They understand how they are connected to the customer, and they look to take on that responsibility. That's just the way it works.

Long ago, Hypertherm moved far beyond creating a culture of continuous improvement and a program of waste elimination and instead turned its focus and efforts to business growth. "We look for Operational Excellence to provide us with a competitive advantage," said Evan Smith, the vice president/general manager of Hypertherm. He went on:

> That's different from being a manufacturing-focused company that focuses on efficiency to the factory. We want to be a customer-focused company. We want to be excellent at meeting customer needs, and there is a big difference between the two.

Hypertherm does many good things in its operation that have resulted in sustained business growth, and it does these things naturally. Operational Excellence is embedded in its culture. To get a better feel for how this culture has been developed and how Hypertherm has applied the principles of Operational Excellence, we will take a look at a number of areas around Hypertherm that have affected the organization. We will look at the shop floor, the office, something very distinctive called the Hypertherm Technical Training Institute, the supply chain, management intervention, and the company's commitment to research and new product development, all of which work together in synergy with the theme of Operational Excellence to provide Hypertherm with sustained business growth.

THE SHOP FLOOR

On the shop floor, Hypertherm seemed to have a natural sense early on of how to establish flow in production without the need for heavy management. The ideas and operating principles simply "made sense" and took root organically in the late 1990s. The goal was to have the associates on the floor play a key role in delivering product to the customer. This task was challenging, as Hypertherm's operation is vertically integrated, with a mix of final assembly and test as well as machining and fabrication. The company began by establishing cells to build product at the rate of customer demand, but as its business evolved and grew, it could only go so far with cells, and it needed to extend this thinking to its end-to-end value streams. Because of the complexity of its operation, Hypertherm sought more in-depth education on topics such as mixed-model flow and creating flow through shared resources.

After receiving this education, Hypertherm implemented the principles of flow through all areas of its operation, from the receiving deck through fabrication, assembly, and shipping. It did this with the intent of having end-to-end value streams in its operation running the same way its cells did: without management intervention. It was successful, but it did not stop there. Today, Hypertherm's value streams have evolved to the point where they now operate *without production control*. Fabrication areas with dozens of lathes and turning machines now operate off visual signals, with a minimal amount of management or need for setups. Hypertherm uses "thermometer boards" consisting of green, yellow, and red zones that let the associates at each process know how the flow is progressing. These visual connections between processes also authorize associates on what to work on next and tell them whether a breakdown has occurred or is imminent. Standard responses are used to correct breakdowns in flow if they do happen, and management and Engineering need to become involved only infrequently. There is no production control department at all in the entire company; orders flow directly to the production cells. There are central resources like Planning and Procurement for materials requisition, but production is signaled entirely on the shop floor. There are very few meetings, and rescheduling or reprioritizing orders is isolated to exceptions.

"Operations aren't a fundamental business problem," said Jim Miller, the vice president of manufacturing at Hypertherm. He continued:

> *They're not an issue. What amazes me when I sit through our planning, relative to other firms I've been with, is how very little time we spend discussing Operations-related things. It's really focused on customers; it's focused on markets; it's focused on strategy. Operations gets time; it's not ignored. It's not like we don't want to talk about it. It's that we don't have to talk about it.*

In order to achieve this, Hypertherm knew early on that managers had to remove themselves from running the operation. As a result, there is almost no management for a 600-associate production staff. Miller continued:

> *There are business team leaders, and they have Operations responsibilities. However, that is not where they spend the*

*majority of their time. They're able to spend their time on busi-
ness strategy and continuous improvement. There is no need for
a breakthrough to cut lead time or something else, because those
things are already happening naturally. Each associate knows the
system and wants to contribute in order to grow the business.*

So robust is the design of flow that is self-managed and self-im-
proving that associates see and correct anything that contributes to
the failure of flow, without approval from management. They just do
it. For example, in one value stream, products need to be transported
from a swaging process into a FIFO lane that feeds machining. Parts
are moved using large rolling racks, and occasionally one of the parts
might fall off. An associate had the idea of attaching a Plexiglas door
to the rolling rack to prevent parts from falling out, and this was done
without any approval from upper management. There were no *kaizen*
events run to fix the problem. The leaders of the company didn't need
to sign off on the improvement because the associates understand
that any improvements they make on the shop floor must be geared
toward improving the overall flow of product in order to better
serve the customer. The associates at Hypertherm are not beholden
to management directives even when it comes to improving flow in
the operation. Instead, they understand the principles and guidelines
of flow and realize that any improvements in the operation must be
done in order to better meet the needs of the customer.

THE OFFICE

By the late 1990s, Hypertherm employed more than 500 associates and was experiencing continuously increasing levels of annual
growth. Dick Couch, one of the company's founders and its current
president, set out to redesign and expand the facility to support his
growing business. When the architectural firm he hired came back
with its first draft of the new proposed layout, Couch noticed something in the drawing that didn't seem right.

Each functional area of the company had been color-coded for easy identification on the plan, but each department was completely segregated from the others. On the drawing, there was an isolated patch of purple for Marketing, a swath of yellow for Sales, and orange elsewhere for Production. There was no integration, no inherent flow between the different areas of the organization. Couch, an engineer by training, wanted the respective functionalities to intertwine and flow with one another as much as possible. Just as the company's plasma cutters were designed to work a certain way to deliver their functionality to the end user, so too, he reasoned, should the company function in a certain way to satisfy its customers. With this insight, he set out to restructure the company in a way that would support the continuously increasing growth that he saw coming down the line.

To achieve this new look, a key change occurred at Hypertherm. On the functional side, the company was reorganized into business teams. Each of its three main product lines (manual plasma cutters, mechanized plasma cutters, and consumable products) was now led by someone who had responsibility for Operations, Research and Development, and Sales and Marketing for that product line. Previously, these functionalities had been separated into traditional departments. Assigning these functionalities separately to each of the three business units and charging one person with overseeing them within each business unit enabled a robust flow and integration of information and knowledge between what had previously been separate areas of the company. This enabled the service side of the business to focus on the operational needs of the organization and the service needs of the customer—one of Dick Couch's original goals.

This reorganization also enabled Hypertherm to streamline its ability to respond to customers within each of its three main business segments. With one person in charge of a business segment's operation (which takes care of what the business unit currently produces), sales and marketing (which handles how to project the business unit's products to customers), and research and development (which handles the future direction of the business unit's products), the company was able to respond to both current and future customer and marketplace needs quickly and efficiently.

Since the 1990s, this insight has evolved into the ability for everyone involved in the office to see customer needs. It evolved naturally, first to create flow in the office, then to make that flow visual. As at Parker IPDE, a visual display is provided in the customer service department with the current incoming workload and "red zones" that designate when the workload becomes abnormal. Once the flow became visual, Hypertherm set up a process in which the associates who work in the flow would see it and react accordingly. "The same words and concepts we use on the shop floor when we talk about flow and designing flow were used to create what we have in our offices today," said Charlie Hackett, Ph.D., corporate improvement team leader.

THE KEY RESOURCE—THE ASSOCIATES

Hypertherm believes that its number one asset is its associates. The company tries to give every associate 24 hours of training per year, which includes shop floor training but also health and well-being and even financial training to help foster greater personal development. It has had an Employee Stock Ownership Plan since 2001 and a no-layoff policy since the founding of the company, *to which it has held for all of its more than 40 years of existence.* This philosophy holds true even when times are tough; even during the most punishing months of the recession, the company never thought about abandoning its no-layoff policy. According to Miller, Hypertherm "had a tremendous number of excess production resources" during this time. At the end of 2008 and the beginning of 2009, based on Hypertherm's production capacity models, the company had more than 100 production associates who were "not needed" to meet its manufacturing requirements. At that point in time, there were approximately 600 associates working in production, which means that the workforce was nearly 20 percent larger than it needed to be given the sharp decrease in demand that Hypertherm (and most other manufacturing companies) had experienced during the recession.

For most manufacturing companies, carrying a 20 percent excess of production resources during such a downturn would have been unthinkable and would probably have translated into painful layoffs. But the response at Hypertherm was different. The associates are a key part in delivering product to the customer, so the company found ways to keep these associates employed even during tough times. Miller explained what Hypertherm did with its "excess" resources during the recent economic downturn:

> We had been on a fast growth pace for so long, and it seemed like we could not do continuous improvement at the pace we desired. We viewed the economic downturn during the recession as our opportunity to make up for lost time. We focused on doing continuous improvement at an accelerated pace. We did this by dedicating the right number of associates to meet customer demand, then dedicating others to improvement efforts.

While some associates worked on improving Hypertherm's already strong system of flow without management, other production associates were redeployed into different production support areas such as the lab to help with the testing of new consumable products. But even with all of these adjustments, there were still many associates left "unutilized." So, Hypertherm took the unusual step of insourcing much of the contract work needed to support its facility. "Outside contractors were virtually eliminated in 2009," said Miller. Through a volunteer program, associates were temporarily redeployed into nonproduction positions like landscaping, grass cutting, snow shoveling, and even drywall work (one associate had run his own drywall business before joining the company). Essentially, every effort was made to hold true to the no-layoff policy, even when some lateral thinking had to be applied. The value of retaining skilled associates during tough times proved to be a good thing for everyone, as it enabled Hypertherm to accelerate its recovery more than a year ahead of its own schedule and at a rate twice that of its competitors.

The company emerged so strongly from the recession at the end of 2009 that it was even able to pay an annual profit-sharing bonus equal to 6 percent of each associate's annual base compensation during the economic downturn. "Our goal is dynamic growth, growth that continually renews a company environment of challenge and opportunity," said Smith. Today, Hypertherm operates three production shifts 24 hours a day, 5 days a week, even including two or three extra shifts per weekend just to meet its demand. In fact, in one area of production, the company went to a 24 hours a day, 7 days a week schedule for the first time in its history because of the need for extra production capacity, all to meet its increasing growth.

HTTI—THE HYPERTHERM TECHNICAL TRAINING INSTITUTE

Hypertherm's accelerating growth provided it with new challenges, one of them being the local labor market for qualified associates for its machining areas. In and around Hanover, New Hampshire, an area known as the Upper Valley, a large industrial manufacturing base does not exist. Because of this, skilled machine operators are in short supply, and these are precisely the manufacturing personnel that are needed to support the rapid growth in Hypertherm's consumable business unit, since the vast majority of components are machined in-house. Prospective machine operators need to have skills like CNC programming and blueprint reading, and there simply weren't enough people with these skills to support the growth forecasted in the consumable business unit at Hypertherm around 2006–2007.

The small pool of skilled machinists was one challenge, but a number of other pressures existed at this time, too, mostly driven by Hypertherm's forecasted growth. The company anticipated that it would need to hire somewhere between 40 and 60 machine operators *per year* because of anticipated growth and the need to fill positions because of attrition (which, at Hypertherm, typically means that someone has received a promotion and transferred out of Production). For a sense of proportion, at the end of 2006, the total number of associates at Hypertherm was 817, and the total number of production associates was approximately 430, so adding 40 to 60 machine operators per year represented a significant percentage increase in the total production staff year over year.

Traditional hiring methods weren't working, Miller remembered. Job fairs and classified ads in newspapers were hit or miss, because a strong cultural fit with the Hypertherm company ethic was seen as paramount in hiring new associates. Prospective associates had to like working in teams, enjoy an ownership culture, and want to take the initiative. Combine this with the number of associates that Hypertherm needed to hire and the robust technical skill that those associates had to possess, and it is easy to see the daunting task the company faced. A funnel of labor meeting these criteria in the numbers required simply did not exist in the Upper Valley.

Following the trend in most U.S. companies, an easy solution to Hypertherm's problems would have been to outsource its consumable production to other machine shops. While Hypertherm believes in developing suppliers (as we will see in the next section), this was never really an option for this type of machining. The parts produced are extremely technical and contain intellectual property. Hypertherm also knew that it would be more competitive if it produced the parts in-house rather than having a supplier produce them; the company knew that if it outsourced a part, it would pay a premium price for that part.

With this in mind, Hypertherm's market growth and the increasing complexity of its product line still left the operation in great need of skilled machine operators. To combat all of these pressures and challenges, the company created the Hypertherm Technical

Training Institute (HTTI) in partnership with a local college. The HTTI can be thought of as something like a college for machine operators. Its goal is to be able to take anyone with the right cultural fit and a basic set of skills, like a certain level of hand-eye coordination and basic mathematical ability, and train that person to be capable of operating a CNC machine to produce consumable products effectively. The class runs eight hours a day, five days a week, for ten weeks, with eight hours of homework on both weekend days. The credits earned at the HTTI can even be used toward earning an associate degree. "It was very intense," said John Topolewski, a machine operator at Hypertherm who has been through the top-level training at the HTTI. "Ten weeks, really intense, really tough."

Machine operators who graduate not only master how to produce Hypertherm's technical parts but also learn to work on offense activities. The training and knowledge that they acquire at the HTTI enables them to assist the engineers as they develop and test new consumable products. An engineer may have written the original CNC program to machine the new consumable product, but the more associates who are capable of writing and executing programs at a high level to test new designs, the faster the pace of technology development can take place. Increasing the speed of this development cycle is one of the reasons that Hypertherm never really considered outsourcing its consumable production. Doing so would have solved its capacity issue, but it would have done nothing to increase the speed or effectiveness of its product and technology development cycle, and this would have dulled the company's competitive edge and run counter to its philosophy of leveraging operations for business growth.

The HTTI helped with other issues that translated into business growth, too. During one year, for example, there were more than a thousand requests for support on machines that were down for various reasons. A machine operator would issue a request for assistance when something happened, and help would come from a central organizational resource like Engineering. But today, through autonomous maintenance, machine operators are able to fix many of these problems on their own. Training the machine operators to handle issues that otherwise would have gone to Engineering enables Hypertherm to be more productive *overall as a company*, not just more productive on the shop floor. Once the machine operators became capable of handling certain problems, not only could production resume more quickly, but the engineers and other associates who had previously responded to the problems now had more time to spend on product and technology development, a much better and more offense-focused use of their time.

Of course, none of this would have been possible had it not been for the time and working capital freed up as a result of implementing the principles of flow. Miller, the current vice president of manufacturing and the director of operations for the consumable business unit in 2006–2007, was Hypertherm's lead contact and developer of the HTTI. He led the effort to create the HTTI and invested much of his time in doing so. Both he and the leadership team knew that it was the right thing to do, so that was where he focused his time. Because he was not actively involved in managing the flow of product to the customer each day, Miller was able to work closely with the college to develop the curriculum needed to support Hypertherm's technical needs. With the help and support of other leaders and associates, the HTTI was successfully created and solved the issue of finding qualified associates for Hypertherm's machining areas, enabling accelerated growth. This was an endeavor in which the then-director of operations for the consumable business unit spent a lot of his time, instead of running the day-to-day operation.

THE SUPPLY CHAIN

With the principles of Operational Excellence applied on the shop floor and in the office, and with the development of the associates focused on delivering product to the customer without management,

Hypertherm turned its attention to the supply chain, the area where most manufacturing companies struggle. The company began by strategically selecting suppliers who were located only a few hours' drive from Hanover. It then worked closely with these suppliers and instituted a formal process to share knowledge, and it created a material delivery system with the suppliers that ensures that the right raw material for today is delivered on time, every time. In times of high demand, no additional inventory or floor space is needed; instead, deliveries are made more frequently through a signaling system.

This signaling happens automatically right from the production floor. The signals are authorizations for the supplier to perform work and for the material delivery to happen more frequently. In addition to the structure of the supply chain, the associates at Hypertherm are authorized to work with suppliers to improve the flow in their operation in order to better serve their customers. A group of associates on the shop floor worked with one of Hypertherm's key suppliers to design a crating system to deliver a kit of parts to the assembly line in the order, sequence, configuration, and even height (relative to the current build) in which each part is needed. All of this was designed and driven by the associates on the floor, with the approval of the company leaders, in order to leverage the supply chain to better support flow in Hypertherm's operation.

While Hypertherm has successfully implemented supply-chain connections with many of its suppliers, its supply of electronic components has been affected just like that of many other companies. Miller explained:

> When customer demand did pick back up, we were able to meet that need with most of our suppliers. However, we have a huge issue in the electronics industry. Capacity was cut, a lot of things were cut back, and they're not easy to put back in place. It seems everyone has double the demand for what their output capacity is, and this is one issue we need to work through.

As the company works through these issues with its supply chain, it is learning every step of the way. It understands the need to strengthen this area of the supply chain or protect against the possibility of limited supply as it grow its business. Once again, Miller explained:

> As our business grew, we were able to increase our output double what was forecast, and our demand was even greater than that. Most of our supply chain responded. However, electronic components became an issue. We were not working directly with the supplier, as these go through a distributor. It was a good learning point for us, and we look for opportunities like this to evolve our operations further.

MANAGEMENT INTERVENTION

With an operation that consistently delivers product without a problem, an office that sees customer needs and reacts accordingly, and a supply chain that contains robust connections to Hypertherm's changing customer demand, the amount of management time needed in the operation has changed considerably. Gordon Rice, the vice president/general manager of the consumable business unit and one of the business unit leaders that Miller referred to earlier, estimates that he used to spend from 90 to 99 percent of his time dealing with the operation back before Hypertherm was reorganized in the late 1990s. But since the redesign according to the principles of flow, he now spends very little of his time on the operational side of his business unit. He is in charge of it, but it runs so effectively on its own that he rarely needs to step in and give direction or "muscle the flow." Hypertherm has more than 220,000 plasma cutting units in the field, all of which require consumable products, and yet Rice spends almost none of his time with the operation responsible for continuously resupplying every one of those products in the field.

Today, when management does get involved in the operation, it is via regular walks throughout the business to recognize and celebrate associate improvements, which strengthens an already vibrant and supportive relationship among all levels of the organization. "I think of my and [Dr. Hackett's] job as being one of education," said Miller. He continued:

> It's our job to educate the associates on how making improvements within the principles of flow ultimately makes the business more successful. With Hypertherm's philosophy of shared rewards throughout all levels of the organization, this is very easy to do. All of our associates understand that improvements made to the business will directly affect their compensation in a positive way.

PRODUCT DEVELOPMENT

Because of the lack of management time needed to run the operation, Hypertherm has been able to devote significant amounts of its time and resources to being more competitive in the marketplace through the development of new products and technology. Hypertherm holds more than 80 patents relating to plasma cutting technology and continues to innovate more new ideas every year. One of the concrete results from Hypertherm's devotion to offense occurs every year when the consumable business unit "war-games" different scenarios with its sales associates. Associates in Marketing develop storyboards for several real-life competitors, and a few external sales associates, along with representatives from Marketing, Engineering, and even Operations, "become" Hypertherm's competition and develop hypothetical strategies to counter Hypertherm as a business. This gives Hypertherm insight into what its competitors might do in the future, which feeds into the business unit's annual SWOT (strengths, weaknesses, opportunities, and threats) analysis, from which Rice estimates that the company generates about 90 percent of the critical items that it ends up working on during the following year.

This war-gaming exercise is only two or three years old, but the company has already seen payback from it. Some of the competitive strategies that the sales associates developed during these sessions playing Hypertherm's competitors have actually come to fruition in real life. As a result of the war-gaming, the company started developing a product to counter a potential threat that was looming on the horizon. "[The competitor's] product was released a little bit before ours, but if we hadn't foreseen that, we could have been in a little bit of trouble," said Rice.

So committed is Hypertherm to research and development that even during the worst of the recession, the company maintained a full focus on product and technology development. "In 2009, our revenue was actually down 36 percent, but our research and development spending went up 20 percent," said Smith. More products were developed during 2009 than in any other one-year period in the company's history. "This helped us keep our new product development pace, which we maintained through the recession," said Miller. "And when things picked up, we were ready with new products. That's part of the reason we were able to rebound so quickly."

Dave Laprade, the vice president/general manager of the mechanized business unit, sounded a similar note:

> There wasn't any discussion around should we slow down our engineering spending. That discussion never even happened. In a time when our competitors were cutting investments, we actually increased [investment] and did more product launches. We have gained market share as a result, and as things improve, it's just a bigger gain that's going to accrue for us because we have a bigger piece of the pie. You can turn the corner more rapidly to meet the rising demand. Having that continuity is key to our competitive success.

Smith added: "The first signs of life were probably in September of 2009. When we compare ourselves with the public benchmarks available of players in our industry who are publicly owned, we've probably doubled their growth over the same time." At the time of this writing near the end of 2010, sales at Hypertherm are already back to June 2007 levels, and according to internal company forecasts, they are about one year ahead of schedule from where the company had predicted they would be.

THE RESULTS

The focus on flow without management throughout the organization, and the ability of each associate to work on some form of offense, resulted in a sales increase of seven times from 2002 to 2008 (see Figure 27.1). Yet, with the company's natural evolution to Operational Excellence, Hypertherm still produces its products from its campus setting in Hanover, New Hampshire.

During the 2009 recession, like almost all businesses, Hypertherm saw the demand for its products drop. However, with no layoffs of associates and a focus on growth, its sales quickly recovered to a path of growth. Figure 27.2 demonstrates how quickly Hypertherm has rebounded from the recent economic downturn; it is nearly back to the peak sales it experienced before the recession took hold.

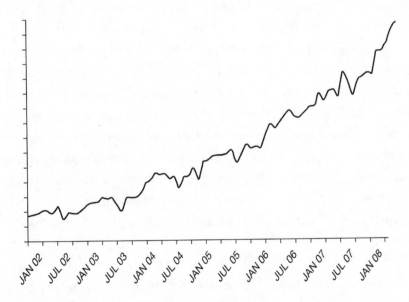

Figure 27.1 *Hypertherm Sales Graph (Prerecession)*

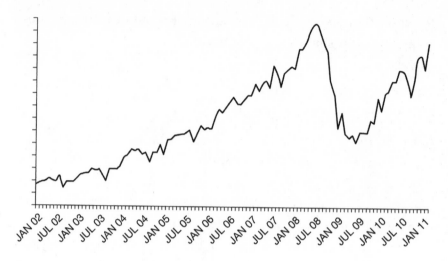

Figure 27.2 *Hypertherm Sales Graph (Postrecession)*

Hypertherm's growth includes a good amount of sales to an area into which most U.S. companies that produce domestically have not been able to expand: Asia. While the trend in American factories is to import low-cost components from a global source, assemble the product using these components, and then sell the product in North America, Hypertherm does just the opposite. Its manufacturing facility in New Hampshire *sells and delivers nearly 25 percent of its products to Asia and almost 30 percent to Europe* with very little inventory in the pipeline. It competes with low-cost overseas producers right in its own backyard with products made in New Hampshire, a testament to its products' functionality and also the ability of its operation to deliver that functionality to customers on a global basis.

In terms of Operational Excellence, Hypertherm just does it naturally. It's just the way the company sees things. The operation was designed to focus on the customer early on. The design evolved to developing end-to-end flow and removing management from operations. Hypertherm's focus on the customer *and* its strong commitment to each associate has allowed it to create Operational Excellence and grow its business. All of this is done with tremendous humility, as if nothing out of the ordinary is taking place at Hypertherm and the way it does things is just the natural way things should happen. "Our mission statement is to provide our customers with the best thermal metal-cutting equipment in the world and to provide for the development and well-being of our associates," said Miller. He went on:

> Going forward, we're going to keep pushing the envelope for how autonomous our operations can be in terms of not relying on management for their day-to-day functioning. We want to be focused on our customers and the needs of our business so we can continue to grow globally and challenge our associates.

Designing an operation that flows product seamlessly to the customer without management was the insight that Hypertherm's founder had in the late 1990s. He instilled this design early on, and as the company grew and more associates were brought in, each of them learned it as well. The design evolved with formal education to support a global customer base from Hanover, New Hampshire. The design still holds true today, and it still works.

Conclusion: Our Blueprint for Growth

Only by following a design for Operational Excellence can we truly achieve a systematic, sustained approach to business growth. Just like our aircraft in flight, our business is *designed to be in motion*. It is designed to flow a product or a service to the customer, without management intervention. There are design principles that create this robust flow and provide performance parameters. We make the flow visual, allowing everyone (even a visitor) to see it. We provide checklists to ensure that we are getting the performance we need from our flow. And we have checklists for what to do when the flow becomes abnormal. Like the airline company that has entrusted the "value-added" part of its service (the actual flight) to the pilots and crew members, we have entrusted the flow of the product or service that we provide to the employees who work in the flow. They are the ones who carry out the value-added activities. By doing so, we are able to focus our time and effort on offense, or business growth. We create a design or formal process to do this as well. We put the activities that create offense in flow. This creates a perpetual system of business growth by making our customers successful, allowing us to break into new markets. All of this is funded through the improvements we have made in our operations, with no additional cost or financial investment. The investment is just of the time and effort that have been freed up from our operations.

This is a blueprint for a design that works. It's a proven design, as we found in the case studies. It's a design that a few progressive companies have used and applied to achieve sustained business growth.

This design can be applied to any business entity, including manu-facturers, service providers, financial companies, hospitals, and even governments.

The successful implementation of the design is dependent upon leaders who know exactly where the operation is going and the de-tailed design for getting there. These leaders don't inspire people to find a way to achieve management goals; they provide and teach a process. They drive this process through formal education, and then ask questions to ensure that the knowledge is retained. The process is one of education, then application, followed by more education. There are no shortcuts; we build Operational Excellence by follow-ing design guidelines, by following the blueprint. There is no brain-storming where to improve next, no searching for low-hanging fruit. Operational Excellence is achieved by following a design, through structure and process—from our operations to market share.

The end result is a business that is designed to grow, *and the design works.*

Notes

Chapter 1

1. Flow is the progressive achievement of tasks along the value stream so that a product proceeds from design to launch, order to delivery, and raw materials into the hands of the customer with no stoppages, scrap, or backflows. James P. Womack and Daniel T. Jones, *Lean Thinking* (New York: Simon & Schuster, 1996), p. 306.

Chapter 4

1. This definition comes from the masters program in Business Operational Excellence at the Ohio State University Fischer College of Business, Columbus, Ohio, 2010–2011.

2. SMED (Single-Minute Exchange of Dies) is a program that teaches us how to reduce setup time on a machine or process.

3. Poka-yoke is mistake-proofing.

4. Traditionally, 5S is a method of workplace organization and stands for Sort, Set in order, Shine, Standardize, and Sustain.

5. A value stream is defined as all the activities, both value-added and non-value-added, that are required to bring product from raw material to the customer. Mike Rother and John Shook, *Learning to See* (Cambridge, Mass.: Lean Enterprise Institute, 2003).

Chapter 5

1. "VIBCO Vibrators: How Do VIBCO Vibrators Help?; http://www.vibco.com/content/about-vibrators.php accessed February 11, 2011.

Chapter 17

1. James P. Womack and Daniel T. Jones, *Lean Thinking* (New York: Simon & Schuster, 1996).

2. Mike Rother and John Shook, *Learning to See* (Cambridge, Mass.: Lean Enterprise Institute, 2003).

3. More information on creating product family matrices can be found in Kevin J. Duggan, *Creating Mixed Model Value Streams: Practical Lean Techniques for Building to Demand* (New York: Productivity Press, 2002).

4. Ibid.

5. *The Office That Grows Your Business: Achieving Operational Excellence in Your Business Processes* (North Kingstown, R.I.: Institute for Operational Excellence, 2009).

Chapter 19

1. Mike Rother and John Shook, *Learning to See* (Cambridge, Mass.: Lean Enterprise Institute, 2003).

Chapter 25

1. "Parker Instrumentation Innovations," Parker Hannifin Web site; http://www.ipde-innovations.com/ accessed January 17, 2011.

Chapter 26

1. "About IDEX," IDEX Web site; http://www.idexcorp.com/about/about_about.asp, accessed December 20, 2010.
2. Ibid.
3. "Strategy," IDEX Web site; http://www.idexcorp.com/about/about_strategy.asp, accessed December 20, 2010.
4. Ibid.
5. "Rheodyne," IDEX Health & Science Web site; http://www.idex-hs.com/Rheodyne.aspx, accessed December 21, 2010.
6. "Micropump," IDEX Health & Science Web site; http://www.micropump.com/about_overview.aspx, accessed December 22, 2010.
7. "BAND-IT" Web site; http://www.band-it-idex.eu/en/index.html, accessed December 22, 2010.

Chapter 27

1. Plasma is the fourth state of matter, defined as superheated, electrically charged gas.
2. Erika Cohen, "Best Companies to Work for 2009: Hypertherm Inc.," *Business New Hampshire Magazine*, December 2009.
3. "SHRM Honors 50 Best Small and Medium Companies," SHRM Web site; http://www.shrm.org/about/news/Pages/CMS_022042.aspx, accessed February 17, 2011; Robert Levering and Milton Moskowitz, "The 100 Best Companies to Work For," *Fortune*, February 4, 2002; http://money.cnn.com/magazines/fortune/fortune_archive/2002/02/04/317486/index.htm, "IW Growing Companies Introduces the IW Growing Companies 25, America's Most Successful Small Manufacturers," *Industry Week*, November 1998.

Index